# THE STRICKEN DEER
## OR
# THE LIFE OF COWPER

WILLIAM COWPER
From the drawing by W. Harvey after L. Abbott
in the National Portrait Gallery

# *The*
# STRICKEN DEER

*or*

## *The Life of Cowper*

*by*

### DAVID CECIL

"I was a stricken deer that left the herd
Long since; with many an arrow deep infixt
My panting side was charged, when I withdrew
To seek a tranquil death in distant shades."

WILLIAM COWPER, *The Task*, Bk. III

INDIANAPOLIS

### THE BOBBS-MERRILL COMPANY

PUBLISHERS

PRESS OF
BRAUNWORTH & CO., INC.
BOOK MANUFACTURERS
BROOKLYN, N. Y.

*To*
**I. P.**

# PREFATORY NOTE

COWPER has already been the subject of many books. But these, when they have not been primarily studies of his literary genius—like those of Mr. Goldwin Smith and Mr. Hugh Fausset—have been definitive and documented biographies—like those of Hayley, Southey, and Mr. Thomas Wright. My purpose is rather, in the light of all the information gathered for us in these more elaborate works and elsewhere, to tell straightforwardly the story of this extraordinary man, with such analysis of his character and those of his friends and his period as may seem necessary to make it clear. We are able during large portions of his life to do this in the most intimate detail. From the mass of poems, letters and reminiscences that have come down to us we can reconstruct, not only the outward ordering of his life down to the way he spent each hour, and every article of furniture in his room, but also the trend and fluctuation of his solitary thought. Only twice during his early manhood and in the period of his second madness are we conscious of a want of sufficient information. But, since history is only interesting as long as it is strictly true, I have not attempted to supply this want except by a few very tentative conjectures. If, therefore, my picture grows at moments hazy, its central figure indistinct, I ask pardon of my readers, and solicit their indulgence.

# CONTENTS

| CHAPTER | | PAGE |
|---|---|---|
| | A PROLOGUE | 13 |
| I | MORNING | 30 |
| II | MADNESS | 57 |
| III | FAITH AND MRS. UNWIN | 93 |
| IV | FAITH AND MR. NEWTON | 127 |
| V | POETRY AND LADY AUSTEN | 166 |
| VI | FAME | 230 |
| VII | GATHERING SHADOWS | 248 |
| VIII | NIGHT | 289 |
| | INDEX | 333 |

# ILLUSTRATIONS

FACING PAGE

WILLIAM COWPER                                          *Frontispiece*
*From the drawing by W. Harvey after L. Abbott in the National Portrait Gallery*

WILLIAM COWPER                                                      28
*After the drawing by Romney in the National Portrait Gallery*

THE TEMPLE IN THE WILDERNESS                                       190
*From "Cowper Illustrated by a Series of Views, etc.," London, 1810*

WESTON LODGE                                                       254
*From "Cowper Illustrated by a Series of Views, etc.," London, 1810*

# THE STRICKEN DEER
## OR
# THE LIFE OF COWPER

# THE STRICKEN DEER

## A PROLOGUE

PAST periods, like foreign countries, become the fashion.
Just as people like one sort of hat because it suits the
type of beauty they admire, so people are attracted to a
particular place or period because it suits their prevailing mood.  Mankind, in its restless search for some ideal
and fairy country which satisfies a fancy, dissatisfied with
that in which it lives, will identify it with the civilization
of some other time or people which appears to possess
the qualities it most values, and to lack those which it
most dislikes.  The ancient world, Corinthian capitals
and Latin inscriptions were the fashion in the Italian
Renaissance; the celestial empire of China, porcelain,
and short moral fables about people with Oriental names
were the fashion in the eighteenth century; the Middle
Ages, Gothic tracery and the *Morte D'Arthur* were the
fashion in the days of the Pre-Raphaelites.  The mode
of a bygone age flourishes again; a curious exotic blooming in the warmth of the admiration of a later day long
after its parent tree is withered and dissolved back into
earth.

But the later day does not confine itself to admiration.
It begins to imitate modes and styles and to adapt them
to its own circumstances.  The Renaissance despots built
classical temples and wrote classical poems and planted

13

classical groves; the powdered dilettanti of 1775 bought English chinoiserie vases and French chinoiserie hangings and Chippendale chinoiserie chairs. The nineteenth century, thorough in everything, was thoroughly Gothic. Its connoisseurs made Gothic summer-houses, Gothic bathrooms, Gothic umbrella stands. They filled the house with stained-glass windows and even called their children by Gothic names—Blanche, Hubert, Edith.

But these imitations only serve to bring out in a stronger light the difference between the period they interpret and their interpretation of it. They recreate it in the image of their own desire; they intensify the elements that charm them; they modify those that offend against their conventions. And the result is a blend of the style they are imitating and their own, that, by its very indication of what they admired, is an exquisitely characteristic example of their own civilization.

There is nothing more typical of the English eighteenth century than an eighteenth-century chinoiserie chair, with all the flowering graces of Pekin tamed into the delicate regularity of Bath. Nothing brings back the feel and atmosphere of the first French empire like an empire sofa, with its rigid sphinx heads and garlands, and bundles of fasces copied exactly from an ancient sarcophagus, in brass and mahogany, and upholstered in red ribbed silk. How Victorian are the Rowenas and Rebeccas of the paintings illustrating Scott's novels that covered the walls of the Royal Academy from 1825 to 1850, with their sloping shoulders and downcast eyes and jet-black hair *en bandeaux;* and the Arcadian shepherd of Elizabethan pastoral, dressed in a mantle of blue silk, his hair stuck with gilly-flowers, spouting conceits; and the scholastic-tongued sages of antiquity of Dante's *Inferno;* and the sultans that strut in so Parisian a minuet through the tragedies of Voltaire! How precisely, how intensely, they bring their age before us by their every word and gesture! These corporate creations, the spirit of one age expressed in the dress of another, possess a fanciful charm of their own: bouquets whose scent mingles many flowers, music whose harmony is made by a peculiar combination of instruments. But they derive this charm from the vivid way in which the unwonted dress reveals the individuality of its wearer. The period appears more clearly itself because it is vainly trying to look like something else.

To-day the eighteenth century is the fashion; we print eighteenth-century memoirs; we reprint eighteenth-century novels; we anthologize eighteenth-century poems; we translate eighteenth-century romances. On weekdays we perform eighteenth-century ballad operas; on Sundays eighteenth-century comedies. Our most up-to-date writers eulogize Baroque and Rococo; our most Olympian critics prefer Mozart's operas to Wagner's. And, like earlier ages, we imitate as well as admire. Modern architects design in a severely classical style, all pilaster and pediment. Modern story-tellers emulate the grammatical nakedness of Defoe.

But we are as much the creatures of the time we live in as were the people of other periods; and our interpretation of the eighteenth century is no more like the reality than a Renaissance statue of Apollo is like a Greek statue of Apollo, or the Houses of Parliament are like a Gothic cathedral. People like the eighteenth century because they see it as the Golden Age of the qualities they value; and so they conceive it as possessing these qualities and no others. They like its sensibility because they dislike emotion, and it seems to express itself in emotions so deliberate as hardly to deserve the

# 16 *The Stricken Deer*

name at all.  They profess to like pure form, whatever
that may mean; and the eighteenth century had a talent
for form.  So they represent its music as all form and no
matter, its novels all form and no morals, and its religion
all form and no faith.  Finally, they dislike the nineteenth century, and they see the eighteenth century as its
opposite, and therefore their idea of it exaggerates
everything in which this opposition lies: its elegance,
its cynicism, its impropriety, its frankness of speech, its
foppishness of manner.  The eighteenth century of their
imagination is a series of salons, where people with snuff-
boxes and worldly-wise outlook make *mots* in a mood
of urbane skepticism born of an extensive experience of
the brighter side of life in the capitals of Europe.

It is the land of their dreams; but it is not at all
like the England of the eighteenth century, the teeming,
clamoring, irregular, enthralling England of the eighteenth century.  In order to mold the age they love
nearer to their heart's desire, they have successfully
shattered it to bits.  For one thing, their idea is too
homogeneous.  Only countries of the mind are so much
of a piece.  The past does not, any more than the
present, escape that incompleteness, that inconsistency
which is the essential characteristic of life as we know it,
as opposed to life as we should like it to be. An historical
period is not a water-tight compartment, containing only
what it has itself created, sharing nothing with what has
gone before and what comes after.  It is a tangle of
movements and forces, of various origin, sometimes in-
tertwined and sometimes running parallel, some beginning, some in their prime, some in decay; streaked by
anomalies and freaks of nature; colored by physical con-
ditions, by national characteristics, by personalities;
struck across by unexpected, inexplicable stirrings of the

spirit of God or of man; yet with every strand part of what is past or what is to come: a great river ever fed by new streams, its course continuous and abrupt, checkered and unfaltering, now thundering over a sudden cataract, now partially diverted into a back-water, and carrying on its mysterious surface fragments of wreckage, survivals of an earlier day not yet dissolved into oblivion.

To describe any period, then, as all of a piece is as inaccurate as to paint a picture of its streets with all the houses of the same age and style. Even if the eighteenth-century spirit as we imagine it was really prevalent in the eighteenth century, it would be as false to imagine it as exclusively prevalent, as to imagine all the furniture was made by Sheraton and all the decoration done by Adam. But it was very far from prevailing; it is altogether too much made up of modishness and mockery. Of course, some of the typical figures of the eighteenth century are modish and mocking—Casanova, Voltaire, Lord Chesterfield. But though unlike in other respects, they were alike in outraging most of their contemporaries very much. Casanova succeeded in shocking visitors to Venice even more broad-minded than those of our own day. Lord Chesterfield was looked upon by the ordinary man as having, in the words of Johnson, "The manners of a dancing master and the morals of a whore." While to imagine that Voltaire expressed the general opinion of his time is as sensible as to imagine that Jonah expressed the general opinion of Nineveh. He represents a characteristic and important aspect of eighteenth-century thought, a vivid thread in its tangled skein, but any one who thinks that it is the only aspect, above all in England, has a conception of the period that is wrong from start to finish.

For how many-sided the eighteenth century was can be seen by any one who looks at the mass of novels, plays, poems, sermons, memoirs, letters and speeches that go to make up a library of the period. If we would find the true spirit of the eighteenth century we must leave the eighteenth century of to-day, the eighteenth century of the stage, of the book illustrator, even of the historian; and seek it in its own books.

For a happy moment let us shut the door on the modern world and retire in fancy to some Augustan library. The curtains are drawn, the fire is lit; outside the silence is broken only by the faint crackling whisper of the winter frost. How the firelight gleams and flickers on the fluted moldings of the bookcases, on the faded calf and tarnished gold of the serried rows of books: the slim duodecimo poems and plays; the decent two-volumed octavo novels; the portly quarto sermons, six volumes, eight volumes, ten volumes; the unity of brown, broken now and again by a large tome of correspondence, green or plum or crimson, only given to the public in our own time. The whole eighteenth century is packed into these white or yellowing pages; all its multifarious aspects, its types, its moods, its morals, self-revealed; the indefinable, unforgettable perfume of the period breathing from every line of print. For the shortest, dullest letter really written in a past age can bring its atmosphere home to you as the most vivid historian of a later time can never do.

Here, through this long line of volumes, of correspondence, crystallized into a diamond immortality by the fragile brilliance of Horace Walpole's style, streams the life of that small dazzling Whig world that ruled England, with its habits and fashions and whims, its political secrets and its private scandals, its heroes, its

buffoons and its beauties. It is the world of the nobleman who was educated till he was eleven at his ancestral
home by a tutor who was also the chaplain; who, after
a severely classical four years at Eton, left England for
the Grand Tour in his berline; who was speechless
with shyness at Madame du Deffand's parties in Paris,
who bought Guido Renis in Bologna; who admired Frederick William I's Guards in Potsdam, stepping together
like giant marionettes controlled by one hand; who came
back to England; married the daughter of a nobleman
as Whig as himself; sat for a pocket borough belonging
to himself or a relation; attacked Walpole or maybe
Carteret; played loo; made rotund orations, studded with
Latin quotations; collected curious antiquities; laid out
his gardens in accordance with the grandiloquent plans of
Capability Brown; who spent half the year lounging in
the windows of Brooks's and half among the oaks and
elms of his country seat; who was painted in youth by
Allan Ramsay, and in age by Romney; who was brought
up to like Pope, but grew to prefer Ossian; who patron-
ized Doctor Johnson; who talked and wrote voluminous
letters and composed compliments in verse; who laughed
at the royal family and drank too much port and died.

It was a society at once narrow and cosmopolitan, as
much at home in Paris as in London, but knowing few
people in either. It knew every aspect of its world, but
that world was small. It liked painting and politics, but
painting meant Leonardo and Raphael, and nothing else,
and politics meant the Whig cause and the balance of
power, and nothing else. Even the classical learning from
which it quoted so freely was more Roman than Greek,
and more French than Roman: precise and rhetorical,
a collection of apothegms, full of patrician independence
and uninsular patriotism. It was conventional, too; luke-

warm in religion, but scrupulous about going to church; slack about morals, strict about the proprieties; often republican in theory, always aristocratic in practise.

But though it was outwardly so formal and so cosmopolitan, it was really very English, impulsive, copious, untidy, full of exceptions to the rule, of eccentric characters, excited by sudden gusts of enthusiasm, that make it as different from that contemporary French society to which its conventions gave it an outward likeness as a portrait by Gainsborough is unlike a pastel of Latour. No Frenchman would have suddenly put up a ruined castle in his garden, like Lord Holland, or had fully grown cedar trees planted by torchlight, like Lord Chatham.

It was, indeed, the most original, as it was far and away the most amusing and attractive, society England has ever known. For its unquestioning acceptance of the conventional structure of life left its whole energy free to develop the individual. It was because their world was so small that they could touch so many sides of it, because they took the facts of existence for granted that they could cultivate its graces, because they never doubted they were born to rule that they could say, with Pitt, "I believe I can save the country, and no one else can."

But eighteenth-century England is not only its aristocracy. Take down this volume of Fielding. Here you may see the life of the middle classes, the life that we see in Smollett and Gillray and *The Beggar's Opera,* whose painter was Hogarth, not Reynolds, whose engraver was not Bartolozzi, but Rowlandson; a life spent among tradespeople in the town and squires in the country, the life of the road and the tavern; with its virtuous side lived in those decorous, irreligious, classical churches with large-cushioned box pews and a sounding-board over the pulpit; and its vicious among the pimps and pickpockets, the gambing-hells and disorderly houses behind Drury Lane. It was a life sensible, coarse and moral; in high spirits, but with its feet planted firmly on the earth; the life of the plain man, in a decent brown-stuff suit and shoes with steel buckles, who lived over his shop, and went to Vauxhall on a holiday and sat under Seed or Jortin on Sunday; who gave money to an orphanage and took his wife to see an execution.

For its conception of morality is that expressed in Hogarth's prints of the idle and industrious apprentice. The idle apprentice is hanged, the industrious apprentice becomes Lord Mayor. You might fall into an occasional lapse among the rosy, frankly bosomed trollops or doxies of Covent Garden, but it was soon proved to you by a sober and unenthusiastic clergyman that respectability was the best policy.

It had its adventurous side, too, that adventurous side of life which filled eighteenth-century literature from the novels of Defoe onward. Adventure was undertaken in a very matter-of-fact spirit, drawing its excitement from its incidents alone, and not from any romantic light shed on them by the temperament of its hero; the adventures of the young men who were pressed for sailors, or taken by pirates, like Captain Singleton; or who explored New Zealand with Captain Cook; or were shipped off as incorrigible rakes at eighteen years old, to make fortunes as Indian nabobs, like William Hickey. It is a whimsical contrast between the dying Mogul empire, still illumined by gleams of fantastic splendor, shadowed by omens, wrapped in all the immemorial and colored mystery of the East, and its prosaic red-faced conquerors with an unappeasable thirst for good living, and without a nerve in their bodies.

But the eighteenth century was not altogether without nerves. Look at that fat collection of paper-bound three-volume novels about fashionable life. They are the expression of that neurasthenia that at its worst produced the vapors and at its best *Clarissa Harlowe;* the condition of mind of the languid ladies, with waxen hands and small caps poised dizzily on a tall fan of hair, that droop at one so pensively out of the canvases of the Reverend William Peters. Their nerves affected not their imaginations, but their feelings. Natural sentiments—filial love, maternal love, conjugal love—swelled to such an extent under the tender and unrelaxed attention of their owners as to endanger their healths. If one is to believe the novelists who describe them, these ladies spent whole days writing letters, seated on elegant, uncomfortable chairs except when they walked, muffled in swan's-down, to the willow tree on which the loved one had carved their names. How absurd and morbid and unreal it reads to us! But from time to time the sentences melt into a delicate beauty for which in the works of the robust and healthy-minded we search in vain.

For Beauty in eighteenth-century literature always comes as an expression of the feelings. Look at those long, unread, unreadable shelves of poetry. The descriptions of Nature by Thompson or Crabbe are exact, but they are untouched by the light that never was on land or sea, but which illuminates all great poetry. They would convey no pleasure to a reader who did not know the English scenery they were describing and therefore could not recognize how accurate the description was. Only when the heart of the poet is touched does his poem glow into real beauty, the sentiment gaining an added ring of pathos from the formal language in which it is expressed.

For who, to dumb forgetfulness a prey.
This pleasing anxious being e'er resign'd,
Left the warm precincts of the cheerful day,
Nor cast one longing, lingering look behind ?

On some fond breast the parting soul relies,
Some pious drops the closing eye requires,
Ev'n from the tomb the voice of nature cries,
Ev'n in our ashes live their wonted fires.

Horace Walpole, Fielding, Hickey, Richardson, Gray, what differences of outlook do these names conjure up! I can not think of a single quality common to them all, except a uniform unlikeness to the modern idea of the eighteenth century. And they do not exhaust the varieties of the eighteenth-century scene. There are the astrologers and magicians, Cagliostro and Mesmer, whose practises quiver with a lurid light round the French monarchy in its decay. The Jacobites, shabby, silly, romantic; the miners of Cornwall, howling and foaming at the mouth under the eloquence of the Methodists; the bishops, whose dioceses were in Wales and whose residences were in London, and who edited, with dignity, the more scabrous classical authors.

But there is another strain in the skein of the period, that can not be so briefly dismissed. I mean that literary intelligentsia which derived from Addison and reached its zenith in the Club; that centered round Burke and Garrick and Goldsmith and Miss Burney, but which could extend to include Gibbon on the one hand and Mrs. Barbauld on the other; the circle whose greatest figure is Doctor Johnson, and whose spirit, lingering on into a new century, flowered once more, a late autumnal blooming, in the chaste talent of Jane Austen.

If eighteenth-century England must have typical representatives, these are the typical representatives of the

English eighteenth century. The essential characteristic of their point of view was a disbelief in extremes. They were gregarious but not giddy, stay-at-home but not solitary, often devout but never mystical; if urban in their tastes, not modish; if rural, without any transcendental sentiment about Nature; plain-spoken but not salacious, domestic without sentimentality. They disliked the paradoxical, the ecstatic, because they thought them false. What was the value of an idea, however entertaining or original, if its conclusions could not be carried out in ordinary life, or of an emotion, however intoxicating, that could not stand the wear and tear of prosaic every day? But they were not cynical. Indeed, their distrust of the extreme arose from their deep belief in the moral purpose of existence, and their consequent distrust of any fancy or feeling that might distract them from this purpose. You lived in order to be good; theories and feelings were valuable in so far as they helped you in this, and no further. They despised all speculation that was not practicable, all emotion that was not durable. With a robust and rational capacity for enjoying themselves, they thought self-pity and self-depreciation neither sensible nor healthy. But they looked at life with open eyes, and they were too honest and too clear-sighted to expect very much from it.

The shelf of their works is long indeed, and the best books of their time are on it. They wrote the best biography, the best history, the best political pamphlets, and they rocked the cradle of the domestic novel. And they gave the literary tone to other writers whose lives were lived far from their company and according to ideas not theirs. Of these not the least distinguished was William Cowper, the poet, whose story is the subject of this book.

His poems are not much read now. Bound in solid

leather and adorned with the sober magnificence of gilt
lettering, they rest upon the upper shelves of old-
fashioned libraries, unread from year's end to year's end,
their backs growing drab, drained of hue and luster by
the strong destroying sunlight.  They are become merely
furniture, less valued because less noticeable than the
globes and grandfather clocks and graying mezzotints
that crowd the room around them.  When, on tiptoe,
one drags a volume from its place and opens it, *pouf!*—
the page is clouded for a moment by the shaking out of
the dust that has accumulated for so long there.  And
the words seem dusty and faded as the paper on which
they are printed.  Pedantic epigram, antiquated compliment, pompous, didactic apostrophe, follow one another,
as lifeless as the half-obliterated signs on an ancient and
undeciphered papyrus.  It seems impossible to believe
that this was ever the genuine expression, however formal,
of a living person's mind.

And then suddenly one's attention is caught by a
chance word; the page stirs to life; a bit of the English
countryside appears before one's mental eye as vividly
and exactly as though one really saw it; or an ephemeral
trifle, a copy of verses addressed to Miss M. or Mr.
D., laughs out of the page with the pleasant colloquial
intimacy of a voice heard over the teacups in the next
room.  And now and again, as if from the strings of a
tarnished, disused harp stumbled against in one's rambles
round the library, there rises from the old book a strain
of music, simple, plangent, and of a piercing pathos, that
fairly clutches at the heart.

> To me the waves that ceaseless broke
> Upon the dangerous coast
> Hoarsely and ominously spoke
> Of all my treasure lost.

Your sea of troubles you have past
And found the peaceful shore,
I tempest-tossed and wrecked at last
Come home to port no more.

Here is no Byronic pessimism, rhetorical, exaggerated, the expression of a posture or at best a passing mood. Through these quiet verses trembles the true voice of despair.

And the contrast between them and the wooden versification in which they are embedded is not more striking than it is between them and the poems of Nature or of home in which, alone of all his other work, Cowper rises to real poetry. These are the parallels in verse of *Cranford* and *Our Village* in prose. He paints with simple pathos and gentle humor the home life of country gentlemen and doctors and clergyman in the late eighteenth and early nineteenth centuries; peaceful, cozy, friendly, civilized, full of small excitements, and family jokes, and innocent enjoyments; knitting and sketching and playing on the pianoforte and reading aloud and cribbage and a little harmless gossip; easily shocked, easily amused; enacted in studies and drawing-rooms furnished with Heppelwhite chairs, the walls hung with silhouettes and samplers, and the tightly shut windows with curtains of striped chintz.

Now stir the fire, and close the shutters fast,
Let fall the curtains, wheel the sofa round,
And while the bubbling and loud hissing urn
Throws up a steamy column, and the cups
That cheer but not inebriate, wait on each,
So let us welcome peaceful evening in.

And his Nature poetry describes the same life outdoors. It is authentic English landscape; not the wild

naked landscape of the North, but the tamed country
of the Home Counties, coated with human associations.
And Cowper's mood is tamed too, amused, contempla-
tive, passive; observant of everything, carried away by
nothing. He might know more about plants and trees
than the ladies and gentlemen of his acquaintance, but
that is because they are in his line, as hunting or painting on silk might be in theirs.

> Ye fallen avenues! once more I mourn
> Your fate unmerited, once more rejoice
> That yet a remnant of your race survives.
> How airy and how light the graceful arch,
> Yet awful as the consecrated roof
> Re-echoing pious anthems! While beneath
> The chequered earth seems restless as the flood
> Brushed by the wind, so sportive is the light
> Shot through the boughs, it dances as they dance
> Shadow and sunshine intermingling quick,
> And darkening and enlightening, as the leaves
> Play wanton, every moment, every spot.

What is there in common between the last two quotations and the overpowering grief, without alleviation
and without hope, of the first? What sort of man was
he that could write all three? What sort of life that
could embrace three such different moods? We look
at his portrait, and the same anomaly strikes us. The
face is a plain, every-day sort of face, with ruddy,
weather-beaten cheeks, and a wide gentle mouth. The
set of the lips, precise yet kindly, shows refinement, but
it is an old-maidish kind of refinement; and the impression
of old-maidishness is added to by the poet's curious head-
gear—a sort of homely English version of a turban,
finished off on top with a neat white bow.

But out of this face glance a pair of eyes which change its whole expression; startled, speaking eyes, fixed on something outside the picture which we can not see, in fear, in horror, in frenzy; luminous, dilated orbs; the eyes of an artist, of a seer, can it be of a madman?

This duality is the central fact of Cowper's life. We search the little heap of dingy volumes, the few faded bundles of correspondence, that are all that remain to us of the endless, thrilling panorama of his earthly existence; all the evidence, conscious or unconscious, that we can gather from his own entrancing letters, the pompous panegyrics of his friends, the chance words of his acquaintances, the long-winded exhortations of his spiritual directors. And there emerges a drama whose action is as simple, as strange, and as terrible, as that of a classical tragedy. It took place in a small circle in the soberest and most peaceful section of the sober, peaceful, professional class of the day, its humdrum cheerfulness much further removed from tragedy than the glittering whirl of fashionable society or the harsh and unremitting struggles of the very poor. And Cowper himself, in his virtues and limitations, is the very epitome of his environment: scrupulous, timid, a little provincial, weak on the logical side; but candid, constant, cultivated, humorous, skilled in the small tactfulness, the minor charities of domestic life. He felt more intensely and expressed himself with greater brilliance than the people round him; but what he felt was what they felt; and his superior sensitiveness and brilliance only helped him to express it more exactly.

But he was under a curse. From his earliest years there loomed over him, born in disease, nurtured in fanaticism, the frightful specter of religious madness. And his life resolved itself into a struggle, fought to the

WILLIAM COWPER

After the drawing by Romney in the
National Portrait Gallery

death, between the daylit serenity of his natural circumstances and the powers of darkness hidden in his heart.
For a time it seemed that they would be defeated. Yet
even when the light shone most brightly on his face,
the shadow lurked behind his back; around the sunny,
grassy meadows crouched the black armies of horror
and despair. At a moment's weakness they would ad-
vance; inch by inch they gained ground; till, with a
last scream of anguish, his tortured spirit sank, overwhelmed.

# CHAPTER I

FROM the first the atmosphere in which Cowper passed his life was domestic. He was born in the country; but the country was the country of Hertfordshire, even in those days the least sequestered of all the districts in England not confessedly urban. The small green Hertfordshire landscape, with its flattish fields and leafy coppices and well-kept canals, with here and there the blue smoke of a chimney rising from one of the placid redbrick cottages with which the country is speckled, was the first view of the world that he saw from the sash-windows of his father's rectory of Great Berkhamstead.

And his life in that sleepy, well-to-do little town was as comfortable and quiet as the scenery surrounding it. The Cowpers were a large respectable family, connected, though distantly, with an earl, and boasting among their most recent members a Speaker of the House of Commons. And on his mother's side William was connected with the Donnes, a family honorably known all over Norfolk, who traced their pedigree back as far as the great Dean Donne of St. Paul's. It is a whimsical thought that this eccentric sixteenth-century divine, alone of Cowper's family, could have truly understood and expressed the pity and terror of his spiritual tragedy.

On both sides his relations were numerous, though legitimate; and much of Cowper's memories of his early

30

years was concerned with visits to and from little Donnes
and Cowpers—racing round the garden with them, picking currants in the orchard, giggling in the parlor.  But
he was a shy child; his affections were concentrated on
what he was most used to; and the dominating fact of
his early life was his mother.  His father, a prosperous
Anglican clergyman, innocent of mysticism, did not play
much part in his existence.  Few children's fathers are
intimate with them till they are ten years old at least; and
intimacy to Cowper implied that caressing confidence,
those small endearments, which are peculiarly maternal.
His father was always the papa of Anne and Jane
Taylor's poems; whom one was fond of as one was fond
of one's old home, but who, like one's old home, formed
part of the background of life, and took his walks and
wrote his sermons and, if he was Mr. Cowper, composed
ballads, with the unnoticed regularity of the seasons.

He felt a more personal interest in his brother.  But
the deepest affection of which his heart was capable was
poured out on that mother from whom he had inherited
his eyes and his mouth and his temperament.  It is a great
mistake to think that people's characters alter as they
grow older; though different circumstances may bring
different sides of them into prominence.  Cowper the
child was like Cowper the man: a defeatist, hating decisions, frightened of the unknown; the creature, not the
creator, of his destiny; liking some one or something on
which to lean.  But he had a genius for affection, and
would devote himself to any one he loved with all the
strength of a nature humble, steadfast, exquisitely tender
and nearly selfless.

His mother satisfied all his needs; he worshiped her,
and she sheltered him from the onslaught of an existence
he was not coarse or self-confident enough to face by

himself. It was she who showed him how to prick out a paper pattern of pinks, violets and jessamine from the figured brocade of her gown; who came to say good night to him in bed; who, when he was old enough to do lessons, wrapped him up in his red cap and velvet cloak and sent him off to learn his book at the dame's school down the street; who waited, smiling, with "a biscuit or confectionery plum" for him on his return; who soothed his brows with lavender water when he had a headache. And it was from her homely piety he learned the elements of that faith which was to bring him the few fleeting moments of ecstasy he was ever to know.

For these first six years of his life were the only unshadowed ones. As time went on his mother's figure shone forth in his memory as the beneficent and omnipotent goddess of that golden age when he was absolutely happy. Forty-seven years later he writes: "I can truly say that not a week passes, perhaps I might with equal veracity say a day, in which I do not think of her." And when, a gray-headed man of fifty-nine, scarred with agony and achievement, he was given her picture, he was in a tremor; passionately kissed it; and hung it at the end of his bed, that it might be the first thing on which his eye alighted when he woke.

But when he was six the evil fate that was to pursue him through life struck its first blow. His mother died. He watched from his nursery window the funeral cavalcade trail off; and as he turned away in tears, his nurse, to comfort him, told him his mother was coming back to-morrow. But to-morrow came, and another, and another, and she never came back. The first of his life's illusions was shattered.

It was tragic, for no one was less qualified than Cowper to live the independent life of an orphan. The sup-

port round which his shy clinging nature had wound itself
had been suddenly taken away; the old idyllic life at "pastoral" Berkhamstead was over for ever when its center
was gone. But a worse blow was to follow. His father,
uncertain what to do with him at home, sent him to
school at the small town of Market Street, about seven
miles from Berkhamstead.

Going away to school for the first time is as purely
painful an experience as there is in most men's lives. It
is like a rehearsal of one's execution. Strung up by two
or three weeks' agonized and helpless anticipation, relentlessly, inevitably, the day arrives when one is plunged
into a world probably hostile and certainly unknown,
without a single link to bind one to the world of one's
experience. But such a fate, cruel in any case, was for
Cowper especially cruel. By temperament he fastened
himself with a peculiarly tenacious hold to the people and
places to which he was accustomed, and now, when he
was already tottering under the loss of a mother around
whom his whole world revolved, his last roots were cut
from beneath him, and he was deposited, bruised and
bleeding, in a place where there was not a face, not a
tree, not a smell, he had ever known before.

And it was a place of torment. Boys have never been
humane; nor did the robust axioms that governed eighteenth-century education believe in protecting people
from the natural discipline administered to them by their
contemporaries. Cowper, shrinking, lonely, six years old,
was quite incapable of standing up for himself, with the
consequence that within a short time of his arrival he
had become a mere quivering jelly of fear. He was so
abjectly terrified of his chief tormentor, an overgrown
lout of fifteen, that he only recognized him by his buckled
shoes; he had never dared to lift his eyes to his face.

Such a situation could not go on for long even in those days; his tormentor was expelled. But Cowper's nervous system was ruined for life.

Such sufferings alone would be quite enough to account for it. But obscure hints reach us of a more somber cause for Cowper's youthful sufferings. It is alleged that he suffered from an intimate deformity, and from early years the thought of it preyed on his mind. The whole subject is mysterious. In later life his emotional experience was normal and developed perfectly spontaneously. On the other hand, he never was a passionate man; and there are certain facts in his later life for which such a deformity would offer a convincing explanation. If he was deformed there is no doubt that he must have learned about it early, possibly from the deriding lips of his tormentors. The effect on him must inevitably have been disastrous. Boys dislike above all things to be different from other people; nor was Cowper of an age to estimate coolly the relative importance of his abnormality.

At any rate, from whatever cause, he left Market Street with the rooted feeling that he was different from other people, different from no fault of his own, but differing for the worse. It was morbid of him, because no one had more in common with his fellow men, and for the rest of his life he was unusually attractive to every type, every age and both sexes. But there remained buried in the hidden foundations of his mind the idea that he was under a dark and shameful curse; that other people could not help him, for he was not as they were; that he started life with the dice loaded against him, and come what might, in the end he would lose the game. He was despondent by nature, and his first experience of the world had proved to him that his despondency was justified.

But his strange sufferings were visited by consolations not less remote from the ordinary child's experience. One day he was huddling on a bench in the deserted classroom, free for one short moment from that terrible pair of feet—cruel, purposeful feet; heard on the stairs, in his bedroom, in the garden, now creeping, now scampering, now climbing, but always in pursuit of him; awful, headless feet, who haunted him in his dreams, who might even now be stealing up behind him to trample on his raw and shuddering spirit. His dazed mind wandered back to that happy home life, so distant that it seemed like a story told long ago and now forgotten. He saw in his mind's eye his mother, and himself sitting beside her while she read to him. Suddenly there flashed into his mind a fragment of the Bible, heard often in those days, but now fraught with a new and tremendous significance: "I fear nothing that man can do unto me." His whole being was filled with a strange spiritual exaltation, far more intense than the happiness of his early childhood, for that arose only from the absence of sorrow, and this vanquished sorrow in her extremest citadel. The forlorn child, hiding away from his bullying schoolfellows, turned and faced his fate with the unearthly serenity of the mystic and the martyr. What did it matter what man could do to him? His soul was inviolate, at one with itself, at one with the Divine Spirit from which it sprang.

It was only for a moment—and then he was back in the schoolroom, miserable, homesick; in fear, above all, of those terrible feet. But that moment had made as deep an impression on him as the sufferings that preceded it. He never forgot what he had felt. In the brief prologue of his first school-time, the two protagonists of his mental tragedy, the demon of his despair and the angel of his consolation, had both made their appearance on the stage.

Having made their bow, they retired; and the scene changes to comedy. For the next fourteen years his life returned to its ordinary, comfortable, daylight key. Buried in the recesses of his memory, the incident of his first school was to all appearance forgotten. In the light of his common day, nightmare and vision soon grew equally dreamlike, the recollection of a life vague, painful, and utterly unconnected with present normal existence.

Children look forward, not back; their spirits are so resilient that whatever inward bruises their nervous systems have sustained are hidden, and they seem perfectly well again. The obscene, crawling beasts had sunk to sleep in the furthest corners of Cowper's spirit. Later on they might bestir themselves and come forward and pounce. But for the present all was soothing and unshadowed, at the house of Mr. Disney, the oculist, where Cowper was sent to be cured of some specks on his eyes. Mrs. Disney was an oculist too; no one seemed certain which one went to consult. But they were both very amiable people, though they did not have family prayers. And the days passed in an easy round of treatment, walks and a few mild lessons.

There were holidays too: rambles alone, or trotting by his father through the woods and commons round Berkhamstead, already heavy with sentimental associations for him; and visits to his Donne cousins in Norfolk, where he made the still, autumnal garden ring with his and Harriet's shouts, and chattered to Castres, and rocked tiny Rose on his knee and, when the curtains were drawn and the candles lit, recited Gay's fable of *The Hare with Many Friends,* in a high treble voice, to the assembled company.

The years rolled by; his eyes got better; and he was sent to Westminster. He must have seen the gate of his second school chilled with apprehension, remembering his experience at his first. But if he did, he was agreeably surprised. The easy flow of his days was not interrupted. Westminster was as pleasant as Berkhamstead or the house of Mr. Disney.

All around him surged and roared the palpitating, many-colored London of 1741. Nightly the torch-lit coaches jostled one another on the way to masquerade and rout; weekly the crowds swarmed to Tyburn to see a woman hanged for stealing a yard of silk; Fielding, his aquiline nose bent over the paper, finished *Joseph Andrews;* Peg Woffington took the town by storm in the peruke and satin breeches of Sir Harry Wildair; Horace Walpole, just back from France, arranged objects of virtu in his house in Arlington Street; while every night, only a few hundred yards from where Cowper worked, old Sir Robert, tottering to his fall after his long ascendency of twenty years, defended himself with dogged shrewdness against the fiery eloquence of the Boys and the Patriots. But the even tenor of Westminster existence was little disturbed by the thundering tide of life that ebbed and flowed around it. Governments might rise and fall, men commit crimes and be hanged for them, waistcoats get longer or shorter, but the boys and masters of Westminster pursued with an undeviating regularity the curriculum prescribed for them in the days of Queen Elizabeth. Like the pool in the middle of a cyclone, the school seemed all the calmer for the swirling rush surrounding it on every side. Every morning the deep bell sounded, the boys toiled or skimmed through their Latin prose, prayed in Westminster Abbey, played knuckle-taw if they were small, or cricket if they were bigger, under the green or fading plane trees.

The little world had its incidents, too.  Young Lord Higham Ferrers and his friends kept the school alive by their pranks.  Every one talked of how he had visited the school dressed as a lady of title and was carried up the great hall in a sedan-chair, followed by the giggling boys, and preceded by the obsequiously bowing head master; or of how the little Duke of Richmond had set "Vinny" Bourne, the classical master's wig alight in order to have the pleasure of boxing his ears to put the flames out.  Or Cowper himself did a good copy of Latin verses that were passed round, to the admiration of the masters, and rewarded with a silver groat.  He liked school very well; he was by nature a scholar.  To the end of his life his genius was not creative except under the stress of intense emotion.  He had not a sufficiently strong imagination.  But though he could not weave, he could embroider.  He had an agreeable individual fancy and a capacity for painstaking and exact work; given a subject, he could make a very pretty thing of it.  This was just what was wanted for success in the scholarship of his day.  Cowper's verses followed the best models, and yet were adorned by that touch of originality which marked them as his own.

His classical style was formed by kind, untidy, talented Vinny Bourne, of whom he grew very fond.  At Westminster Cowper tasted the sweets of friendship for the first time.  The boys were a distinguished lot.  Looking down the packed lines of the assembled school, besides the humorous, gentle countenance of Cowper, one's eye would have lighted on the faces of Colman, Elijah Impey and the pale cheek and lofty brow of Warren Hastings.  The impression made by the great before their great-ness is known is a fascinating study.  Did Hastings move among his schoolfellows stamped with the solemn seal of one whose destiny it was to direct the fate of millions under an alien sun? Was Cowper himself marked by his closest friends as possessing a mysterious, individual something which, had they known it, implied that power of expression which alone can communicate with future generations and achieve for its owner a printed immortality? Idle speculations! Down what obscure vistas do they lead us! Far from Cowper laughing with Legge and Lloyd and dear Russell and the rest of his friends.

How he loved them! What fun he had with them, playing cricket—he was good at cricket—or arguing about the right way to translate Homer or, on his leave-out days, examining the glittering weapons on the walls of the Tower or staring at the lunatics at Bedlam! "I was not altogether insensible of the misery of these poor captives," he wrote, "but the madness of them had such a humorous air, and displayed itself in so many whimsical freaks, that it was impossible not to be entertained; at the same time that I was angry with myself for being so." Poor Cowper! He was not always to laugh so easily at madness. Sometimes they would go farther afield and spend a day in the country, so close to London then; and return home tired and hungry, their mouths stained with the blackberries and "sloes austere" which were all they had had to eat during the day. Though he liked Westminster, Cowper was a countryman by taste and education. He had lived the happiest days of his life there, and he was happiest there still.

He had his solitary pleasures, too. He loved animals: they provided a channel for his flow of natural tenderness. He bought a mouse. However, it ate its children, and he got rid of it in disgust. Later, he took to writing verses, mostly little occasional pieces for his friends on *A Lady's Shoe Lost at Bath,* or some such subject. But when he was in a more serious mood his mind returned irresistibly to the woods and lanes he loved, and whose leafy silence afforded such balm to his sensitive spirit.

All this tended to make him more cheerful. Children have very little humor, even if their lives are happy; and Cowper's, as we have seen, was only partially that. Nor does humor flourish in solitude. One must take oneself seriously alone. But in the social warmth of his friends' company his spirit expanded and flowered into a delicious self-deprecating irony which lights up the few scraps of his writing that survive from this part of his life, and which, except at his very gloomiest, was to shimmer round every sentence he wrote.

But he was not at peace, for he was continually worried by small fears. Sometimes they were of something concrete: that he was going to get into trouble at school. In consequence he grew as skilful as most public-school boys at telling a ready and convincing lie. But generally his fears were more subjective. When he was eleven he was possessed by the idea that he had got consumption. He was too shy to ask any one about it, so that for years the horrible idea lingered in his thoughts, and would suddenly cross his mind when he was sitting, talking or writing, and strike a chill to his heart.

But worse than the fear of illness was the fear of death. One evening he was picking his way among the grave-stones of St. Margaret's on his way home to bed. A blanket of darkness enveloped the world. It was a moonless, starless night. The great buildings that crowded him in on every side might have been a hundred miles away for all he could see of them. The only sound that broke the stillness was the recurring crunch of the sexton's spade digging a grave. Suddenly Cowper felt his leg struck by a round object; he bent down to examine it by the light of the dark lantern he carried in his hand. The light shone on the eyeless sockets, the smooth, repulsive contours of a human skull. With a sickening stab of fear he realized the transitoriness of human life. What good was it to avoid other dangers when here was a danger that could never be avoided? Every minute, every day, every year that one lived, was only a year, a day, a minute nearer this. Friends, books, what were they? Insubstantial masks conjured up by man to hide this bald, grinning horror that was the only reality. Distract oneself as one might, forget it if one could, this was what one came to in the end. The joys of life turned to ashes in his mouth, and he rushed shuddering home.

His horror was followed by a strange reaction. With exhilaration he felt that whatever happened to other people, he, William Cowper, was fated never to die. But this feeling did not last. The terror of death was added to the other terrors of existence.

The truth was that at the bottom he had no confidence in life. By nature nervous and despondent, only an untroubled upbringing and the undivided personal attention of some one he loved and trusted could have persuaded him into anything like optimism. He needed the support of a solid foundation of realized happiness before he could meet the world with any confidence. But at the very outset of his life he had received two violent shocks. The first, the loss of his mother, by removing the corner-stone of his childish existence removed also his belief in the stability of human happiness, and taught him to feel that one must not trust in the continuance of the most assured source of protection. The second, the torments he suffered at his first school, convinced him

that life was even crueler than he had feared, and that
he was the specially selected object of its cruelty. As
time passed he ceased to think of his youthful sufferings;
at times even forgot them. But he had lost his nerve.
Underneath the ebb and flow of his daily thoughts there
was always the half-conscious feeling that life was trying
to hurt him and it was no use relying on any earthly defense, however strong it might seem. It was not just
that he could not stand a row. If he had not a real cause
for fear he invented one; and as fast as he freed himself
from that, he fell a prey to another. For they frightened
him not in themselves, but as the changing manifesta-
tions of a constant distrust of life.

For such ills religion was the only real remedy. The
work and play of ordinary mundane existence might distract him from his hidden fears, but they could not remove them; for they moved on a different plane. In
the light of common day his terrors would have looked
shadowy indeed, but it was of their nature that they never
saw such a light. He might feel perfectly at ease when
he was running about the school yard; but when the lights
were extinguished and he was alone in bed the nameless
horrors would return, the more frightful for their short
oblivion. But religion did not only drive them to their
lairs; it rounded them up and cleared them out. Alone
it met them on their own ground; armed Cowper with a
spiritual sword to combat the enemies of the spirit; prescribed a celestial antidote to the poisonous fear of dis-
honor, disease and death. The ultimate source of all
happiness was the soul; and over the soul they had no
power.

He had felt this that morning in Market Street; and
now and again, notably during the time he was being
prepared for confirmation, he felt it still. For a moment

it seemed to be of no consequence if he did lose his name or his health or his life. The only treasure worth having was laid up in Heaven, and that was his for ever.

Unluckily his anxious mind, searching suspiciously for the thorn beneath every rose, soon began to detect as much cause for alarm in the question of his spiritual as of his material salvation. He felt that his moments of religious comfort were vouchsafed to him in order to win him to the Christian life, by showing him a glimpse of the Heaven it was in his power to attain to. But it is not easy to live a life of austere devotion if you are a growing boy, enjoying yourself at a public school; and Cowper's life followed much the same course as it would have done if he had had no religion at all.

The result was that the whole subject grew as disquieting to him as the fear it was its function to dispel. He felt he would never be able to live up to his beliefs. Would Heaven then withdraw its comforts in this world? Very likely. And in the next, worse punishment might follow. Uneasily he diverted his mind from the subject.

However, it is foolish to emphasize the importance of these youthful worries. Cowper's nervous system was never so deranged as to render his views abnormal and deluded, not to be treated as those of a reasonable man. Life is precarious, tragic, surrounded by dangers; and if delicate and highly strung people are peculiarly conscious of this, it is because they alone are fully alive to their true situation, and are not, like the healthy, the dupes of their own good digestions. Youth, unacquainted with the world, dazzled by the enchanting prospect before it, is proverbially unaware of the possibility of failure and death; and Cowper's only abnormality is his premature delivery from the illusions of youth. Indeed, his nervous troubles were little more than the crises

every imaginative boy goes through between the ages of
twelve and twenty. And they occupied a very small part
of his time. For one agitated night, he passed thirty in
comfortable sleep; and from the worst fear he could be
distracted by any ephemeral pleasure. On the whole he
was very happy. The only formidable fact in his mental
condition was that his happiness was founded on nothing
stronger than the natural energy and spirits of boyhood;
so that, if later he was attacked by a serious trouble,
he had no settled confidence in the probability of ultimate
happiness, with which to withstand its assault; which,
coupled with his early acquired sense of the danger of
human existence, might, in a temperament like his, lead
to a catastrophe.

The years passed. Walpole was succeeded by Pelham;
Ranelagh began to supplant Vauxhall as a center of
fashion; and Cowper left Westminster. He went to
live with Mr. Chapman, a solicitor of Ely Place, Hol-
born, to learn law. But the coloring of his life did not
alter very much. He was a young man, and not a boy;
he used to drink port with his friends, dressed in small
clothes in the evening by way of recreation, instead of
eating blackberries with them, dressed in jackets in the
afternoon; and he worked when he liked. But the friends
themselves and the subjects they talked about were the
same as at Westminster.

Cowper was not the sort of character that sows wild
oats. Apart from his natural sobriety, his mind continued absorbed by the subjects which had occupied most
of its attention at school. He was a scholar; and that
is to say that his school work was the beginning of the
work he did when he grew up, not a preparation for it.
He estimated a man's ability by his scholastic attain-
ments. Nothing else seemed to him so worth doing.

Law bored him extremely; and he spent most of the time he was supposed to be working at it in writing Latin verses. For the rest he argued and laughed with Colman and Thornton and Russell about Homer and Horace just as he had done at Westminster. Only now one had delicious conversations that could go on as long as one liked and where one liked, without being called away to go to bed or to apply one's mind to some dreary subject in which one took no interest.

He did not only talk about scholarship. Politics stirred him deeply. He had all the full-blooded eighteenth-century belief in the superiority of England to every foreign country in every respect. And beyond this, he just liked talking about the world around him. In this, too, he was of his period. The men of the eighteenth century always aspired to be men of the world, restricted in its dimensions though that world might be. It was not then the mark of a distinguished man to devote himself exclusively to one interest, and count the world well lost. Men of fashion knew about literature; artists discussed politics. For, as everybody accepted the general lines on which society was constructed, they would have thought a man eccentric who rejected any activity that lay within them.

But Cowper would have been interested in the world around him wherever he had lived. He was a born friend; always more interested in the man he was talking to than in the subject he was talking about; vigilant to follow his friend's mood, careless where it led him. And his interest therefore naturally played round such of his experience as he and his friends shared together. He was quick to notice all he saw in their company: the types and oddities of London; the fops and the pedants; the feeble young man who was dominated by his mother;

the spoiled child who told tales of the servants; or, when he had gone on a visit to the country, the decaying village churches whose cracked bells had ceased to ring; the worldly farmers' wives who came to church to show off their fine silk clothes. He began to make new friends. There was a young man called Thurlow also working with Mr. Chapman. He was much better at law than Cowper, but very merry and communicative. Easy-going Mr. Chapman did not bother them much; and they used to sit for hours, two excited boys in the decorous dress of 1752, discussing books and people and how best to dispose of money in charity; and going off into fits of laughter and then growing very serious again, while the evening sky darkened to night behind the worn traceries of St. Etheldreda's, Ely Place, and the bending trees in its churchyard.

But other friendships began to dwindle to a small place in his thoughts compared with that which grew up between him and his uncle's family in Southampton Row. Cowper made and liked men friends; he was so gregarious and so affectionate that he made a friend of an animal if he could not find a human being. But his natural *milieu* was a domestic circle. It gave him what he really cared for in converse with his fellow creatures: intimacy, the delicious sweetness of mutually enjoyed pleasures, an interest shared with some one else, a sorrow sympathized with by some one else, a joke laughed at with some one else. And it gave these to him enhanced by a thousand small graces that the most affectionate man friend could never provide. Cowper was always happy with women. They liked his warm heart, his charming interest in little things, his good sense, his delicate, unremitting care for the feelings of the individual; while they alone were soft-hearted and refined enough never to jar on his sensitive taste. But he did not like meeting them at parties. He was shy, and liked knowing people well, if he knew them at all. Nothing else fitted in with all his wants so well as family life; and it was doubly attractive to him as he had never had it except in that remote, sunlit past when he was happy with his mother. He grew to love all the little incidents and institutions of that cheerful, respectable Southampton Row household: the little parties, courteous and informal, for a few friends; the little excursions to the country for a few weeks; the tea-drinkings and wool-windings and readings aloud and nicknames; the family jokes lasting for weeks that he bandied with his cousins.

They were the magnet that drew him to the house. He was fond of his Uncle Ashley, a little man so like a mushroom in his big white hat with its yellow lining. But he was not Harriet or Theodora. Harriet was the beauty of the family; a very Georgian beauty, dark-haired, with a blooming complexion, arched eyebrows and a decided mouth. When Cowper went to Ranelagh with her, all the young men turned to look at her. She had the ways of a beauty, too: little caprices and coquetries; the desire to please; the confidence that she could do so. And she was clever, vivacious and well-read, with a fund of high spirits and high-spirited humor. Not that she was unconventional. No, her ideas were those of the sensible, respectable society in which she lived, though perhaps she expressed them with more enthusiasm and force. She believed in living a decent, reasonable life, not without the pleasures that a decent, reasonable man allows himself. She approved of a decent, reasonable church; took a decent, though less reasonable interest in the royal family. These are the ideas that emerge from her well-written, underlined, entertaining letters. Cowper was very fond of her. How they used to laugh together! How well they understood each other! "So much as I love you," he wrote to her once, "I wonder how the deuce it has happened I was never in love with you." It was not really such a wonder as he said. One can not be in love with two people at once; and he was in love with her sister Theodora.

Compared with her sister's vivid and definite individuality, her personality seems curiously undefined. Her poignant figure glows through Cowper's story with a lambent light of its own: but a tender mist of love floats round it, blurring its outlines. Our rare glimpses of her detect her in some beautiful attitude of regret or tenderness; but we can not distinguish her features. Through the haze her eyes shine out like stars; yet we fail to discern their shape and color. Perhaps love inevitably thus cloaks its object. How many of all the love poems that fill the libraries of the world convey to their readers the impression of a living individual? What human being, indeed, can possess such transcendent qualities as to single her out and set her above all others? She is not loved for what she is, but because for one moment she incarnates to her lover the essential spirit of beauty, not found on earth, and partakes of its mystery. The end of that mystery is the end of love.

It may be that this is why we learn so little of Theodora from Cowper's poems and letters. And alas, time has silenced her own voice. We have none of her letters. Her one reported remark is facetious, but cryptic. Her father asked her what she would do if she married Cowper. "Wash all day," she replied, "and ride on the great dog all night." From what we can gather, she must have been vivacious, like her sister, enjoying a joke and an argument, able to treat Cowper with the ortho-

dox caprice of a mistress. And, more than this, she felt
for him a deep and touching sentiment. She loved him
better than he loved her. To him she was attractive
largely as the expression of that gay secure domesticity
which he desired. When in later life he gave up all idea
of this, he never seems to have thought of her again.
But she did not so easily forget him. She never married;
secretly she followed all the events of his career: helped
to support him, though he never knew it; and—pathetic
illusion—as an old woman mistook a slight love poem
appearing anonymously in the newspaper for one of Cowper's own, and rejoiced to think that his mind was still
constant to that boy-and-girl romance that had ended
nearly forty years before.

However, all that was a long way away. For the
moment Cowper gradually spent more and more of his
time in Southampton Row, till at last he only slept at
Mr. Chapman's. All through the hot July days, and
through those of winter when the windows were never
opened he used to sit with the sisters, and sometimes
Thurlow, "giggling and making giggle." He was gawky
and ill-dressed at first, but Theodora took him in hand,
and improved his clothes and taught him how to come
into a room, and how to talk and how to walk and how
to dance, till, as he said, "No dancing bear was so genteel
or half so *dégagé.*"

Whatever his real feeling, he certainly enjoyed being
in love with her, quarreling with her and making it up,
writing poems and letters to her, thinking of her. When
he went to stay with his cousins, the Donnes, in Norfolk,
and they drove him about in a whiskum snivel, he thought
of Theodora. When he went out shooting, the coveys
flew over his head unnoticed; he thought of Theodora.
He used to sit with a book on his knees for hours read-

ing some pages again and again, and knowing no more about it at the end than at the beginning; he was thinking of Theodora. "Let her say," he wrote,

> Let her say why so fixed and so steady my look
> Without ever regarding the person who spoke,
> Still affecting to laugh without hearing the joke;
>
> Or why when with pleasure her praises I hear,
> That sweetest of melodies sure to my ear,
> I attend and at once inattentive appear.

Meanwhile his time with Mr. Chapman came to an end. In 1752 he went into residence at the Middle Temple. And now within a few months a depression began to overcast his spirit. It was partly due to his age. The poison had always been there. But it had been counteracted by the routine of school life and the irresponsibility of youth. He forgot every worry as quickly as he could; and he had so much to do that he forgot them very soon. But adolescence breaks up the whole fabric of habit built up in childhood. Restlessly one reviews every element of past experience. One must understand; one must, if possible, assign each its proper place in the order of life. Even at twenty-one one tries to coordinate the different aspects of existence. One can no longer forget a real trouble under the spell of a momentary pleasure; especially if, like Cowper, one is by nature introspective and dejected. The melancholy induced by temperament, increased by early experience, latent throughout boyhood, bestirred itself and came into the forefront of his thoughts.

Any natural tendency to depression was increased by his manner of life. The Temple was a melancholy place. It was gay enough on a summer evening, when the fig

trees were in leaf and the leading Counsel were taking
the air, in ruffles and cocked hats, by the side of the
Thames, gleaming in the level rays of the setting sun;
or in Doctor Johnson's chambers over the way, where
the pithy, brilliant talk flowed on till the candles flickered
yellow in the pallid dawn. But to Cowper, who was not
a leading Counsel, and did not know Doctor Johnson,
the Temple meant solitude in a dusty set of chambers up
a flight of dustier stairs.

Nor was he, as at school, distracted and occupied by
the routine of daily work. In the Temple there was no
routine, and very little work. He was without briefs;
and such work as he chose to do he could do when he
liked and how he liked. None of this would have mat-
tered if he could have cared for his profession, if he
could have looked on his present inertia as the inevitable
prelude to an absorbing career. But he had only become
a lawyer because his father had wanted him to; he disliked the subject and showed no talent for it whatsoever.
He used to sit through the long days, with nothing to
do but to brood over his future.

How dark it must have seemed! Cursed from birth,
pursued by misfortune in childhood, he had now taken up
a profession which he hated, and in which he could not
but fail. Yet there was no other that he liked better;
and he was too poor to do nothing at all. Where was he
to look for encouragement? To love? The amiable
sentiment he felt for Theodora was not serious or passionate enough to take him out of himself. Was it not
rather another cause of trouble? Physique and poverty
alike might prevent him from marrying her. Nor could
the thought of his friends much console him. What did
the most intimate friend know of the viewless maladies
of the soul? And how could he heal them if he did know

of them? The very classics lost their power to appeal
to Cowper. He began to hate himself for the value he
had set on these stony pagan pages.

As the months dragged on his depression deepened to
anguish. With extravagant self-deprecation he cursed
his weakness and incompetence. But his old sense that
fate was his enemy made him hopeless of curing himself
of them. In the lonely silence of his chambers he cried
aloud in his misery. At last he turned to religion. It
had helped him once, it might help him again. But religion he approached shaken by all the terrors of a conscience that felt he had neglected it. As he nerved himself
to face a righteous God, his poor, pitiful little sins, his
petty schoolboy lies, the Sundays he had not gone to
church, assumed in his mind the proportions of great
crimes. But God was always merciful; He cared for
the poor in spirit, the failures, those for whom the world
was too hard. Perhaps He would listen to him if he
were sorry for his great sinfulness. He flung himself
upon his knees; but his spirit was too numb to pray.
Like Christina Rossetti, he longed for a heart of flesh
instead of a heart of stone. He could not feel; he could
only suffer.

One day he picked up a book of George Herbert's.
The language was "rude and Gothick." Yet the spirit
of fresh, untroubled piety that arose from the pages
stole into his heart, and breathed there the first whispers
of that spiritual consolation that more direct methods
had been unable to entice. He was still in torture; but
these simple verses, like a cold compress on an aching
wound, brought momentary alleviation, and taught him
to hope once more. From them he learned of a world
innocent and secure, where the light of faith shone
steadily, unshaken by storms; where, across the little

fields, the bells called clearly to church beneath a serene
sky. Herbert taught him that the state of mind he
longed to attain was attainable by a human being. Under
his influence he grew more composed; his heart warmed
and softened; he felt he could pray once more. For
twelve months he lived in the Temple alone, fleeing the
world; still convinced that he was fated to misery, but
deriving a little comfort from a self-appointed régime
of devotion; praying, writing prayers, reading Herbert.

It was an odd life for a young man of twenty-one. A
great deal too odd it seemed to one of his relations who
came to see how he was. With a misunderstanding of
the situation typical of the anxious relative, he attributed
all the trouble to Herbert, and urged Cowper to put the
book away. "It encourages all that is worst in your
condition," he said. In reality it had so far improved
Cowper's condition that he was able to leave the Temple
to go on a visit to Southampton with a Mr. Thomas
Hesketh, who was engaged to his cousin Harriet.

Cowper's disgust with life did not disappear at once.
But insensibly it grew more bearable. For one thing,
he could not feel so gloomy in the country. His mind
was unable to concentrate on its own woe, as it could
in the stuffy solitudes of the Temple, if he was out all
day rambling on the cliffs or lounging on the hard sands.
He could not lie awake all night in restless self-torment
if he went to bed filled with that delicious aching lassitude that comes from a day spent in the open air. And
his companions were most tonic in their influence. Mr.
Hesketh used to take "meo considine," as he called Cowper, bathing and sailing. Cowper liked the bathing better than the sailing. He wore sailor's trousers and tried
to enter into the spirit of the thing; but he felt cramped.
Still, even this distracted his mind from more ethereal

woes. With Harriet, who joined them, Cowper used to walk and read and incessantly to talk. His spirits began to rise. The life which he now led, the pleasant prosaic summer holiday, full of small events and fundamental peace, provided a sort of counter-attack to his mental terrors. How could he feel that he was the lonely victim of an awful fate when he was animatedly discussing the most agreeable "scheme" for passing the next day with Harriet and Mr. Hesketh? And as the ordinary daylight of the mental atmosphere surrounded him, his fears began to appear the insubstantial figments of a diseased brain.

One day after he had been in Hampshire for a few weeks a decisive change came. It was a beautiful cloudless day, and he had walked out to a hill overlooking the sea. Suddenly, silently, as at the bidding of a divine gesture, the clouds that had hung over his mind for so long that they had come to seem an inevitable condition of existence rolled away, and the sun shone out in a clear sky. Sitting there, his cheek caressed by the salt breeze, and far below him the shimmering sea, he was overcome with an indescribable sense of peace. Awful as the period of its dominion had been, his melancholy had not lasted for ever. It was not invincible, it could not ultimately stand between him and happiness. How could he ever thank the God who had not left him comfortless? A gush of intense emotion, in which exaltation, gratitude and an exquisite sense of relief mingled like instruments in an orchestra, welled up in his heart and filled his eyes with tears.

As the days went on his troubles dwindled to still smaller proportions in his mind. He felt that they had been too trivial to be dignified by the name of spiritual; they were the result of some physical weakness. Ac-

centuated by his cloistered life in the Temple, they had
been banished by a change of air and scene. If he could
lead a more normal existence, see more people and have
more occupation he could easily keep them from troub-
ling him. His spirits rose higher every day. He laughed
with Harriet till his sides ached; and after a few cheerful
months drove back to London, burned the prayers he
had written, and sallied out to find his friends.

The fit was past. Once again, as at school, the vitality
of youth had routed the shadowy battalions of his
nervous fears. And he now hoped that by resolutely
averting his mind from such subjects he could keep them
at bay for ever. Sometimes when he was alone in his
chambers dark thoughts would begin to steal back into
his mind. Hurriedly he would take up his pen and paper
and begin a letter:

> 'Tis not that I presume to rob
> Thee of thy birthright, gentle Bob, . . .
> That I presume to address the muse;
> But to divert a fierce banditti
> (Sworn foes to everything that's witty),
> That, with a black infernal train,
> Make cruel inroads on my brain,
> And daily threaten to drive thence
> My little garrison of sense:
> The fierce banditti that I mean
> Are gloomy thoughts led on by spleen.

That was what he must hold on to. His gloomy thoughts
had no rational foundation; they were the result of
spleen.

For the moment this method of dealing with them was
successful enough. The dark mists that had shrouded
his spirit were dissipated. Already beside the sunny

realities of his holiday life they had shrunk to a cloud
no bigger than a man's hand. A varied existence of
work and play, with no time left for moping, would surely make them vanish altogether. Perhaps after a few
busy, happy, normal years he would look back on his
troubles of 1751 as a trivial green sickness of nerves,
such as any young man might pass through in the difficult
first years of maturity. Perhaps——

# CHAPTER II

MADNESS

> "September 2nd, 1762.
> "YOUR letter has taken me just in the crisis; to-morrow
> I set off for Brighthelmstone, and there I stay till work
> brings all to town again. The world is a shabby fellow
> and uses us ill: but a few years hence there will be no dif-
> ference between us and our fathers of the tenth genera-
> tion upwards. I could be as splenetic as you, and with
> more reason . . . but my resolution is never to be
> melancholic while I have a £100 in the world to keep
> up my spirits. God knows how long that will be, but in
> the meantime 10 Triumphe! If a great man struggling
> with misfortunes is a noble object, a little one who de-
> spises them is no contemptible one; and that is all the
> philosophy I have in the world at present. . . . Did you
> ever know a man who was guided in the general course
> of his actions by anything but his natural temper? And
> yet we blame each other's conduct as freely as if that
> temper was the most tractable beast in the world, and
> we had nothing to do but to twitch the rein to the right
> or the left. . . . This is a strange epistle, nor can I
> imagine how the devil I came to write it; but here it is,
> such as it is, and much good may you do with it. I have
> no estate, as it happens, so if it should fall into bad
> hands I shall be in no danger of a commission of lunacy.
> Adieu.
>
> > "Yours ever,
> > "WILLIAM COWPER."

*The Stricken Deer*

The Cowper who sat writing these words to his friend, Clotworthy Rowley, was now thirty-one. With the passage of time his features had set: the mold of the big nose and the fine lips was now defined; little lines of laughter had drawn themselves at the corner of mouth and eyes. But otherwise he and his situation had altered little. He was still in the Temple, still without briefs, still as far from real peace of mind as before. Indeed, Clotworthy Rowley, or any one else who cared to read between the lines of this letter of September, could see that it was written by a man who, for all his boasted stoicism, was profoundly discouraged about life.

Of course he was never likely to shake himself free from a constitutional depression by simply refusing to think about it; for that method left the roots of his melancholy untouched. He was still afraid of it. Occupy himself as he might, he could not rid himself of the unspoken conviction that he was diverting his mind from a dark tangle of horrible shadows, which he must not think of lest it should make him mad. And his fears were still mysterious fears. He had never had the courage to turn them out and examine them in the light of day; so he had never been able to reconstruct his scheme of existence to include and control them. They remained anomalous to it, a nameless blackness whose origin he had not traced and whose powers he could not gage. As long as they kept quiet he was happy enough; but if they became active he understood them too little and feared them too much to do anything but succumb.

Yet they would only keep quiet as long as his life was untroubled. For as he had made no rational attempt to discover their true strength, his only weapon against them was to maintain a cheerful vigor—vigor in the light of which mental terrors appeared trivial and without substance. To a temperament like Cowper's such a mood was only possible as long as his horizon was unclouded. But the perspective of his past life down which he gazed as he leaned back in his armchair in the Temple room was a gray one, undisturbed by any shattering grief, but unillumined by any lasting joy—an image of failure, of vacuity, of the sad futile fleetingness of human life.

In 1756 he lost his father, and with him the last link that bound him to his happy childhood, to his mother and the green meadows of Berkhamstead. He went down to the funeral. "Then, and not till then," he wrote, "I felt for the first time that I and my native place were disunited forever. I sighed a long adieu to fields and woods from which I once thought I should never be parted, and was never so sensible of their beauties as when I left them all behind me to return no more."

He had lost Theodora. The long courtship had dragged on two years, three years, four years, and at the end her father, for reasons of health or of money, had said that it could not be. Perhaps they had never expected it would come to anything. But it had been a delicious dream while it lasted. Now the dream was broken, and it seemed to Cowper that he must for ever climb life's rough path alone. He had loved her, and she had adored him; but their stars were contrary, and they must part. And with Theodora went the chief charm of that sunny life in Southampton Row which had proved itself so sturdy a bulwark against his melancholy.

He turned more and more to his men friends. Within a year Russell, closest of all since Westminster days, was accidentally drowned. This third blow struck Cowper hard. Friendship without intimacy meant nothing to him; and it seemed as if fate was determined to deprive

him of all those with whom he was intimate. He be-
came moody and silent, and unable to talk in company.
"Doomed as I am in solitude," he wrote to Harriet
Hesketh, "To waste

> The present moment and regret the past
> Deprived of every joy I value most,
> My friend torn from me and my mistress lost:
> Call not this gloom I wear, this anxious mien,
> The dull effect of humour or of spleen.
> Still, still I mourn with each returning day
> Him snatched by fate in early youth away
> And her through tedious years of doubt and pain
> Fixed in her choice and faithful—but in vain."

That was five years ago now, and time had a little
dulled the edge of his grief. But he had never altogether recovered his spirits; and lately a more mundane
trouble had begun to disturb him. Cowper had never
been rich; now he was becoming poorer. And poverty,
though it may not be so desolating at any given moment
as the loss of friends, is more persistently worrying to
the nerves. It shuts one in on every side. If Cowper
felt downcast he could not go abroad or keep open house
at home. He was not rich enough.

But the difficulties imposed by having little money now
were nothing compared to those raised by having less in
the future. He was not luxurious, and, like all timid
people, he could easily learn to put up with any sort of
life if he felt it to be safe and certain. But he was
proportionately more upset by not knowing what was
going to happen to him. He must find some way of in-
creasing his income. But what? He had been a failure
as a lawyer. He loathed it, and had never tried to work

at it properly. Perhaps if he made an effort now—but at the thought a sort of impotence seized him. The more important he felt it to be that he should work, the less he seemed able to do it. He had followed the idle bendings of his inclination so long, had become such a slave to chance desire, that he could not make himself work regularly—especially if it was at something he disliked. Indeed, though he did not realize it, lack of regular work was one of the subtlest causes of his depression.

If you are working hard all day at a given task you can not become the victim of your own moods. You are just part of a machine; and if you are to perform your function properly you must attend to it, and not to your own mental condition. This forcible diversion from your own thoughts saves you from succumbing to them; it clamps you to reality. But if, like Cowper, you have no regular work, you judge the value of all you do or see by what you feel about it. Nothing has any objective value, outside the emotional response it rouses in you. And as the same emotional response can never be aroused for long by the same stimulus, nothing seems to have a constant, solid value on which you can rely. Life flits by you without purpose or arrangement, like a series of airy pictures, that must not be looked at too closely lest they should fade.

And without regular occupation the will, too, ceases to function. You lose the habit of making yourself do something at a definite time, with the consequence that when an occasion arises when it is necessary to act at once, the spring of action is rusty and will not move. Cowper simply was not able to work at law. But he felt he was getting too old for anything else.

And this reflection merged in a more general and a

more fundamental melancholy, born of the flight of youth. Youth can not take a consistently pessimistic view of its lot, for it thinks of its mode of existence, not as real life, but as the preparation for it. So that, however much it may deplore the present, it is hopeful about the future, which must be different, and will probably be pleasanter. But with maturity hope begins to flag. One has grown up and settled to a profession and made one's friends, and the course one's life will wend is clear before one. If one is still weighed down by the burdens of youth, it seems likely that one will carry them to the grave. Cowper was now thirty-one; he had been ten years a member of his profession. And he had as much experience as falls to many men in their whole lifetime. He had lived in a great capital; he had made many friends; he was a scholar; he had loved. But he had found no lasting source of happiness, and the lack of confidence that had tormented him in youth was as strong at thirty-one as at twenty-one.

Nor could he hope to throw it off as he had hoped then. When he had come back to London in 1754, in high feather at recovering from his first fit of despair, he had thrown himself into a thousand activities: written poems, pamphlets, political ballads; founded a dining club, the "Nonsense Club"; contributed to a magazine, the *Connoisseur*. How his heart had swelled when Wolfe took Quebec! How it had beaten with admiration and excitement when he first read Sir Charles Grandison! But now his interest in books, in social life, in political events seemed nothing but a vain attempt to fill a life essentially futile and void. They moved him when they were new and he was young; but in the clear sunless light of advancing age he began to see how little real hold they had on him. His youth was over,

and he had done nothing. He began to wonder if he
ever would. One evening, drinking tea with Thurlow,
now a successful lawyer, he suddenly exclaimed, "Thurlow, I'm nobody, and I shall always be nobody, and you
will be Lord Chancellor."

He loathed himself for his ineffectiveness. And yet
he could not feel he was really to blame. He had tried
to do what he thought right as hard as most men he
knew. But Fate had been against him. It was a thought
that struck a responsive chord in the deepest fibers of
his nature. His old distrust of destiny revived with a
doubled and compelling force. It had never been wholly
latent. At twenty-one, in the first rosy dawn of his love
for Theodora, he could write to her

> Fated to ills beyond redress,
>   We must endure our woe;
> The days allowed us to possess
>   'Tis madness to forego.

And his experience since then had confirmed his gloomiest
forebodings. One by one the objects on which he had set
his affections had borne sad witness to the nature of their
mortality. His mother was dead, Russell was dead, his
home was sold, Theodora lost to him for ever, and youth
itself was passing. Nor were his present prospects
brighter. He was poor, and seemed likely to become
poorer; he had failed in his profession; yet he felt incapable of making an effort at that or anything else.
Fate had dogged his footsteps with disaster. Fate had
created him powerless to drive it away.

He should, as in 1752, have sought consolation in his
religion. But, unluckily, religion had become nothing but
an added sort of discomfort to him. As at school, he
felt that he did not live up to it sufficiently to be rewarded

for it. If Christian doctrine was true, then in order to be saved one ought to dedicate oneself to the Christian life. But he lived a life which, though not vicious, was solely concerned with the ambitions and pleasures of the world. Nor did he feel equal to changing it now. In spite of his theoretical acceptance of orthodox Christianity, it had not since 1752 been able to raise the feeblest spark of response in his emotions. He made the worst of both worlds. He passionately wished religion to be true, as only by its help could he extricate himself from the ruthless mechanism of Nature. But if it was true, then his neglect of its precepts was in a fair way to lead him to eternal perdition.

Noisily and persistently, almost as if he wished to persuade himself that he was as sure of them as he said he was, he would assert his beliefs amid companions infected with the skepticism fashionable among intellectual young men of the period. One evening when he had defended the austere tenets of the Church till late into the night over the guttering candles and the wine-stained cloth, the man he was addressing said with a note of asperity, "Well, if what you say is true, you are damned by your own showing." At these words an access of self-loathing swept over him. What a contemptible creature he was! Unable to do right, able only to talk about it, and to render his views ridiculous by his inability to act on them. God Himself had called him, yet he could not tear himself away from pleasures he did not really enjoy to follow the call.

As he ruthlessly scanned his life, his self-disgust attached itself not to spiritual shortcomings alone, it merged into a general revulsion from his whole moral character. Had he been a professing hedonist he would not have been so unhappy. His life, though confined, was peaceful; he could enjoy the passing hour and wander at his will. Indeed, his nerves were too fragile to stand a career of strenuous well-doing. But the Puritan ideas among which he had grown up, and to which, it must be admitted, he had taken only too readily, taught him that no moment of one's existence is justified unless it furthers a moral purpose. His moral ideals were too high for his nervous system; with the consequence that he lived in a state of war with his own nature, disapproving of it as it was, but without power or inclination to turn it into what he thought it ought to be.

If he could only have faith, if he could be actively convinced of the truth of the Gospel, he felt he might be able to change his life. But at the thought of making any effort to induce it his distrust of destiny crept in and blighted his spiritual, as it blighted his material, hopes. Perhaps he was doomed not to believe. Fate was against him in this world; would not Fate be against him in the next? He brushed the idea aside, but it had made religion a painful subject to him. Like his past and his future and his own character, it was one of those things he must try not to think about.

It is over religion, above all, that people nowadays so often fail to understand a past age. Their historical imagination fails them. They can not, as it were, fit the religious pieces into the rest of the evidence about a historical character so as to make up a convincing human being. Cowper's religious ideas seem to them incongruous both with the period he lived in and with the other sides of his own personality. His letters, were they not so well written, might be written to-day. They reveal a character as educated, as sensitive and as complex as our own. We do not feel, as we do when we open a medieval, or even a Renaissance book, that we have left the ordinary daylight of modern life for another atmosphere, alien, crude and mysterious. Yet suddenly Cowper will make a remark revealing that in some respects his ideas are those of the Middle Ages, literal, limited, anthropomorphic. He sees nothing improbable in prophetic dreams and special providences; he believes he is deliberately pursued by a conscious and malevolent fate.

But human beings were quite as consistent then as they are now. It is just in their attitude toward such subjects that the difference between them and us lies. Their view of the physical world was still that held in the Middle Ages. They believed in a fixed order of the universe. Theists and atheists alike thought that the world and everything in it was originally created exactly the same as it is now, except in so far as the conscious reason of man has impelled him to alter it. If this were generally assumed, their very rationalism would lead them to think that such a complex scheme of things must be the deliberate creation of a conscious Will. And if every individual man is the result of an act of conscious Will, it seems likely that that Will will continue to follow and control his destiny.

But since the eighteenth century the developments of natural science have completely altered that conception of the nature of the universe which, vague and unquestioned, underlies the ideas of the average person. The earth is conceived of as a minute atom, among millions of other atoms, evolving from no one knows what, in a manner no one knows how, and in a direction no one knows whither; while man himself, sadly fallen from his former dignity, is become merely an animal, like other animals, a late, haphazard and ephemeral development of some automatic principle of life unknown.

The consequence is that religious ideas are now confined to religion. His reason working on his usual assumptions about life no longer leads a man to search for a religious explanation of any phenomenon he does not understand. But it did in the eighteenth century. The visitation of God seemed to him the most probable explanation of an epidemic, as defective sanitation might seem the most probable explanation to us. A hundred and fifty years ago even those who rejected Christianity believed in a first cause. Voltaire himself would have been surprised at some of the views held by an orthodox clergyman of the Church of England in 1930. Cowper's conviction of God's personal interest in him, and his fears of immediate damnation if he disregarded it, may have been morbid, but they were not unreasonable. And they were perfectly consistent with the conception of the cosmos held by every one of his day.

With the failure of religion the last solid ground between him and disillusionment split and subsided. Whichever way he looked he saw no stable fact or idea to which he could pin his hopes or on which he could build his life. Love, youth, friendship, the things of the mind, the things of the body, they all passed. Nothing was constant but his disillusionment and the dim fears that for ever prowled in the background of his consciousness.

For experience that had destroyed his belief in the reality of everything else had left these untouched. Indeed, it had laid him more open to their attack. He could no longer restore his inner life to its true proportion in the scheme of things by comparing it to the world outside. For in his present mood he could no more use the world outside as a standard by which to measure the reality of his inner experience than he could use a cloud as a standard to measure the size of a building. He believed in the actuality of nothing but himself, the secret drama of his own soul; and about that nothing could seem incredible.

He was not acutely miserable, but he was without a moment of genuine happiness. Sometimes for a short time, as he sat at his open window and watched the branches feathery against the sky and listened to the water splashing and gurgling from the pumps in the court below, he could fancy he was in the country, and be for a little soothed. But when he turned back into his dingy room, the dreary realities of life would sweep back into his mind again, all the more painful for his moment of forgetfulness.

He used to try to comfort himself with trite maxims: "Never despair," "The best way to meet misfortune is to scorn it." But he did not believe them, and he knew he did not. Was he not painfully aware that the only strong feeling left in him was superstitious fear of the future? The army of his thoughts kept a semblance of marching order. But their morale was gone. At any shock they would become a rout.

Such, as far as we can judge, were the main facts of his mental condition at thirty-one. And they must be kept in mind if we are to have any understanding of the terrible, the momentous events that followed. Cowper had reached the turning-point of his life. In a short ten months his personality was to undergo a change only less catastrophic than death. The nervous, scholarly barrister of the Temple was to die in a lurid agony of despair and madness, and be born anew in another place, stripped of worldly possessions and worldly interests, but strong, single-minded and sustained by inspiration from an unseen world.

This is the fact, the astounding, terrific fact. But the process of its accomplishment is mysterious. Tracing a man's history through the records time and chance have left to us is like reading a novel from which important pages have been torn out at random. Characters appear in the front of the stage; clearly they are to play some significant part in the story; but the next pages are missing, and when we take up the tale again these characters have left it for ever. A few years pass blank and unmentioned. Suddenly a brilliant light is turned on to the scene. We see the chief persons at a crucial moment in their lives; every detail of their every day is revealed with the graphic meticulousness of truth. But before we have realized the full purport of the drama the light is withdrawn as suddenly as it appeared, and we see no more.

In vain we scan the imperfect records left to us in an effort to understand the real origin of Cowper's catastrophe: the slim volume of confessions he wrote when he recovered; a few chance references in later letters; a handful of gossip collected from contemporaries by his first biographers. But though some episodes are lit up in vivid detail, though the mystery is checkered by many gleams, clues to revelation, we never see the event in the round, are never certain that we have had a full view of all its features. We must guess, draw our conclusions, put two and two together, if our portrait of Cowper is to have that completeness which is as necessary to history as to other arts. But it is a difficult task; much of the evidence makes the event not less, but more mysterious. The ostensible causes seem so much too slight to have produced so great a catastrophe. It is here that a realization of Cowper's nervous condition helps us. This condition was already such as to make some catastrophe inevitable. As we have seen, any shock would be enough to upset him altogether; and it was impossible that he should live an ordinary life in an ordinary world without experiencing some sort of shock some time. His inner life was now his only standard of reality, so the most severe shock would be one that stirred up his inner fears. And thus it might well be given by some event that will appear trivial to the outside observer.

It was, in fact, given by an effort to relieve the most pressing of his cares. By the convenient system of government appointment prevalent in the eighteenth century, his cousin, Major Cowper, had the right to present to the post of Clerk of the House of Lords and to those of Reading Clerk and Clerk of Committees to the House of Commons; and he had always promised to offer one or more of them to Cowper. This promise had been Cowper's one hope of improving his financial position, and he had often laughingly lamented the long life of their present occupants, and said how he wished they would die. Now at last one of them did; while soon after, the other two resigned. And one February morning his cousin arrived in Cowper's chambers, offered him both the Clerkship of Committees and the Reading Clerkship, the two most lucrative of all the posts within his presentation.

It was the end of Cowper's financial troubles, and it should have awakened a glow of happiness in his heart. But, strangely, it did not. He returned to his rooms filled with a sense of anticlimax, of doubt, even of depression. A thousand difficulties began to trouble his mind. What would be expected of him in his new occupation? Would he be equal to it? Did he deserve it? And here his conscience, inflamed by years of introspection, began to worry him. He remembered that he had wished for the poor Clerk's death in order that he might take his place; and now he had died, and he was going to. He felt that he was no better than a murderer. No good could come of an advantage gained in such circumstances. He longed to ask his cousin for the House of Lords Clerkship instead of the other two, even though it was worth less. But this idea brought its attendant anxiety. If he took the less lucrative post, people might accuse his cousin of keeping the others back in order to sell them to the highest bidder; he would be injuring his own benefactor.

In spite of this, after some weeks of painful indecision he made up his mind to ask him. But though Major Cowper lived just over the way, Cowper did not go to see him, but wrote him a long letter explaining what he wanted. It was granted. And for a moment Cowper felt relieved, even hopeful. It was not for long. The anxiety he had experienced was far too unreasonable to be stilled by the mere removal of its occasion. The conscience that made itself guilty of the Clerk's death, the state of mind that led him to compose an elaborate letter to a relation living next door, were not likely to leave their possessor long at rest. After the first sensation of relief had worn off Cowper began to grow as anxious about his new post as he had been about his old.

And, unlucky day, circumstances now arose which gave him a legitimate cause for anxiety. The Clerkship of the House of Lords had especially attracted Cowper, as he could take it up without passing a public test or in any way exhibiting his shrinking figure before the eyes of strangers. But in the summer of 1763 he was horror-stuck to hear rumors that a party hostile to his family connection was forming against them, and was ready to go to any length to get the Cowper nominee rejected. The rumor proved true, and the intrigues of this mysterious party succeeded in persuading whatever authority decided such things to decree that the candidates for the Clerkship must pass a public examination. Picture Cowper's horror. He had always been agonizingly shy in public, and now if he was to retrieve his fallen fortunes and be a credit to his benefactor he must stand up and submit to a *viva voce* examination by the whole House of Lords: a House of Lords many of whose members would be trying to trip him up in favor of another candidate. All the chords of his nervous system, already stretched to breaking-point during the last few years, were set trembling and vibrating. His fatalism convinced him he would fail. His inability to work stopped him from acquiring the information required to prevent his failing; his horror of the unknown conjured up a thousand new obstacles which the opposing party might put in his way; while the fear of persecution, latent in him since Market Street, filled him with panic at the very fact of opposition.

He had little reason to feel it. He would have to prove utterly ignorant before his cousin's choice could be quashed, and it would be quite easy for any man of sense to learn what was required in five months. But Cowper was no longer a man of sense. He could not sleep, he could not think, he could not work. The journal books in which he was to be examined were thrown open to him, and every day he went down to the office to read them. The clerks there were in his opponents' interest, and did nothing to help him; but he was far too agitated to have profited by their help had they been willing to offer it. His pulse beating in his ears, his head heavy like lead, he read and reread the same page without understanding a word of it. Every morning when he arrived at the office he said he "had all the sensations of a criminal arriving at the foot of the scaffold." And every morning that passed was a morning nearer the examination.

At last, after three months, remembering his experience of 1752, he decided to try a change of scene, and went to Margate for August and September. For the time being it certainly did do him good. He was practised at putting aside unpleasant thoughts by now, if he was helped by any sort of distraction. As he lay on the sand, watching the irregular line of wave break sparkling, and recede, and break again, as far as eye could reach, his troubled spirit sank into a kind of tranquillity. A mist rose up between him and London. With a heart nominally at peace he lounged on the beach, and walked amid the false Gothic ruins, lancet window and chantry chapel open to the sky, which Lord Holland had erected in the dells of Sandgate Park: absurd castle of Udolpho, where perhaps Charles Fox, a swarthy boy of fifteen, was rambling at the same time—Charles Fox reckless and highhearted; Cowper expectant only of despair.

But his outward agitation alone was stilled; the trouble that caused it was still as formidable to him as before. Though he could put them behind him as long as he was occupied, his sleep was disturbed by bad dreams. And when he woke in the morning and his vitality was low, there was nothing to come between him and his fears, he was in anguish. "I looked forward to the approaching winter," he says, "and regretted the flight of every moment which brought it nearer; like a man borne away by a rapid torrent into a stormy sea where he sees no possibility of returning and where he sees he cannot submit."

How little good Margate had done him became clear the moment he got back to London. When he returned to his work at the House of Lords Office all his old agitation came back, rendered worse by the consciousness that he had tried the only remedy he knew of, and that it had been found wanting. He was in a trap. If he went through with his ordeal he must be publicly humiliated; if he gave it up he would injure a benefactor to whom he owed every gratitude. And a failure in loyalty and affection was especially hateful to him. He felt he would never be able to go through the examination; and yet how decently could he get out of it? Alone in the maddening silence of his chambers, his mind turned round upon itself like a squirrel in a cage.

From henceforward the story is clouded by the smoke, distorted by the lurid light of madness. Horrible hints reach us as to the nature of the fears that tormented him. In the hurricane that was sweeping over him the depths of his personality were stirred up and obscene monsters that had slept there for years came to the surface. He believed, it is said, that his enemies had discovered his secret deformity and were threatening to expose it. It is an unlikely story. How could it help them? Why should such a deformity prevent a man being made Clerk of the House of Lords? On the other hand, there may well have been a more intimate reason for such a catastrophe as overtook him than the mere fear of making an exhibition of himself. And if it is true he was deformed it is possible that, already suffering from some kind of persecution mania, he now associated it with the shameful secret which had done so much to infect him with his fundamental distrust of life.

In his despair he cut himself off from his friends. Aloud in his solitary chambers he cursed the hour of his birth. If he was weak, he was no worse than many other men. He had tried to be good. What had he done to deserve this frightful crucifixion? To ease his pain he began taking drugs. But they only numbed, they did not remove it. And such comfort as they gave was neutralized by the awful awakening, when he looked out wretchedly into the dawn, livid over the Temple roofs, and realized that the relief of the night before had been an illusion.

Once more he turned to prayer. But it was as the last resort of an anguished soul, not as the result of any religious impulse. And the spirit which had been rendered incapable of prayer by the youthful melancholy of 1754 was now far beyond concentration on any world but its own. He soon gave up the attempt.

Physical and spiritual remedies had both failed him. And every day the thought of his examination grew more intolerable. He would never be able to face it, never, never. He would go mad first. And he only hoped madness would come as soon as possible. But day followed day, each more swiftly than the last; and he remained horribly sane, his mind working with exquisite clearness; his sensibilities sharpened to the finest point; his eyes fixed, open and fascinated, upon the doom that was advancing on him. God was even going to refuse him the terrible mercy of madness: he must drink his bitter cup. But he could not, he would not.

And now the idea of suicide began to steal into his thoughts. Death, which had thrown a faint, persistent shadow over his whole outlook on existence ever since he had first realized it in St. Margaret's churchyard twenty years before, now appeared infinitely desirable, a cool dark pool of refuge where he might rest in peace his bruised and burning spirit. The God of his faith had indeed forbidden a man to kill himself. But Cowper's faith had been too much a thing of words, the result rather of a will to believe than of a genuine conviction, to influence his actions in such a crisis. Maybe there was no God. If there was, no hell to which He could consign him could be worse than his present life. But what did he know of God? Perhaps He did not condemn suicide. The great men of antiquity, the idols of that classical scholarship by which all Cowper's young ideas had been molded, had all praised, and some of them committed, it. Why, his own father had not thought it wrong. He remembered well a curious occasion about eighteen years before when his father asked him his opinion on the subject. He had ardently declared against it, but his father had looked at him with a strange expression, and had not applauded what he said. The real reason for this had been that an old friend of Mr. Cowper's had just killed himself, and he did not wish to speak harshly of him. But young Cowper had not known this; and the incident stuck in his mind, and now exercised a powerful effect on his judgment. For he had become so obsessed by one idea that he saw the rest of existence only in relation to it, and its incidents only as arguments for and against self-murder. The slightest fact or the lightest word was to him an indication of that fate predestined for him in Heaven, and against which it was useless for him to struggle.

One evening, at a coffee-house, a gentleman entered into conversation with him and, strangely enough, the conversation turned on suicide. Stranger still, the gentleman, a respectable elderly man, advocated it. Another day, at the little chop-house near the Temple where Cowper took most of his meals, a stranger began to talk to him, and again argued strongly in favor of suicide.

It seemed as if he were being directly pointed to it by some higher power. It could not be by the God of his childhood. But Cowper's very atheism was superstitious. He was so religious by temperament that if he forswore a Christian Providence, it was only to direct his life in accordance with the dictates of some dark amoral totem of his imagination.

These two conversations finally decided him; and one dark evening he went into a chemist's, and in a voice as natural and unconcerned as he was able to muster, asked for laudanum. The chemist looked at him curiously, appeared to hesitate for a moment, and then gave him what he wanted. But there was a week before his examination, and he shrank from taking it at once. For seven long days, alone in his chambers, he waited and waited, his fingers pressed to the cold laudanum bottle in his pocket, hoping that something would happen to stop the examination. But of course it did not. Two days, three days, four days, five days passed; and now before the day after to-morrow he must choose between death and humiliation.

At eight o'clock he woke, threw on his clothes, and dragged himself to Richard's coffee-house to get some breakfast. He picked up a newspaper. The first thing on which his eyes rested was a letter advocating suicide. This last touch was too much for his already tottering self-control. It seemed to him that the author must have known of his case and was writing about it. Crying out, "Your cruelty shall be gratified, you shall have your revenge," he rushed from the room. He meant to go to the deserted fields that lay round London in order to put an end to himself in some ditch. But before he had gone far his mind began to waver. There was no necessity for him to die. He could sell what he had in the funds in a few hours and take a boat for France, there become a Roman Catholic and, cutting himself absolutely off from England, pass the rest of his life in the cloistered peace of a monastery.

He hurried back to his chambers to pack; but he had hardly got back when his mind underwent a reaction. His thoughts fell back into their former proportion and he felt that only death could assure him of peace. It could only be cowardice that had stopped him before, that cowardice which was perhaps the most hateful and contemptible of all the weaknesses that had dogged him throughout his mortal life. He must kill himself at once. But again a wave of indecision swept him. Where should he do it? He was sure to be interrupted in his chambers. He made up his mind to take a coach to Tower Wharf and do it there. But when he arrived, the first object he saw was a porter seated waiting on a pile of goods, as if sent there to prevent him. He got back into the coach and told the driver to go back to the Temple.

"I drew up the shutters," he writes, "once more had recourse to the laudanum and did determine to drink it off directly, but God had otherwise ordained. A conflict that shook me to pieces suddenly took place, not properly trembling, but a convulsive agitation which deprived me in a manner of the use of my limbs, and my mind was as much shaken as my body. Distracted between the desire of death and the dread of it, twenty times I had the phial to my mouth and as often received an irresistible check, and even at the time it seemed to me that an invisible hand swayed the bottle downwards. I well remember that I took notice of this circumstance with some surprise, though it effected no change in my purpose. Panting for breath and in a horrible agony, I flung myself back into the corner of the coach. A few drops of laudanum, which had touched my lips, besides the fumes of it, began to have a stupefying effect on me. Regretting the loss of so fair an opportunity, yet utterly unable to avail myself of it, I determined not to live; and already half dead with anguish, returned to the Temple. Instantly I repaired to my room, and having shut both the inner and the outer doors, prepared myself for the last scene of the tragedy. I poured the laudanum into a small basin, set it on a chair by the bedside, half undressed myself, and lay down between the blankets, shuddering with horror at what I was about to perpetrate —I reproached myself bitterly with rank cowardice at having suffered the pain of death to influence me as it had done, but still something seemed to over-rule me and to say 'Think what you are doing, consider and live.' At length, however, with the most confirmed resolution, I reached forth my hand towards the basin, when the fingers of both hands were as closely contracted as if bound with a cord, and became entirely useless. Still, indeed, I could have made shift with both hands, dead and lifeless as they were, to have raised the basin to my mouth, for my arms were not at all affected, but this new difficulty struck me with wonder; it had the air of a divine interposition. I lay down in bed to muse upon it, and while thus employed heard the key turn in the outer door, and my laundress's husband came in. By this time the use of my fingers was restored to me. I started up hastily, dressed myself, hid the basin, and affecting as composed an air as I could, walked out into the dining-room. In a few minutes I was left alone. The man had just shut the door behind him when a total alteration in my sentiments took place. The horror of the crime was immediately exhibited to me in so strong a light that, being seized with a kind of furious indignation, I snatched up the basin, poured away the laudanum into a phial of foul water, and not content with that, flung the phial out of the window. . . . The sense of the enormity of the crime which I had just experienced soon entirely left me."

Day dawned, chill November day; and now there was only one more night between Cowper and his examination. He still meant to kill himself, for there seemed no other way of escape. But the mental torture which he had undergone the previous night had left him for the moment without the power of doing anything. His mind dazed, his nerves numb, he passed the day in a stupor of misery. Automatically he got up, dressed himself, took his meals, went out, came in again. The sun rose, reached its zenith, declined, set: there were only twelve hours left.

"That evening a most intimate friend called upon me, and felicitated me upon a happy resolution which he heard I had taken, to stand the brunt and keep the office. I knew not whence this intelligence arose, but did not contradict it. We conversed a while with a real cheerfulness on his part and an affected one on my own; and when he left me I said in my heart, 'I shall see thee no more.' I went to bed as I thought to take my last sleep in this world. I slept as usual, and woke about three o'clock. Immediately I arose and, by the help of a rushlight, found my penknife, took it into bed with me, and lay with it for some hours, directly pointed against my heart. Twice or thrice I placed it upright under my left breast, leaning all my weight upon it: but the point was broken off and would not penetrate. In this manner the time passed till the day began to break. I heard the clock strike seven, and instantly it occurred to me there was no time to be lost: the chambers would soon be opened, and my friend would call upon me to take me with him to Westminster. Now is the time, thought I, no more dallying with love of life. I arose and as I thought bolted the inner door of my chambers. I was mistaken. My touch deceived me, and I left it as I found it. Not one hesitating thought now remained, and I fell greedily to the execution of my purpose. My garter was made of a broad scarlet binding, with a sliding buckle being sewn together at the ends: by the help of the buckle I made a noose and fixed it about my neck, straining it so tight that I hardly left a passage for my breath, or for the blood to circulate. At each corner of the bed was placed a wreath of carved work, fastened by an iron pin. The other part of the garter which made a loop I slipped over one of these and hung by it some seconds, drawing up my feet under me that they might not touch the floor; but the iron bent, the carved work slipped off and the garter with it. I then fastened it round the frame of the tester, winding it round and tying it in a strong knot; the frame broke short and let me down again. The third effort was more likely to succeed. I set the door open, which reached within a foot of the ceiling, and by the help of a chair I could command the top of it, and the loop being large enough to admit a large angle of the door, was easily fixed so as not to slip off again. I pushed away the chair with my feet and hung my full length. While I hung there I distinctly heard a voice say three times, ' 'Tis over.' Though I am sure of the fact, it did not alarm me. I hung so long I lost all sense, all consciousness of existence. When I came to myself again I thought I was in Hell: the sound of my own dreadful groans was all that I heard, and a feeling like that of flashes was just beginning to seize upon my body. In a few seconds I found myself fall over with my face to the floor." In a minute or two he rose, stumbled across the room and flung himself on the bed. He did not try to kill himself again.

Indeed, his attempts had not been very successful. It was worthy of notice that either his decision weakened just when it should have been put into effect, or when at last he was forced to take action he was unable to carry it through. In later years he put this sequence of failure down to the hand of God, who had always intervened, as he thought, to save him from committing a mortal sin. But at the bottom his horror of death was as strong as ever, and except in moments of intensest agony, when anything seemed preferable to what he was going through, he never can really have meant to do it. There was no reason why he should not have killed himself in his chambers. But his whole being revolted from the act, and he unconsciously invented some excuse so as not to have to do it. And at the last, when he finally decided on death, his hand faltered. To return to the story. The laundress had heard him fall, and now came in to see if he had been seized with a sudden fit. "I sent her to a friend, to whom I had related the whole affair, and despatched unto my kinsman at the coffee-house. As soon as the latter arrived, I pointed to the broken garter which lay in the middle of the room; and apprized him also of the attempt I had been making. His words were, 'My dear Mr. Cowper, you terrify me. To be sure you can't hold the office at this rate. Where is the deputation?' I gave him the key of the drawers where it was deposited. He took it away with him, and thus ended all my connection with the Parliament house."

The fear which had tormented him since July was removed. But it had provided the single shock needed to overturn the tottering structure of his nervous system. And once it was overturned the harm was done. He was deranged; and the removal of any extraneous cause for his mania only forced him to search for another in himself. It was not difficult to find one. As often happens after a great strain, he was seized with a violent revulsion from the act he had tried to perform. His superstitious terror, his consciousness of sin, the fear of God's wrath which had tormented him since Westminster, overwhelmed him as never before when he thought of the crime he had so nearly succeeded in committing. And the horror he felt was even more unbearable than his horror at the prospect of examination from the House of Lords. That had only made him feel that he was predestined to unhappiness in this world; this shut him off from hope in the next as well. With every advantage of upbringing, and no real provocation, he had deliberately tried to commit the heinous sin of self-murder, the sort of sin he had read about in the lives of great criminals and shuddered at when a child. Damnation, probable before, was now certain. He was the deserving object of God's righteous wrath, a reprobate from whom any decent man would shrink in disgust.

He began to fancy they did. Roaming wild-eyed about the streets, he would sometimes come across an acquaintance, and it seemed to his suspicious eye that he was avoiding him; or, if not, he read covert allusions to his sin into every sentence he spoke. And as he turned his back surely did he not hear him break into a peal of mocking laughter. Nor was it only his acquaintance whom he suspected. As he listened to the ragged ballad-singers who filled the streets with their strident shouting, he began to imagine that they, too, were speaking of him, that his sin was the chief among the tales of sordid crime they were crying for sale. The whole world knew about him, the whole world was against him, the whole world mocked him. And he deserved every bit he got.

Sometimes he tried to distract himself by reading. But even the voices of the dead accused him. He opened Tillotson's *Sermons*, to find a reference to the barren fig-tree. As he read it seemed to him that the parable must have been written about him. In his thirty-three years what had he produced but leaves—showy, rustling leaves of good intention, but never the fruit of works? And how had he been cursed? Another day he picked up a volume of Beaumont and Fletcher's plays that was lying on the window-sill. His eyes wandered over the page and was caught by the line:

> The justice of the gods is in it.

Surely words so applicable to his own case could not be there by chance. No; God had damned him, and God was announcing it to him through every one of His created works.

Brooding day after day on his past existence, gradually its purport became clear to him. Like the rest of mankind, he had been offered the choice between good and evil, between the world and God. From childhood he had chosen the world. But God, in His particular mercy, had made one last effort. He had plunged him in a melancholy when he was twenty-one, had turned his thoughts to religion, and filled him with the divine grace. After this supreme favor Cowper had, with open eyes, returned to wallowing in his mire. Now he was reaping his punishment. For the last ten years he had been increasingly anxious about his spiritual condition; but had beaten down his fears. At last, bereft of false consolation, he saw himself as he was.

His last ray of hope was dispelled by a dream. He thought he was standing in the nave of Westminster Abbey. From within the choir came the sound of the organ, and the ethereal voices of the choir-boys uplifted in a hymn. He walked up in order to join in the service. When he reached the door of the choir the iron gates were clanged in his face; and he awoke. Such a dream could only be a message of his damnation. He must drag on his life, more unbearable than physical torture, till death should consign him to an eternity compared with which all pains of present existence would seem pleasurable. Spasms of terror ran through him, so acute that sometimes he could not stand, but staggered about the room like a drunken man; for a moment he could see nothing but darkness, and then, as it were, whorls and tongues of leaping flame.

Seated at that writing-table where in other days he had penned urbane articles for the papers, playful letters to Harriet, with trembling hand he now poured out in a strange Sapphic meter the torrent of his anguish.

> Hatred and vengeance, my eternal portion
> Scarce can endure delay of execution,
> Wait with impatient readiness to seize my
>     Soul in a moment.

> Damned below Judas ; more abhorred than he was,
> Who for a few pence sold his holy Master!
> Twice betrayed, Jesus me, the last delinquent,
>     Deems the profanest.

> Man disavows, and Deity disowns me,
> Hell might afford my miseries a shelter;
> Therefore Hell keeps her ever-hungry mouths all
>     Bolted against me.

Hard lot ! encompass'd with a thousand dangers;
Weary, faint, trembling with a thousand terrors,
I'm call'd, if vanquish'd, to receive a sentence
    Worse than Abiram's.

Him the vindictive rod of angry justice
Sent quick and howling to the centre headlong;
I, fed with judgment, in a fleshy tomb, am
    Buried above ground.

The monotonous round of his melancholy was broken into by his brother, now a don at Cambridge, whom he had written to just after he had given up the idea of suicide. John Cowper had a family likeness to his brother. He was scholarly and good-natured and fanciful. But he was saner and sleepier, and his nerves, though not strong, were less strained. Perhaps this was owing to his profession. Anxiety is foreign to the academic life. Picture the horror of this placid don when confronted with a brother, white-faced and wild-eyed, who before he had time to speak ushered him with twitching hands into a chair, and assured him with a flood of incoherent and unconvincing detail that he was damned. He settled in London for the time being and devoted himself to trying to cure his brother. Hour after hour he reasoned with him. It was no use arguing with a madman. Reasoning supposes a common basis of argument, and the central feature of such a madness as Cowper's is that the victim imagines that he is in a different condition from any one else, so that no analogy from ordinary life will be true of his own. Every day his agony of mind increased. One day he found himself saying, "Evil, be thou my good." He wondered if it was his soul involuntarily declaring its true nature. He began to set himself traps to find the way it was tending.

He got out of bed one night and tried to pray; but the words did not come. He tried to say the creed to himself; but a fog seemed to descend upon his memory, and he could not get beyond the first clause. This last experience was too much for his self-control. His brother opened the door to find him stretched on the floor howling with terror. "Brother," he gasped, "think of eternity; then think what it is to be damned."

John Cowper was at his wits' end as to how to reassure him. The voice of his decorous academic religion could never make itself heard amid his brother's ravings. Perhaps his cousin, Martin Madan, a member of the new Evangelical party, would do better. He distrusted what he had heard of his religion; but he felt he ought to try everything. Martin Madan arrived, seated himself at Cowper's bedside, and in a melodious voice, vibrant with an unquestioning faith, assured Cowper of his certain salvation, if he would repent. Cowper was too dazed to understand his words exactly; but the fire behind them stirred, for the first time, a movement of hope within him. "Ah," he sighed, "if I could only be sure!"

A seed had fallen which was to bear fruit later. But for the moment his soul was too petrified with suffering to let it sink in. After Madan's visit he relapsed into his former gloom. Events now moved swiftly to their climax. "Then did the pains of Hell get hold of me. A numbness seized the extremities of my body, my hands and feet became cold and stiff. A cold sweat stood upon my forehead. My heart seemed at every pulse to beat its last. No convicted criminal ever feared death more, or was more assured of dying. When I traversed the apartment in the most horrible dismay of soul, expecting every moment that the earth would open and swallow me, my conscience scaring me, the Avenger of Blood pursuing me, and the City of Refuge out of reach and out of sight, a strange and horrible darkness fell upon me. If it were possible that a heavy blow could light on the brain without touching the skull, such was the sensation I felt. I clapped my hand to my forehead and cried aloud with the pain it gave me. At every stroke my thought and expressions became more wild and incoherent; all that remained clear was the sense of sin and the expectation of punishment." His wish of ten months back was terribly fulfilled. He was a gibbering, raving maniac.

The next five months passed in an incoherent agony, first in London, and then in Doctor Cotton's Home for Madmen at St. Albans. Harriet Hesketh came to see him before he left the Temple; but he turned his face away. He was far past her homely ministrations now. Nor could the jolting journey through the lanes of Herefordshire rouse him. His whole mind was dominated by the thought of his damnation; he believed that God at any moment might strike him dead. And, faced with such a prospect, the episodes of outward life passed remote and unnoticed as the noise of a distant street to a man working in an upper room. Day after day he lay upon his bed at Doctor Cotton's, bound, for fear he should kill himself, with the words "I am damned" repeating themselves in his head like the insistent tap of a drum. Suddenly their full implication would flash upon him. He felt the flames licking his feet, he heard the wails of those who would be his companions for eternity. And then, the spasm past, he would fall back into a stupor, broken only by the incessant reiteration of his damnation.

The powers of Darkness had beaten him. The fragile, intricate cocoon of taste and habit that he had so vigilantly spun around himself was stripped off; Cowper, the scholar and the friend, with his intimacy and urbanity and self-restraint, was gone; and in his stead was only a poor shivering creature bereft even of reason, forcibly fed, forcibly detained, whimpering and cowering from the bogies of his imagination.

But it was not the end. For there is in the human spirit an upward thrust of vitality that can only be defeated by death. Torn up by the roots, trodden under foot, cast upon the dust-heap, the soul will yet, after a little time, again revive, and stretch its tendrils upward, and put forth leaves to the sunlight. Cowper's spirit, so fragile, so tenacious, so bruised, so resilient, once more began to climb from the abyss into which it had fallen. But it was led by other lights than those which had played round the happiness of his earlier years. The homely serenity of normal every day had failed him; the story of his life had changed from a Trollopean comedy of domestic manners to the soul tragedy of a Dostoyefsky. And he was to rise from hell borne on the sublime ecstasies of an Alyosha Karamazof.

In the quiet of the country the fury of his despair died down, and he began to look on his future with a certain resignation. With a curious revulsion from his former self-upbraiding, he wished at moments that he had committed more sins, since, anyway, he was going to be punished everlastingly. However, his damnation did not seem likely to be immediate, so he felt that he had better make the best of what time he had left on earth. The course of his life became more normal. He began to eat and drink with appetite and to laugh at kind old Doctor Cotton's jokes.

Winter softened to spring, spring glowed into summer, and in July his brother came to see how he was. At first he was disappointed. William eyed him with dejection. After an awkward pause John asked how he felt; but he only replied, "As much better as despair can make me." For the last time John burst out in protest; urged, argued, insisted that it was all a delusion. At these words William felt the heavy load that had weighed down his mind so long stir in its place. Could his brother's words be true? Was it conceivably, marvelously possible that he should yet live to look back on all that he had gone through as an unsubstantial nightmare? His returning vitality leaped out to meet the thought. "Oh," he cried, and as he spoke his breath caught in a sob of emotion, "oh, if this be a delusion, then am I the happiest of men!" And he burst into tears.

But though his brother's visit had unsealed the fountain of his hope, there was as yet no channel through which the stream might flow. He felt ready for happiness, but he had no intellectual conviction with which to justify such a feeling. As he paced the sunlit garden he trembled with expectancy; whether of joy or sorrow he could scarcely tell. But every moment, and with a growing persistence, something whispered in his heart that there was mercy for him. His spirits were further raised by a dream. He thought that a child about four years old came dancing up to his bedside, radiant and beautiful as an angel from Heaven; and that at the sight of it an indescribable sense of peace and freshness stole into his heart. He awoke, but the memory of the dream had spilled a perfume of happiness over his thoughts that lingered there all day. Like his fall, his recovery imaged itself in dreams: flowers of an imagination blossoming in sleep, or intimations from another world, who can tell?

A few days later, walking in the garden, he came
upon a Bible lying on a bench. He opened it at the
twelfth chapter of St. John's Gospel, and read the account of the raising of Lazarus. The beauty and pathos
of the story moved him profoundly. Could there be any
bottom to the depths of a compassion that was able to
vanquish death itself? Might it not extend even to him?
Within a few hours he received his answer.

"Having risen with somewhat of a more cheerful
feeling, I repaired to my room, where breakfast waited
for me. While I sat at table I found the cloud of horror
which had so long hung over me was every moment passing away. I flung myself into a chair near the window,
and seeing a Bible there, ventured once more to apply
to it for comfort and instruction. The first verse I saw
was the 25th of the III Romans, 'Whom God hath set
forth to be a propitiation through faith in his blood, to
declare his righteousness for the remission of sins that
are passed through the forbearance of God.' Immediately I received strength to believe it, and the full beams of
the Sun's righteousness shone upon me. I saw the
sufficiency of the Atonement he had made, my pardon
sealed in his blood, and all the fulness and completeness
of his justification. In a moment I believed and received
the Gospel. Whatever my friend Madan had said to
me long before revived in all its clearness the demonstration of the spirit and with power. Unless the Almighty arms had been under me I think I should have
died of gratitude and joy. My eyes filled with tears, and
my voice choked with transport, and I could only look
up to Heaven in silent fear, overwhelmed with love and
wonder."

The fears and pains of his troubled thirty years had
fallen off him like rags. Sin and sorrow and disillusion,

madness itself, were nothing and less than nothing in the transcendent glory of his spiritual reconciliation. But the supreme moments of religious ecstasy, like the supreme moments of esthetic experience, are not to be expressed in words. Dante measured hell and purgatory, described their smallest detail with a meticulous exactitude; but when he reached the final circle of Paradise, and was face to face with that Divine Spirit by whose will the whole huge system lived and moved and had its being, he was conscious only of a blinding light.

# CHAPTER III

## FAITH AND MRS. UNWIN

THE Evangelical movement stands out in violent contrast to the prevailing thought of its time—a black, melodramatic silhouette against the precise, freshly hued color print of eighteenth-century England. Where the prevailing thought believed that religious feeling should be disciplined by common sense or refined by sensibility, it believed that only at its rawest and most violent was it sincere. Where the prevailing aim was to develop you on every side, the Evangelical said that all activities not directly connected with religion should be shunned. Where the prevailing theological opinion emphasized the moral aspects of religion, the Evangelical rejected these as worthless except in so far as they were signs of a healthy spiritual condition. For, excluded from other systems of thought, there poured into the narrow channel of Evangelicalism all the mystical and transcendental emotion of the period.

In its early decades, the Church, tired with two centuries of religious strife, had fallen into a polite lethargy. Its faults can be, and have been, exaggerated. It was learned, rational and dignified. It did not, as in earlier times, occupy itself with persecution, nor, as in modern times, with hysterical bickering over trivialities of form and ceremonial. But it removed religion from common life; it did not touch the heart, nor gratify the

93

longings of the soul to penetrate beyond the veil of its mortality. Mankind, however, a stranger on the earth, bears these longings within him, an integral part of his nature; and if the religious system in which he is educated does not cater for them, he will change it for one that does. Unsatisfied by Bishop Berkeley on the one hand and Parson Adams on the other, the spiritually minded person turned to Wesley and Whitefield.

Their movement started about 1730. Most of its early work was done among the very poor, and took the form of revivalism, with its accompanying faults of theatrical emotionalism. The Church at first looked askance at it; and its first founders broke with the Church. But the fire of their spirit gradually permeated all the religious life of the time; it took firm hold of the middle classes, and penetrated up into the aristocracy. The more distressing eccentricities of the early movement were removed, and by the second half of the century Methodism, pruned, tamed and polished into Evangelicalism, was the animating force behind the most active, if not the most numerous, party in the Church of England.

Their religion was an exclusively emotional one. The movement really came from a sense that the good life is not merely the fulfilling of an ethical code, but the achievement of a state of mind, that is at its highest a state of religious ecstasy. And they therefore evolved a theological system according to which the achievement of this ecstasy was the only aim of religion. Mankind, they held, has by his own act become utterly depraved, incapable of a good action or even of a good intention. The laws of divine justice demanded that he should be punished for his wickedness. But God, by an act of ineffable love, had Himself borne this punishment in the person of His Son, so that now the only thing necessary for a man to be saved was that he should fully realize this—should, in their phrase, "lay hold of his salvation" and be "converted." And they identified this consciousness of conversion with the supreme moment of religious ecstasy.

This consciousness was the sole test of religious life. If you had it, you were saved; but without it a life spent in good acts was of no avail. For any act must necessarily be that of a child of sin, and therefore evil. Such a view of life, logically pursued in practise, would lead man to do nothing but sit and wait for Heaven to convert him. But the Evangelicals were no more logical than other fatalists. And the end of all their teaching was that man must make it the object of every act and thought to attain conversion, to enter into that small band whom the divine love has snatched from the eternal misery which they deserve.

It is not hard to foresee how such a creed would apply itself in practise. Your whole energy is concentrated on achieving the state of grace, and maintaining yourself in it when you have got there. In so far as it helps you to do this, an activity is good, and should be encouraged; in so far as it does not, it is bad and must be avoided. For, as one of their leading divines put it, "A man only stays in the world to do the work of his Creator, as he might stay out in the rain to deliver an important message." The pleasures of the world are particularly to be shunned; for, by presenting you with the image of false good, they distract you from following the true. Nor were learning and reason much better. They were as much within the capacity of a child of wrath as of a child of grace, and encouraged man to forget his incompetence.

To the afflictions of life, on the other hand, the Evangelicals had less objection, for these discouraged man from looking for happiness in this world; while death itself, the final disaster, was to them the highest blessing. For it took a man out of the world altogether. Such worldly activities as he must take part in should be made as far as possible to serve some religious purpose, and so preserved from that taint of sin which is inherent in their nature. If he wrote a letter or paid a call or read a book, he should do so in such a manner as might lead other people to grace.

The form of this creed derived directly from sixteenth-century Calvinism. Indeed, the renunciation of the world under the impulse of religious experience is behind all ascetic religions. But such an impulse generally expresses itself in a corporate organization. The believers band themselves together to abandon the normal way of life in order the better to do the work commanded them by God. But the structure of society was too generally accepted in the early eighteenth century for people to contemplate any corporate break with it. So, in consequence, all this volume of lyrical emotion, this fear of death, this shuddering horror of sin, this faith that would remove mountains, expressed itself not in a Thebaid or a Covenant or a Crusade, but in the ordinary affairs of conventional life. Instead of commanding their followers to forsake their family and their business, and to follow the Cross throughout the world, the Evangelical preachers had to assure them that family life and business, carried on in the right spirit, could be the life of the Cross.

In this incongruous contrast between its motive impulse and the mode of its expression lies the distinguishing characteristic of eighteenth-century Evangelicalism.

In every class of society, in every walk of life, little centers grew up: domestic monasteries, homely outposts of salvation. In nearly every country village there was one family who had prayers morning and evening and went to church three times on Sunday; who read nothing but the Bible and the works of a few "experiential" divines, never wore bright colors, and modeled their conversation on the precepts of some preacher, Mr. Venn or Mr. Romaine, whom they had once "sat under"; who collected money for foreign missions and distributed tracts; who would hardly move out of the house on Sunday and would not dance or play cards on any day of the week at all. In regiment and on battleship, among the Hogarthian naval and military society of the day, the jolly, brutal Commodore Trunnions and Captain Plumes, with their carbuncled faces and brazen voices, their swearing and wenching and drinking, would suddenly appear a man, like one of Cromwell's Ironsides risen from the grave, who never swore or got drunk, who read prayers to his men, and who spent such time as he could spare from the stern performance of his duties in religious meditation. An uneducated serving-boy would be moved by the Spirit and, to the irritation of his employers, hold prayer-meetings for his fellow-servants, like Humphrey Clinker. A peer of the realm, like Lord Dartmouth, would withdraw from rout and race-course and dedicate himself to the fulfilment of his more serious obligations under the guidance of a "faithful" chaplain.

The mixture of religious and conventional life extended itself to the way in which the Evangelicals expressed themselves. In their hymns the mysterious doctrines of atonement and redemption are incongruously packed into the mild dactylic meters of eighteenth-century pastoral and set to the matter-of-fact melodies of eighteenth-century ballads. Their preachers, in well-brushed wig and Geneva gown, would discourse to a respectable London congregation on the wickedness of Sunday travel, in the bloodstained imagery originally used by some half-naked prophet to an Oriental tribe among the precipitous cliffs of a Syrian desert.

This combination of the religious and the conventional had its defects. For one thing it made practise often inconsistent with precept. The austere tenets of Calvinism had to be considerably modified to suit eighteenth-century custom; the rude "Gothic" canvas had to be cut down before it fitted the neat Adams panel. The middle-class Evangelical could not feel it wrong to make money, however little one should enjoy it when it was made; and he would spend Sunday in proclaiming the vanity of earthly riches, and week-days in amassing as much of them as he could. Nor could he allow his conviction of man's equality in sin to imperil the social order. If he and his wife confessed their abject unworthiness to receive earthly honors, they did it from a cushioned pew in the front of the church, while the cook and the foot-boy repeated the same sentiments from a convenient bench at the back. These were not the only defects of Evangelicalism. Its repudiation of the world cut it off from the whole sphere of esthetic achievement. Other religions have bequeathed us cathedrals; Methodism only yellow-brick Little Bethels. Its doctrine of conversion tended to arrogance. Those who considered themselves converted became too familiar with God, too contemptuous of man. And its emphasis on the emotional side of religion often led to false emotionalism: hothouse fruits of the spirit, unctuous soul-confessions, luscious mechanical ecstasies.

And of course the Evangelicals were often highly

ridiculous. They had rejected reason, and reason soon
rejected them. The Reverend Alfred Hutchinson, a
respectable divine, carried his belief in verbal inspiration so far as to hold that Hebrew alone of human lan-
guages had the syntax and grammar competent to
express the mind of God, and that all the possible
discoveries of physical science, mysteriously evaporated
in the process of translation, could be found in the Bible
if read in its original tongue. The Evangelicals could
discern a special Providence in the most trivial occasions.
If a man fell into a puddle, it was because God was
chastening him; if he avoided falling in, because God
had given His angels special charge over him. Their
language is as absurd as their thought. Elderly clerics
write to young ladies to urge them not to use rouge, in a
style which combines, but which does not unite, those of
Jeremiah and the polite letter-writer. Middle-aged
women paint their feelings on meeting a favorite
preacher in the voluptuous imagery of the Song of
Solomon. The world of *Tom Jones* is not most happily
described in the language of the Book of Job. Elijah
among the teacups can not fail to be a comic figure.

Yet in spite of its defects, its absurdities, one can not
refuse the Evangelicals one's admiration. For they imposed a moral order on life. Ignorance and fanaticism
made it an imperfect order; but it was none the less an
order. And to those who believed in it the happenings
of daily life were no longer isolated and purposeless
trifles, but integral parts of the great structure of existence—a structure which, with all its limitations, was
centered around the profoundest elements of man's
nature. It alone among the philosophies of its time
took account of man's spiritual side, wove into the
tapestry of his ordinary life his visions, his enthusiasms,

his exaltations, faced and tried to explain the mystery of his existence, the omnipresence of evil, the inevitability of death. The merchant in the counting-house, the spinner in the factory, the old maid in the village, all felt themselves actors in the great drama of mankind's salvation. Revealed against this tremendous background, their lives assumed heroic proportions. What did the trivialities of mere outward circumstances matter? Their friends were exultations, agonies and love and man's unconquerable mind.

And the compelling power of their faith was shown by their actions. It was they who purified the morals of English society, who founded modern philanthropy, who stopped the slave trade. Nor could any creed less passionately exclusive have so effectively inspired them. You must look only to the Cross to be a successful crusader.

Finally Evangelicalism—and in this also it was unique among the philosophies of its day—could satisfy the temperament of the artist. For it alone set a supreme value on that emotional exaltation in which the greatest art is produced, it alone made the imagination the center of its system, and not a mere decorative appendage to it. An attitude of civilized disillusionment is all very well in its way, but it is not conducive to creative art. Wesley could have understood Dante as Voltaire or even Doctor Johnson could never have done. The Evangelicals may have disliked poetry, but their sublime conception of the universal plan is the most imaginative poem of its day.

Surging and swirling, flowed on the varicolored stream of eighteenth-century life. People were born and grew up; made money or lost it; were serious, were frivolous; yielded to a good impulse, yielded to a bad one; had moments of ecstasy and forgot them; made resolutions and failed to keep them; married and grew old and died—their life an incoherent tangle of hopes and fears, desires and inhibitions, aspirations and apathies; heterogeneous, hand-to-mouth, without order or sequence. But through it moved a small band of people for whom the whole multifarious complex was resolved into a single and majestic action—that conflict which, as long as life lasts, the children of light must wage with the prince of the power of the air. They were sometimes feeble and sometimes erring, for they were mortal; but they never faltered in their effort to measure their every word and act by the highest standard they knew. They did what they thought right whatever trouble it got them into, and whatever pleasure it deprived them of. Indeed, the ephemeral joys and sorrows of the world meant little to them. On their brows lay the shadow of the wings of death, and in their ears chimed ever the bells of paradise.

It was among this band of people that the next eight years of Cowper's life were passed. Their world was a very different one from that of his youth—mildly interested in everything, enthusiastically interested in nothing. But Cowper was a different man. At the outset of his life his nervous system had been infected with a deadly poison. He had tried to expel it by throwing himself into the life around him, trying to identify himself with its interests, its pleasures and its difficulties. The struggle had been long, but in the end he succumbed. After two years his natural vitality reasserted itself and he recovered; but the interests of his old life had lost all value in his eyes. Society, family life, scholarship, public affairs—they had been weighed and found wanting. Indeed, they were inextricably mixed in his mind with failure and disaster. His returning energy rejected them and turned elsewhere to find a worthy object for existence—turned to religion.

He had always had leanings that way. From childhood his fundamental conception of life had been a religious one. The very nervous diseases which had sent him mad had taken the form in his mind of a conviction of damnation; and his rare moments of religious emotion had been the only moments of his life when he was completely free from nervous terror. It is true he had sought consolation from religion without success; yet even when he had felt such consolation furthest from him he had never lost the conviction that it was the highest good, were it possible to achieve it. Now, after his crucifixion of the last ten months, it remained the only good of his early life that had not been spoiled. All other things on which he had set his heart had proved powerless to protect him against the onslaught of his secret enemy. His spirit, filled to overflowing with the gratitude and delight of recovery, saw in religion, and in religion alone, a worthy object on which to pour itself out. And the returning tide of his health, the tremendous reaction of joy after the anguish of the last three years, all the vigor of his restored mind and body, gushed in one irresistible torrent down this single channel. Under its pressure his imaginative life rose to a pitch of intensity never touched before. At last the earthy curtains through which elusive gleams of paradise had penetrated to him were torn down, and he stood forth in the full blaze of the mystic vision.

He must never lose it again; his whole life must be dedicated to its preservation. As people always do under the stress of strong religious impulse, he longed to incarnate his ecstasy, to find some tabulated program of beliefs and duties, some rule and ritual of daily life in which it could have permanent, practical expression. He was a convert, but he needed a Church. It was this need that led him to the Evangelicals. He was not likely to be satisfied with the religion of his childhood. He wanted a new form in which to express a new emotion; and the only new religious form accessible at St. Albans in 1765 was Evangelicalism.

It was peculiarly accessible to Cowper, because Doctor Cotton was an Evangelical, and only too willing to encourage a tendency toward the truth in any one else. But Cowper needed no encouragement. The Evangelical creed might well seem created to suit his particular case. It explained his difficulties so exactly, so perfectly enshrined his aspirations. He knew, none better, the inefficacy of works. For thirty years he had lived a moral and respectable life. Yet he had never known a moment's real peace of mind; and when the powers of evil had attacked him, he had succumbed with hardly a show of resistance. He realized man's inability to save his own soul. Had not the Divine Grace shone forth on him long after he had ceased to struggle against evil, and was lying bereft even of reason? He knew that faith alone justified. The faith inspired by his moment of vision had raised him to a level of spiritual exaltation, that all the vigilant virtue of his youth had never brought him within sight of. In the light of the Evangelical creed, the wretched tangle of his life-history fell into a simple beneficent order—the plan by which an all-wise and all-loving God had reclaimed a soul stubborn to seek its own destruction. He had been born a child of wrath, incapable of a good thought or a good deed, predestined to damnation. Once or twice God had let fall a ray of His grace upon him, but, seduced by the pleasures of the world, he had shut his eyes. On the threshold therefore of his manhood God had plunged him into a melancholia, had overwhelmed him with spiritual fears; and then, as suddenly, had removed them and filled him with spiritual happiness. But again he had neglected His message. Then indeed God, determined to save him in his own despite, had turned to stronger measures. Gradually He removed from his life all that might distract Cowper's soul from the love of Him; He deprived him of his love, friends and family. But just when Cowper, maddened by misfortune, was about to decide his damnation by committing the frightful sin of self-murder, God miraculously rescued him, showed him to himself as the vile creature he really was, and revealed the hell that was in store for him if he proceeded in his evil doings. Finally, when he was still trembling under this newly found consciousness of sin, He turned the full light of His grace upon him. He saw it and was converted.

Seen from this angle, those evils for which he had thought his life was singled out from the rest of mankind ceased to appear evil, or vanished altogether. If he was weak and contemptible, a puppet in the hands of a higher power, so was every other created being. And that higher power was no inexorable, malevolent deity, but a loving and omnipotent Father. Again, happiness was no longer a transitory and precarious condition. His present happiness arose from the fact that he had at last "laid hold of his salvation," and the state of his salvation was of its nature eternal. He was in the hands of God, and no torments could touch him ever any more.

Nor did the ascetic side of Evangelicalism put him off. The pleasures of the world held no attraction for him; and the very idea that they might distract him from the right way was enough to make him give them up. But he had no fears that he would ever be so distracted. He, nervous, apprehensive William Cowper, whose whole existence had been dominated by the desire to avoid real or imagined danger, could now turn and look at life and see only good. No wonder he wished to consecrate his whole life to the God who had so wonderfully blessed him. The span of man's existence seemed all too short to express his joy and gratitude. His ordinary mental condition for months on end was a pitch of ecstasy such as most men experience once or twice in their lives for a single moment. He seemed to live his life to a sound of celestial music, to get up and go to bed, to work and eat and sleep, to the accompaniment of an unseen orchestra of flutes and shawms and violins. Summer bloomed in his heart as it bloomed in the garden outside. Up in the trees the birds were singing, and in his thoughts too the birds of happiness sang and soared and clapped their wings of silver and gold. Every word he spoke, every letter he wrote, was breathless with ecstasy. Lyrically, incoherently, garrulously, he proclaimed and reproclaimed the glory of his redemption. The Hertfordshire garden used to ring with his rhapsodies.

They could not command an adequate audience—it was confined generally to Sam, the kind solid servant who had nursed him through his illness, the cobbler's boy Dick Colman, an open-mouthed urchin of seven years, and Doctor Cotton himself. Poor Doctor Cotton! He sometimes wondered if Cowper saved was much saner than Cowper damned. He was certainly quite as great a strain to talk to. However, Doctor Cotton was an Evangelical, and accustomed to such ordeals, and he strove to calm his patient by giving him a book to read called *Meditations among the Tombs*.

So passed a year. In May, 1765, Cowper was ready to leave St. Albans. But where was he to go? His friends lived mostly in London; but London he held in horror—it was connected indissolubly with his miserable past. It was there he had fallen away in 1753; and there he had passed through his most frightful agony. He wanted to shut the door on his past altogether and settle in some secluded spot where, undisturbed by painful memories and unseduced by worldly pleasures, he could devote himself to religious contemplation. It was exactly the same impulse as makes people go into monasteries. But Cowper's religion provided no monasteries. However, an unofficial hermitage in some country place would do as well. He had always turned for happiness to the country, to rural sights and sounds and silence; and such a change would most effectively cut him off from his old life.

In nothing has English life changed more since 1765 than in the relative positions of town and country. Before the day of trains and motors and newspapers and wireless, country people lived a different world from townspeople, a world that did not center round London at all. They got up at a different time, dined at a different time, did not try to follow town fashions. They heard only such news of London as could be gleaned from a fortnight-old *St. James's Gazette* lent them by the squire. Their very speech was different. Old comedy is full of loutish country squires, Sir Wilful Witwould and Sir Tunbelly Clumsy, who arrive in town to find themselves the butts of the wits for their queer clothes and queerer accents and their ignorance of the outstanding events of the day. And country districts were as remote from one another as from London. To go to live in a different part of the country was like going to live abroad to-day. You had to learn to order your life according to new customs, to call common objects by new names. Nor could you hold much communication with the place you had left when it was distant two or three days' journey in a creaking, stuffy coach over a road like a cart-track, and it cost five shillings to send a letter. Near relations lived within twenty miles of each other without meeting for ten years. Cowper's decision to live in the country meant that he was only likely to see the friends of his youth once or twice again before he died. It was a fitting symbol that he had begun life anew.

His relations, however, did not want him to go beyond all reach of help. In the end it was decided that he should settle, for the time being at any rate, somewhere near Cambridge, so that his brother could keep an eye on him. The nearest place in which his brother could find the cheap quiet lodgings required was Huntingdon. It was over fifteen miles from Cambridge—too far for John Cowper to see William very often—but to William in his present condition solitude meant only more time to be alone with God.

> Far from the world, O Lord, I flee, [he sang]
>  From strife and tumult far;
> From scenes where Satan wages still
>  His most successful war.
>
> The calm retreat, the silent shade,
>  With prayer and praise agree;
> And seem, by Thy sweet bounty made,
>  For those who follow Thee.
>
> There if Thy Spirit touch the soul,
>  And grace her mean abode,
> O with what peace, and joy, and love,
>  She communes with her God !

> There like the nightingale she pours
> Her solitary lays;
> Nor asks a witness of her song,
> Nor thirsts for human praise.

The lodgings were engaged; and on June 17, 1765, he started for Cambridge, where he was to spend a night on the way. He could not forbear a tremor as he got into the coach. For two years he had been virtually out of the world; and now, at his first encounter with it, his natural timidity swept irresistibly over him. Perhaps some one would blaspheme against the God whom he served; and then, fearful thought, it would be his duty to reprove them. Fortunately the coach traveled all the way from St. Albans to Cambridge without a single oath passing any one's lips.

He sat up late that night with his brother, pouring forth the story of his conversion, and exhorting him, in a trembling voice, to follow his example. John Cowper felt embarrassed. His religion was a mild, cultured affair with leanings toward Unitarianism; and he, like Doctor Cotton, thought Cowper's apocalyptic rejoicings only less insane than his apocalyptic despair. On the other hand, he did not wish to hurt William's feelings by speaking against something which had made his brother so happy. He made a few tentative objections, and finally tried to close the discussion by saying that he was sure that at bottom they meant the same thing. William Cowper did not think so at all. He had been talking for hours in order to prove exactly the reverse. He relapsed into a disappointed silence, only comforting himself with the hope that for some good purpose his brother's conversion was being delayed till a later time.

Four days later he left Cambridge and drove over to Huntingdon. At first he could not restrain a slight feel-

ing of depression. It was all very well to praise solitude at Doctor Cotton's, with kind faces and kind voices
within call whenever he should need them; but sitting in
his poky little lodgings in a completely strange town he
could not help feeling rather lonely. There was not a
soul he could talk to within miles. And he was so shy
of making new friends. However, the fire of his faith
was not so easily extinguished. "I walked forth toward
the close of day," he wrote, "in this melancholy frame
of mind, and having wandered about a mile from the
town, I found my heart at length so powerfully drawn
towards the Lord that, having gained a retired and
secret nook in the corner of a field, I kneeled down
under a bank and poured forth my complaints before
Him. It pleased my Saviour to hear me in that this my
depression was taken off and I was enabled to trust in
Him."

On the following day he was confirmed in this quickening of the spirit. It was Sunday; and for the first time
since his illness he went to church. The dignified ceremonial, the stately English of the prayers, the music, the
building, above all the unaccustomed sense of corporate
worship, profoundly stirred a spirit ever open to esthetic
impression. The lesson was the beautiful story of the
Prodigal Son. To Cowper it seemed a fable of his own
life; and as he listened to it his soul was again filled with
the supreme ecstasy of the moment of conversion. He
could hardly restrain his tears; his heart leaped out in
love to the people round him, especially, as he naïvely
puts it, to those in whom he observed "an air of sober
attention." He gazed at a gentleman singing psalms in
his pew, blessed him in his heart and blessed him again.
How foolish had been his despondency! Had it not always been the triumphant boast of his faith that it could
uphold and console him in any circumstances? And had

not this, his first solitary adventure into the world, proved this boast abundantly justified?

However, as the weeks passed he found he did not have to rely solely on spiritual compensation for his loneliness. Life at Huntingdon possessed more mundane sources of comfort. For one thing there were the pleasures of Nature. He did not, indeed, admire the country; nothing could be further from the bosky groves and smiling glades which were what the eighteenth century meant by beautiful scenery than the fens, that strange no man's land between earth and sea, but more like the sea, as it stretched, level, into the distance, with here and there a church sticking up from it like a ship, and over all the vast, varying sky, now gleaming blue, now hidden by driving rain, now troubled with moving masses of cloud; by night swarming with stars, ominous in the red light of the setting sun. Cowper told Lady Hesketh it was merely "flat and insipid." He could not feel in it that sense of space and wind and lonely freedom which it shares with other flat landscape, Holland and Romney Marsh; which blows so poignantly from the canvases of those painters of Norwich who depicted it forty years later. But any country was better than no country; and he enjoyed bathing in the River Ouse and wandering alone among the blue willows on its banks.

Not that he was always alone, either. He made some acquaintances: two clergymen, Mr. Hodson and Mr. Nicholson, who, if not Evangelical, were at least unworldly; and Mr. Pemberton, the woolen draper, who was so kind as to offer to lend him *St. James's Gazette.* And once a week, mounted on the back of a horse, he clattered off to Cambridge to see John.

Still, it became clear that such a mode of existence could only be temporary. From a purely practical point of view Cowper was incapable of managing for himself. Buying meat, for instance, was a terrible problem. First he bought a leg of lamb, and that was too much; then a sheep's heart, and that was too little; then he fell back on liver, but that soon began to pall. "I never knew how to pity poor housekeepers before," he writes pathetically, "but now I ccasc to wonder at that politic cast which their occupation usually gives to their countenance; for it really is a matter full of perplexity." You have to eat even if you are saved. And the worst of the whole affair was that within four months he had spent a year's income.

But over and above all this, he felt the mental strain. Nothing is more wearing than living alone. The ordinary mold of social habit and custom by which life is directed and regulated in any corporate form of existence is removed. You go out when you like, and work when you like, and go to bed when you like. All the thousand trifling acts of daily life become the subjects of decision; and making a decision is the most tiring thing in the world. It was especially tiring to some one like Cowper, who all his life had liked something to lean on. His very dislike of meeting strangers arose in great part from the fact that such meetings involved his taking the social initiative. The only mode of life that exactly suited him, the only mode of life that had ever exactly suited him, was family life; it provided the quiet social circle he liked, and in it all the practical side of life was managed for him. But it was hard to get what he wanted. The obvious way to get family life is to marry and have a family of your own; but Cowper in his present state of mind had no thoughts of marriage. It would have to be some one else's family, and, if he was to be really happy, one that would sympathize with his religious views. What he needed was a family of pleasant, cultivated Evangelicals who would be willing to take a strange young man just out of an asylum and with hardly any money to live with them indefinitely. It seemed an unlikely thing to find, but for once in his life Cowper was lucky. He found it at Huntingdon.

One September morning as he was taking the air under the trees after church, he was accosted by a young man who said that his name was Unwin, and that he had often wanted to speak to Cowper before, but that he had felt too shy, as he had heard that he avoided new acquaintances. Cowper liked the look of him. He had a bright, open, friendly countenance and a forthcoming manner; and Cowper asked him to tea. The meal confirmed his good impression. His new friend was everything he liked best—intelligent, full of youthful spirits, simple, unassuming, and, best of all, a strong Evangelical. Within a short time he had told Cowper all about himself—how his father was a clergyman, and how he was going to be a clergyman too; that he was working at Cambridge, but was living in Huntingdon with his father, mother and sister. On his departure Cowper flung himself on his knees, to ask a blessing on this friendship from the God to whom he had vowed to consecrate all his activities.

Next day he returned Unwin's call, and found the rest of the family as delightful as himself. On arriving he found himself in the little parlor with the daughter. He had never seen her before; but she began conversation in such a friendly, quiet way that soon he felt quite at his ease. The father was a scholarly old parson, "as simple as Parson Adams"; while the mother, much younger than her husband—in fact only eight or nine years older than Cowper—struck him as having "uncom-

mon understanding, and more polite than a duchess." He
enjoyed his visit immensely. He sincerely hoped he
would see more of the Unwins. He did not know that
his connection with them would only be severed by death.

The Unwins were as pleased with Cowper as he with
them. They had originally moved from Grimston and
come to live in Huntingdon because Mrs. Unwin wanted
better company than the sequestered position of Grimston afforded. Huntingdon had not proved very fruitful of good company. The people there were either
stupid or too worldly in their interests for the Evangelical Unwins; and these soon found themselves as much
alone as they had been at Grimston. Imagine their delight on meeting a young man, clever, educated, with
the most charming manners, and even more Evangelical
than themselves.

With such good-will on both sides the acquaintance
could not fail to ripen quickly into friendship. The
Unwins asked him to come whenever he liked. He was
shy at first; but they were so friendly, and he was so
solitary, that they did not have much difficulty in winning
him over. And soon he spent the best part of every day
with them. "Go when I will," he writes, "I find a house
filled with peace and cordiality in all its parts. I am
sure to hear no scandal, but such discourse as we are all
better for. You remember Rousseau's description of an
English morning—such are the mornings I spend with
these good people. The evenings differ from them in
nothing except that they are still more snug and quieter.
Now I know them, I wonder I liked Huntingdon so well,
and am apt to think I should find any place disagreeable
which had not an Unwin belonging to it."

For life at the Unwins' satisfied his desires as no
other could have done. It combined the two things which

in his checkered thirty-three years really won his affection—family life and the Evangelical faith.  From the
very first meeting, the Unwins had looked on him as a
relation, and had not, in the manner of their time, treated
all his visits as ceremonious occasions, but admitted him
to share in their ordinary occupations and conversations
as if he were a brother.  And he enjoyed with them all
the intimacy, the companionship, the cozy fireside fun,
the sense of communal cousinly work and play that he
had hankered after ever since his mother's death, and
that he had tasted for a little with his uncle's family in
Southampton Row.  But here was Southampton Row
purified from all taint of the world, and sanctified by
that faith which since St. Albans had been the lodestar
of his life.

Life at the Unwins' was dedicated to religion.  All
their employments, their conversations, their reading,
their music were religious.  Cowper felt he had forsaken
the world to follow the Lord, and now the Lord had
rewarded him by giving him back all that had made the
world attractive.  The roomy, red-brick house, with its
rambling garden with the pear tree in it, seemed a sort
of earthly paradise to him, in which Mrs. Unwin sat
enthroned—the patron saint.

Gradually, as the weeks went by, she began to stand
out from the others.  All that he loved in the Unwin
household tended to identify itself with her.  As the
weeks went by her name appeared in his correspondence
with growing frequency.  Suddenly at the end of a letter
to Joseph Hill about something quite different, he would
add as a postscript: "And I know no one as like Mrs.
Unwin as my Aunt Madan—I do not mean in person,
but in character."  And again, to Lady Hesketh: "I met
Mrs. Unwin in the street and went home with her.  She

and I walked together nearly two hours in the garden, and I had a conversation which did me more good than I should have received from an audience with the first prince in Europe. That woman is a blessing to me, and I feel every time I see her as being the better for her company." The rest of the family began to recede into the background.

Old Mr. Unwin, indeed, was rather out of the Evangelical picture. He belonged to a less zealous type of eighteenth-century clergyman. Polite and scholarly, he doubted the divinity of Christ, and was incurably idle in the performance of his duties. Grimston was not a large parish, but he seems to have christened, married or buried hardly any one in it. At Huntingdon his duties were even lighter; but there he never performed them at all. His unfortunate parishioners censured him frequently, and even threatened to expel him; in vain. As he began to know him better, Cowper could not reconcile his conscience with whole-hearted approval of Mr. Unwin.

Miss Unwin, too, ceased to occupy much of Cowper's attention after their first interview. He noticed that she was bashful and unwilling to speak when her mother was there. Perhaps she alone of the family did not altogether like the new visitor. For charming, ardent William Unwin, Cowper's affection showed no signs of waning. But he was only twenty-one, and he was not a woman. Cowper's most intimate friends were always women, for they alone could give that particular moral support of interest and sympathy which he most wanted in a friend. As a child he had leaned on his mother; as a youth on his cousins; and now, as a mature man, worn with suffering and ecstasy, he turned to Mrs. Unwin.

She was peculiarly fitted to bear the weight. Like the life of which she was the center, she gave him all he had loved in his old existence, with additional qualities it could not provide. Beside Harriet and Theodora she would, it is true, have seemed a little provincial. Her manners had a country stiffness. Her talk was sprinkled with the curious Biblical phraseology of Evangelicalism. "The Lord Jehovah will be alone exalted when the day of his deliverance comes," she writes of Cowper when he was not well. But she was not unsocial—had she not come to Huntingdon for company?—she had humor, though of the kind that sees rather than makes jokes; and she was well read in a serious Evangelical sort of way. Her distinguishing qualities, however, were to be found not in her mind or in her manners, but in her character.

It was simple, its interest centering exclusively round two objects—the religious and the personal. And it was strong, but with a feminine strength, instinctive, passive, tenacious. In religion she was a disciple, not a leader; and in the outward ordering of her personal life she was chiefly concerned to carry out the wishes of those she cared for. But within her own sphere she acted with the unhurried confidence of supreme determination. She never analyzed her feelings or questioned her beliefs; she thought some things right and did them, and some things wrong and did not do them. If by chance she erred, she made no excuses for herself, but wasted no time in useless self-upbraiding. Her personal feelings were of a piece with the rest of her—strong but not violent, deep but not overflowing. She was not given to outbursts of emotional feeling; but when she did give her heart, it was absolutely and for ever. There was no sacrifice she would not make for some one she loved.

Yet even in regard to them she adhered rigidly to her simple code of right and wrong. She would not allow her affection to blind her to their faults; nor would she tell them she approved of them when she did not, for fear of hurting their feelings. She was at one with herself; and from this her personality drew a calm force which differentiated it from that of the ordinary pious domestic woman. Even now, from the dingy, ill-drawn engraving which is all the portrait we have of her, her eyes gaze out beneath her clear forehead with a serene, direct, sensible expression that soothes us, as it soothed Cowper long ago.

It was no wonder he liked her. For she supplied all the qualities he lacked. He did not mind if she was limited, unsubtle, without ideas of her own. He wanted not guidance, but support; and support was just what she was fitted to give. Strength and sanity and repose were the qualities he always liked in a friend; but he generally found them only in people who thought his religion queer. She believed all the same things as he believed, but with a contented, equable confidence quite beyond his compass. He was certain that whatever doubts and terrors, "flaws and starts, impostors to true fear," he might feel, however much his mood might vary between unreasonable exaltation and unreasonable despair, she would always be the same—firm and safe and sure; that when he came into her room trembling from some qualm of conscience, some horrid vision of the night, she would turn untroubled eyes upon him, lay aside her work, and in quiet tones and unexaggerated terms affirm those consoling truths he was longing to hear. And he would be reassured.

Their intimacy increased all the quicker on account of its peculiar circumstances. Mrs. Unwin's position as

the center of a grown-up family had presented her to
Cowper in a maternal light. It was part of her attraction to one who, ever since he was six years old, had
felt the need of a mother so keenly. And of course it
removed any embarrassment he might naturally have
felt at becoming so intimate with a strange woman. But,
in fact, she was almost the same age as himself; so that
he enjoyed in her company all the understanding and
sense of sympathetic equality that one only gets from
a contemporary. She was, in fact, Theodora and
Harriet and his mother all in one. He supplied her
needs as she supplied his. She was still a comparatively
young woman, but her husband was old and her children
were grown up. Her life was empty; it lacked object,
interest, occupation. And she had no one to guide her
in that Evangelical faith which was beginning to play
such a large part in her life. In Cowper she found some
one who needed her and who could act as her spiritual
director. And the drab, provincial society in which she
had hitherto lived laid her peculiarly open to the charm
he always had for women.

After he had known the Unwins three months, he
went to live with them. Ever since he had met them,
his dislike of living alone had returned with a redoubled
strength. How could he persuade himself he enjoyed
it when he had the pleasures of family life every day
before his eyes? One day it crossed his mind that the
Unwins might take him in as a lodger. He tried to put
the idea out of his thoughts. He felt it the work of the
flesh trying to mold his life according to its selfish desires;
and was it not his creed to purge himself of all selfish
desire, and accept whatever fate God might choose for
him? But he could not silence his longings, and try
as he might he thought of little else for three days.

By the end of the third he had succeeded in fixing his outward attention, at least, on something else. But as he was sitting meditating in his room the words "The Lord of Hosts will do this" came unawares into his mind and began to run in his head like a tune, reiterating themselves, as it seemed, louder and louder and more and more urgently, till at last he began to think that some one was whispering them in his ear. They must be a sign from Heaven; but a sign of what? He turned involuntarily for an explanation to the thought that had never ceased to dominate his subconscious mind. Could it be that God wanted him to live with the Unwins? It should be, it must be so! Joyfully snatching at the idea, he rushed off to see them. They accepted the proposal, and within a few days he had moved in.

He had found his monastery. Here at length was that calm retreat, that silent shade, in which he could consecrate his existence to keeping pure and bright the ethereal flame of spiritual ecstasy that was all that made life worth living to him. Cowper's life with the Unwins is the complete example of the Evangelical idea of the holy home, in the world, but not of it—the religious life lived in conjunction with the customs and comforts of the ordinary eighteenth-century middle-class family. It is a perfect period piece, rising before one's inner eye, as one reads of it, like a series of faded mezzotints after Morland—*The Pious Family in Four Plates: Morning, Noon, Afternoon, Evening*—their titles engraved beneath them in slim copper-plate, in which gentlemen in huge cravats and ladies in voluminous skirts of white muslin read the Bible, and relieve the poor, and take part in family worship, with an expression of discreet benevolence on their small faces.

Cowper's day was mapped out in accordance with a

strict scheme of Evangelical devotion. On waking he
spent a little time in prayer. Breakfast was between
eight and nine, and afterward the family assembled
in the parlor, where Cowper or young Unwin read aloud
the Scriptures or the sermons of some faithful preacher,
while the ladies listened with heads bent and needles
flashing over their work. By a quarter to eleven it was
time to get ready for church, which lasted till twelve.
After that came a break. Dinner was at three, and till
then you could do what you liked. On wet days Cowper
used to sit up in his room reading or writing letters. But
he preferred to be out, riding or walking, or, best of all,
gardening. He had never had a garden before, but
there was something in the occupation at once so innocent
and so civilized, so rural and so domesticated, that was
in harmony with his whole nature. And the steady
manual work was now especially soothing to his weak
nerves and strong body. He spent hours digging and
planting and weeding in the old tangled garden, where
the air was sweet with the scent of jessamine, and the
lime trees stood up leafy beyond the wall. At three
o'clock came dinner; then a little conversation in the
garden till tea, an hour later. And after tea, except in
midwinter, when it had to be taken earlier, came a walk.

This walk was the central point of the day. Cowper
generally went with Mrs. Unwin; they walked four miles
at least, and talked all the time. Can we not picture
them, moving very slowly—for it was impossible to move
quickly in their clothes—Mrs. Unwin dressed neatly,
but a little behind the fashion, her hair parted smoothly
beneath her little cap, and Cowper's lanky figure inclined
toward her in an attitude of old-fashioned courtesy;
while far around stretched the fens, drowsy green in the
summer sun, or a sheet of steel-colored water when the

winter floods were out? After the walk they spent the time in serious talk and reading till supper; or sometimes, gathered together in that quiet sitting-room, with the night shut out by curtains, the little band of believers would lift up their voices in a hymn of praise to the Author of their conversion; while the simple strain echoed itself in the frail precise tones of the harpsichord played by Mrs. Unwin as accompanist. Prayers for the household followed. And then they climbed the stairs to bed, their candles casting ludicrous leaping shadow shapes of themselves on banister and ceiling, so that Cowper pranked round Cowper up the stairs and even Mr. Unwin saw himself fantastic. One last prayer, and Cowper was in bed and asleep before the church clock chimed half past ten.

So passed the day; and so passed every day that followed. Outside, the genteel society of Huntingdon dined and played cards and went to the races. But the Unwin household saw as little of all this as if they lived a hundred miles away. The rigid order of their existence closed them in as with a high wall. For them the passage of the year was marked not by the mundane occasions which marked it for the rest of England, but Moslem-like, by calls to prayer.

They paid as little heed to the serious, as to the frivolous affairs of the world. In 1767 George III, mistakenly anxious to direct the policy of the country himself, dismissed Lord Rockingham's Government; and Huntingdon, in company with the rest of England, was the scene of one of those drinking, brawling, bribing elections that live for us still on the canvases of Hogarth. How Cowper would have thrilled to it in the old days! How he would have argued and shouted and tossed his hat in the air! Now he hardly spared the time to give it a passing contemptuous glance. "Truly I wish it was over," he commented to Hill, "for it occasions the most detestable scene of profligacy and riot that can be conceived."

Corporate activity generates an ardor unattainable alone; and the Evangelical zeal of the little household grew with every day they spent together. Mrs. Unwin's old acquaintances—decent, respectable people who were not above liking their joke—complained when they came to see her that she had lost all her old sprightliness and was grown quite a Methodist. As for Cowper, one would have thought it impossible to become more religious than he was already, but he did—at least more exclusively religious. Ever since his conversion the world had lost its attraction for him, but he had not altogether forgotten its existence. Now, required as he was to concentrate on religious ideas every hour of the day, he ceased to be able to turn his mind to any other. Indeed, to do so was against the principles of his faith. His very recreations grew religious. When he talked it was to discuss some theological point or to recount his religious experiences; when he read, his book was devotional. If he wrote poetry is was a hymn; if prose it was a meditation or the pious chronicle of his spiritual pilgrimage.

His literary style was changing with the change in his ideas. In his letters passages about secular life in the easy, humorous, Addisonian style of his youth alternate with others on religious topics written in the regular Evangelical manner—surging, ejaculatory, riddled with repetitions, stiff with Biblical phrases. "If I were as genteel as I am negligent I should be the most delightful creature in the universe," he would write in one sentence, and then, a few lines later: "A thousand worlds will vanish at the consummation of all things. But the word of God stands fast, and they who trust in Him shall not be confounded."

Every incident of his uneventful life he now examined and judged from an Evangelical point of view. He began to apply a sort of moral microscope to his actions. In the April of 1767 young Unwin went on a visit to Hertfordshire, and Cowper gave him an introduction to a cousin, Mrs. Cowper. It seemed a harmless enough thing to do. But his conscience soon found something to deplore in it; and he felt he ought to make a confession to his cousin. "Though my friend," he wrote to her, "before I was admitted as an inmate here was satisfied that I was not a mere vagabond, yet I could not resist the opportunity of furnishing him with ocular demonstration of it, by introducing him to one of my most splendid connections; that when he hears me called 'that fellow Cowper' he may be able, upon unquestionable evidence, to assert my gentlemanhood and relieve me from the weight of that opprobrious appellation . . . you will be more ready to excuse me than I am to excuse myself. But in good truth it was abominable pride of heart and indignation and vanity."

This Mrs. Cowper was gradually usurping Lady Hesketh's place in Cowper's correspondence. He had never known her well before; but she shared his religious views, and in his present state of mind he cared only to talk of religion. How could he speak of it freely to Lady Hesketh, who would not believe that he had ever been a great sinner, and who showed only too clearly that she considered his present condition dangerously "enthusiastic"? Indeed, for all her seeming virtue, was she not herself a child of wrath predestined to damnation? He hated to believe it, but believe it he must. "How

lovely," he exclaimed wistfully, "must be the spirits of
just men made perfect, since creatures so lovely in our
eyes may yet have the wrath of God abiding on them."
They both felt that an unbridgeable gulf had opened between them; and tacitly, without hard feeling on either
side, their connection lapsed.

He was no happier about Harriet's father than about
Harriet. What was he to think of a man who, at the
age of sixty-six, regardless of the pit of Tophet to which
at any moment he might be consigned, published a volume
of secular poems? And such poems, too! "That holy
and blessed Name to which he bows his head on the
Sabbath is treated with as little reverence as that of
Mahomet. He has, indeed, packed and jumbled them
together in a manner very shocking to a Christian reader." As far as he could see, except for Mrs. Cowper
and the Madans, his whole family were likely to go to
hell. He began even to have doubts about the fate of
his father. Doctor Cowper, it is true, had never so far
forgotten himself as to put the name of his Creator in
an unseemly juxtaposition to that of Mahomet. Cowper
himself admitted that he was "everything that was excellent and praiseworthy towards men." But if he were
not in grace this would avail him nothing. And had he
died in grace? Poor Cowper! He could not but feel
that any doubts on such a subject were unfilial; but in the
exalted atmosphere he now moved in he tended to lose
his sense of natural obligations.

His relations thought that he had lost his sense of
other obligations as well. Cowper had no more money
of his own now than he had before he went mad; and
he was principally supported by a fund made up by his
family. What was their irritation to learn that not
only had he, by sheer mismanagement, exceeded his

yearly income by one hundred and forty pounds, but that he had brought Doctor Cotton's servant—Sam Roberts— and Dick Colman, the cobbler's boy, from St. Albans to live with him. His motive in doing this had been pure benevolence. He believed them to be on the high road to conversion, and wished to keep them with him lest they should be distracted by the temptations of the world. Unluckily he had no money to support them; so that they had to be supported by his unconverted relatives. And to their unenlightened minds it merely looked as if he kept two servants at their expense. They were very angry, and one, Major Cowper, threatened to withdraw his subscription. Cowper explained and apologized profusely, and was so patently innocent of any wish to impose on any one that the storm blew over. The Unwins helped him to reduce his expenditure by letting him off half his rent, and he paid his debts by a small sacrifice of capital. But, try as he might, he never became a good manager. A faith that might remove mountains could not make him economical.

In spite of these small clouds, he was very happy at Huntingdon. His life was beautiful, with the beauty of the cloister, where, far from the aimless hurry of the world, and freed from the pains of expectation and disappointment, man passes his existence in a peaceful round of devotion to God. But it was the cloister without its chill, its unnatural renunciation of natural feelings. On the other hand, it managed to avoid the dowdy unloveliness of the Puritan home. It was more like the Anglican community of Little Gidding than anything else—that community where Crashaw wrote his poems and John Inglesant met Mary Colet. But its spirit differed from that of Little Gidding as the eighteenth century differs from the seventeenth, or the hymns of Charles Wesley from those of Henry Vaughan. It was less jeweled, less soaring, less sacramental, more friendly, easier, more intimate. There was a snatch of morning about it, a nursery freshness, an innocent, lavender-scented sweetness. The very Calvinism it professed so conscientiously had lost its sting. In that kindly atmosphere, superstition and narrowness assumed the character of quaint, almost lovable, foibles. It thought a great number of things wrong, but it did not exult in fierce delight over the probable fate of the sinner; it shunned the vanities of the world, but approved a decent comeliness and order. Its monotony is enlivened by little courtesies, movements of impulsive kindness, flights of gentle humor. As Cowper said, "Such a life is consistent with the utmost enjoyment."

# CHAPTER IV

## FAITH AND MR. NEWTON

ONE day, about two years after Cowper had gone to Huntingdon, old Mr. Unwin fell off his horse and cracked his skull. For four days the family hung over his bed striving to catch, in his delirious mutterings, some trace of that Evangelical faith that alone, in their view, could save him in the world he was about to enter; on the fourth he died. Cowper's life was unavoidably changed. There was no question, indeed, of his separating from Mrs. Unwin. Each had become an indispensable condition of the other's existence. To him she was that rock of support and sympathy for which he had yearned ever since he was a child; while she found in him at last a worthy object on which to pour forth the energy of her devoted, undemonstrative, possessive nature. The personal bond that united them was the closest either was ever to know.

Was it a bond of love? Cowper, fearful of any idea that might interfere with their present perfect intimacy, clung to the view that the relation was filial. "Mrs. Unwin," he assured a correspondent with anxious emphasis, "looks on me completely as a son." But it is not natural to live in a filial relation to a woman only a few years older than yourself, to whom you are not related, and whom you had never seen till you were thirty-three. It could not last. Already Cowper was imperceptibly

127

growing to feel on more equal terms with her. And with a few more years his feelings were to settle into a simple tenderness that had its roots in the very fibers of his being. It was a sentiment of exquisite beauty, vigilant, humble, selfless, and it shines through the mingled gleam and dark of his later years like a clear white flame. Nor was his relation with her without that sense of emotional adventure, that intimacy somehow closer for the very formalities through which it must be expressed, that can only come between persons of different sex. But it never had the distinctive character of passionate love—it lacked the doubts and ardors and jealousies that characterized even so lukewarm an affair as Cowper's youthful sentiment for Theodora. Passion, indeed, was alien to his nature; his deepest feelings were all affections. It is foolish to suppose that a man must be passionately in love with every woman he singles out for intimacy, above all a man of the ethereal, hyper-civilized type of Cowper.

Her feelings were altogether more straightforward. At first, indeed, she can not have thought herself in love, any more than Cowper did, or, with her principles and her strength of character, she would have felt forced to break with him. And to the end of her life she always alluded to "Mr. Cowper" with the decorous formality of an acquaintance. But for his sake she was to show herself prepared to risk the loss of her income, her family and her good name—prepared, in fact, for the loss of anything except Cowper. Him she would not even share with any one else. Her nature was a simple one, not given to fine feelings or fine distinctions. It is unnecessary to try to believe that she was not in love with Cowper.

Mr. Unwin's death, then, did not break up the little

household, but it decided its removal. Now that they
were free to do so, both Cowper and Mrs. Unwin longed
to gratify that dearest of all wishes of the Evangelical
heart, to settle in a "faithful" neighborhood near some
"experiential" divine. From him they would learn how
best to put their faith into practise; and, daily drinking
at the fountain of his enthusiasm, they would grow strong
to brush aside any doubt or despondency the Devil might
whisper to their hearts.

But who was this prophet to be? Where should they
go? Aldwinkle in Northamptonshire? Rivaulx in Yorkshire? Cowper earnestly canvassed the question with
his more serious correspondents. Actually it was settled
by the prophet himself. One day, not long after Mr.
Unwin's death, there arrived at the house an Evangelical
clergyman called Newton, who said that he had been
recommended to call by a friend of Mrs. Unwin. He
was an odd, unclerical-looking little man with a big nose.
But he had a bright, compelling eye, and when he began
to speak, it was with a force and an animation that fairly
flung them off their feet. They had never met such a
dynamic personality. Within a few minutes he had
taken them completely under his wing, was advising them
about their most intimate concerns. And before a week
was out he had written offering them the alternative of
three houses, if they would come and live in his parish
of Olney in Buckinghamshire.

They were not unwilling. Mrs. Unwin had found Newton sympathetic over her husband's death; and Cowper
was dazzled by the flaming certainty of his faith. But
even if they had been unwilling, they would have been
unable to stand up against such a whirlwind. The only
difficulty was that all the possible houses in Olney seemed
to be so far from the church. However, Newton brushed

that aside.  He knew of one, two, three houses nearer;
and if none was available, he would always be ready to
come and hold a service in their house, wherever it might
be.  He had taken a great fancy to them; they were just
the type of people the place needed; they must come.
And come they did.  Within three months their be-
longings had been packed up and bundled across England, and unpacked again at Orchard Side, Olney.

It was not an attractive house.  Its tall façade of dingy
brick, faced with dingier stone, and crowned by a row of
false Gothic battlements, frowned down upon one "like a
prison," thought Cowper, as he caught sight of it, at
the end of the long Olney High Street.  Its garden was
only a narrow strip of about fifty feet by twenty, between
two high walls.  All its rooms looked north, and it abutted
on Silver End, the worst district of the place, whose sordid jollities were a constant offense to Cowper's simple
but fastidious taste.  However, it was near the church,
and it was near Newton.  You had only to open the gate
at the end of the garden, and cross a bit of orchard, and
there you were, looking in at the white-painted sash windows at the back of the Vicarage, still spick and fresh as
a doll's house, for it had been built for Newton by his
patron, Lord Dartmouth, only three years before.

For the rest, Cowper did not take much to Olney; and
never did, though he lived there twenty years.  If it was
at all like it is now, one can understand it.  It is a typical
small country town, with a long straggling High Street
and an avenue down the middle of it, a bow-windowed
inn, and a roomy, perpendicular church.  But it lacks
the cheerful charm associated with such places; its streets
are stagnant, but not peaceful.  On the other hand, Cowper loved the country around.  To us it seems much
of a piece with the town: tame and trivial, a network of

villages and fields, neither flat nor hilly, devoid of distances. But it reminded Cowper of Berkhamstead; it had the same leafy hedgerows and thatched cottages half buried in trees, the same atmosphere of green domesticated peace. And the landscape of Berkhamstead, the first he had ever admired, was still the most beautiful in the world to him. As he gazed pensively south, across the sleepy Ouse toward Hertfordshire, the memory of other days would flood his mind, a thousand forgotten incidents would start before his eyes, and he would feel at home.

Not that he had much time for such unprofitable musings. His life was a very much more strenuous affair now than it had been in Huntingdon. For it was dominated by the extraordinary man who had brought him there. In his later years the Reverend John Newton published, for the edification of his fellow Evangelicals, an account of his life, entitled *An Authentic Narrative of Some Interesting Particulars in the Life of John Newton*. It is a fusty, forbidding little book, and more than half of it is pious platitude; but it enshrines within its stilted sentences one of the most fantastic fairy-tales that was ever the true story of a human being.

John Newton was born in London in 1725, the son of a shipmaster. Even as a child he showed himself possessed of a superstitious, inflammable imagination, and a boiling, dynamic energy, always restlessly searching for an object on which to expend itself. His mother, an old-fashioned Puritan, wished him to become a clergyman, and for the first few years of his life his mind was forced to concentrate itself on religion. From time to time he would be seized with a fit of violent devotion. Once, at the age of fifteen, he was so excited by Beattie's *Church History* that for three months he would not eat

any meat, and hardly opened his mouth, for fear of
letting fall one of those idle words for which he would
have to give account on the Last Day.

However, his mother died. And with adolescence his
virile nature began to react against the ideas to which
he had been brought up. He was incapable of doing
anything by halves; and he became a militant atheist.
His father had sent him to sea; he threw himself with
gusto into the rioting, buccaneering life of the eighteenth-
century sailor, and especially took a fierce delight in blas-
pheming against the God he had so lately delighted to
honor. From time to time, indeed, the convictions of
his childhood would reassert themselves, and visit him
in mysterious stirrings of conscience. Once, for example,
he had a curious dream. It seemed to him that his ship
was riding at anchor for the night in the harbor of
Venice, where he had lately touched: the exquisite,
worthless Venice of Longhi and Goldoni, a strange setting
for the somber fantasies of his Nordic imagination. It
was his watch on deck and as he stood gazing across
the inky waters of the lagoon to where, on the lighted
piazzetta, contessa and cisisbeo stepped masked from
their gondolas to revel at the ridotto, a stranger came up
to him and gave him a ring, which he implored him not to
lose, as he valued his life. This stranger was followed
by another, who as eloquently adjured him to throw the
ring away. And he dropped it overboard. Immediately
the spires of Venice were lit up with a lurid glare; behind them the Euganean hills burst into flame; and his
tempter, turning on him with an expression of triumph,
told him that they were lit for his destruction. But at
this moment a third stranger appeared. As he stepped
on board the flames died away; and he drew the ring
from the water. But he would not give it back to Newton,

saying, with a solemn emphasis, that he should have it at some future time. Shuddering with terror he awoke. The dream seemed to him a parable of his own spiritual life: the ring his salvation, the second stranger the power of evil. He could not get the dream out of his head.

However, it could not for long divert his mind from following its natural course. Already, indeed, it was dominated by a very different theme. His turbulent spirit found it hard to settle to any job, and about a year before he had got a new appointment on a ship bound for Jamaica. A few days before it sailed he went to pay a visit of courtesy on some people called Catlett, to whom his father had given him an introduction. He had hardly been in the house an hour before he had fallen in love with Miss Catlett—a girl of fourteen. His love was of a piece with his religion and his infidelity— a flaming, tearing, devouring passion that burned itself into the very marrow of his being. For the moment time ceased to exist. His ship was due to sail in a few days; and he let it sail, while he sat day after day with his eyes fixed, as in a trance, on the object of his adoration. And when at last he did go to sea, it was only to dream of Miss Catlett, and work with frenzied energy in order to make enough money to marry her.

But now a succession of disasters began to overtake him. Recklessly lounging on Harwich Dock in his sailor's check shirt, he was caught by the press-gang. His vitality enabled him to support his new condition with tolerable ease and cheerfulness. He soon became a midshipman, and he met a fellow-officer who supplied him with many useful new arguments against the existence of God. But when his ship was ordered to New Guinea and he was faced with the prospect of not seeing Miss Catlett for five years, he deserted. He was caught,

brought back in irons, and, in accordance with the savage
penal code of the day, publicly stripped, flogged and degraded to the position of a common seaman.  His rage
knew no bounds.  It was agony to one of his nature to
obey when he had once commanded, and he felt he had
lost his love for ever.  He used to lie for hours, as the
ship made its way through the calm tropical waters,
brooding on his wrongs, till he was half mad.  Sometimes he would decide to kill himself, sometimes the
captain who had misused him, sometimes both.  But
always before he acted the figure of his love, all the
lovelier by contrast with his present circumstances, would
start before him; his heart would be flooded with a softer
emotion; and he would stay his hand.

At last, after weary months, he arrived at Madeira,
where he got exchanged to another ship.  His new captain was kind to him.  But Newton was now so desperate that he became quite unmanageable, insubordinate
to superiors, and given up to every vice.  When they
reached the Platane Islands off the west coast of Africa,
he left the ship and took service with a planter.  One
would have thought it impossible that he should go
through anything much worse than he had already.  But
he did.  His master had a black mistress, who took a
violent dislike to Newton.  For two years he was treated
more harshly than the meanest native slave, under-
clothed, under-fed and over-worked. An attack of tropical
fever, during which he lay untended on the floor without even water to drink, was the final blow.  He became
like an animal, dumb and resigned, incapable of thought
or emotion, or anything but a blind lust to satisfy the
wants of Nature.  Only, now and again, memories of his
early education would stumble into his numbed brain.
He had somehow managed to keep a tattered geometry

in his pocket through all his adventures, and he would steal out by night, half-naked skeleton as he was, and with its help laboriously trace arcs and triangles on the sand in the brilliant light of the African moon.

After a year he got away, and became foreman for another planter in the neighboring islands of the Bananoes. Here his life was supportable save for an occasional pang of regret for Miss Catlett. Such letters as he had written home had brought no reply. And he had given up all hope of getting back. He began more and more to live like the natives, gradually acquiring their habits and superstitions, so that he dared not allow himself to sleep once the moon was above the fronded palm trees. However, after two years and a half, a ship arrived from England with a letter from his father asking him to come home. His first instinct was to refuse. But the thought that he might see Miss Catlett again, though he now had little hope of marrying her, caused him to change his mind.

Newton was now very different from the stormy boy who had sailed from Torbay five years before. His conversation was still reckless and bitter and profane; so much so, indeed, that the horrified captain of the ship on which he traveled home began to fear it would bring a judgment on the ship. But the suffering Newton had undergone had left him with a disgust for the world. Its prizes no longer inspired his ambition, nor its pleasures his desires. Had he not followed the call of his passions wherever they had led him? And what had he got from them but bitterness and misery? But he could not resign himself to inactivity. His dynamic energy still boiled within him, seeking an outlet. He could not find it in worldly ambition or worldly enjoyment. Was there nothing more stable, more satisfying?

Insensibly his mind began to revert for guidance to the
beliefs implanted in it in infancy.

A moment of danger brought it to the point of decision.   Soon after the ship had left Newfoundland a
violent storm got up, and within a few hours the upper
timbers of the ship were torn away, and it was flooded
with water.   Provisions, cargo and some men were lost,
and during two days everybody worked at the pumps.
For a time they seemed to be doing no good.   With a
thrill of fear Newton realized he was probably going to
die.   "If this will not do," he exclaimed unthinkingly,
"the Lord have mercy on us."   The true significance of
his words suddenly came home to him.   He thought,
"If He really exists there will be very little mercy for
me."   In that moment of terrible crisis the whole of
his past life moved in vivid review before him; and it
struck him with overwhelming force that of all the objects that had in turn commanded his allegiance, now, at
the point of death, only the religion of his childhood
retained any value in his eyes.   It alone had not proved
worthless or unattainable: all his sorrows might be dated
from the time that he deserted it.   He resolved if he
were saved to devote the rest of his life to it.   He was
saved.   And for the last few days of the voyage began to put his resolution into practise.   He could not,
indeed, feel a lively faith in Christianity; but he was
convinced that such a faith alone had the slightest chance
of giving him permanent happiness.   And he hoped that,
by consistently living in accordance with Christian precept, he might obtain it.

He arrived in England to find his father away on a
voyage.   But he had made arrangements with a ship-
owner friend of his to offer Newton a job first as mate,
and then as captain, on a line of ships trading in slaves;

so that his future was assured. More pleasing still, he found Miss Catlett still unmarried and still constant. And after his second voyage they were married. In the excitement induced by all these events he tended to forget his pious resolutions, though he still meant to keep them. But on one of his expeditions he saw a young man, an infidel just as he had been, dying in terrible circumstances, friendless in Africa. The fear of death and the terrors of his conscience revived again. A dangerous illness at sea a few months after this finally awakened him from his inertia, and from this time on he entered on a life of rigid study and devotion. Every moment of his day was devoted to some useful employment, and such time as he could spare from his profession and his religion he occupied in teaching himself Latin from a pocket Horace. It must have been a curious scene—the ship moving with sails and rigging aslant against the stars, among the mysterious islands of that equatorial ocean, while the human cargo packed together in the hold sweltered below, and above, the captain paced the deck murmuring to himself the compact urbanities of Horace.

He persevered in this life for five or six years, but without achieving real satisfaction. The fact was that eighteenth-century orthodoxy did not appeal to his imagination, and so could not become that soul-absorbing passion that to his temperament was a necessary condition of happiness. His present religion regulated his life and saved him from the worst sufferings into which he had been led by his infidelity. But what he wanted was a doctrine that would demand the absolute surrender of every energy of his mind and body. One evening in 1754 when his ship was at anchor in the port of St. Christopher he came across a Captain Clunie, who told him about

Evangelicalism. Before the evening was out Newton had given himself up to this new creed as he had to his love for Miss Catlett. Here was the religion he wanted—a creed that spoke to the heart, that commanded the undivided allegiance of the whole personality, that fired the imagination and gave scope to the desire for action. It was the turning-point of his life. He had found what he had been looking for ever since he was ten years old.

For the remaining forty years of his life every thought, feeling and action was dedicated, without a faltering, to the faith of his choice. His life on board ship took on the ascetic rigor of a Trappist monastery. Every moment he was not working or sleeping he spent in prayer or reading the Bible, or instructing his crew in religion. His Latin studies were laid aside as useless frivolities. If he had female slaves on board he ate no meat, for fear it might strengthen his flesh to lust after them. After a time he made up his mind to give up his profession; not, oddly enough, because he thought slavery wrong, but because it was too interesting: it made him think too much about secular subjects.

For five years he was a tide surveyor at Liverpool, where he continued his religious studies, and where he managed to get to know Whitefield and Wesley and other Evangelical leaders. Then in 1758 he decided to take orders. But here was a difficulty. He was not at all the sort of man who appealed to a Georgian bishop. Not only was he enthusiastic, and not quite a gentleman, but it was rumored that he thought a nonconformist had as good a chance of Heaven as a member of the Established Church of England. Every bishop he asked refused to ordain him. Irritated at the rebuffs he received, Newton had thoughts of becoming a Congregationalist minister. But Lord Dartmouth, the good angel of Evangelicalism, stepped in, procured his ordination, and himself presented him to the living of Olney.

Conversion had given Newton incentive, ordination gave him scope. All that virile vitality that had carried him triumphant through so many changes of fortune, that had enabled him to endure slavery, defeat sickness and defy the Navy of England, now poured itself with irresistible force into the avocations of an Evangelical minister. He preached, taught, visited, held prayer-meetings; he wrote hymns and pamphlets; even began a history of the whole world since the creation, from the Evangelical point of view, in order to combat the subversive interpretations of Gibbon and Hume. But his most characteristic activity was his religious letters. All over England, with people of every sort—soldiers, politicians, school-masters, young ladies—Newton kept up a voluminous correspondence, in which he advised them about every detail of their moral and spiritual lives. His advice was always long and generally impassioned; and when, as sometimes happened, it was given unasked, it was not well received. But on the converted it made a tremendous impression. And by the time he met Cowper, Olney was already one of the centers of the Evangelical world.

Newton's character is sufficiently shown forth by his story. He was primarily a man of action. If he thought he should do a thing he did it; and he often did it without thinking about it at all. Nor did thought mean anything to him except in so far as it told him how to act. He was incapable of speculation or self-analysis. Reason was to him a weapon which he used, not very effectively, to confute his opponents. His own acts and opinion were directed not by reason, but by unanalyzed instinct. He became an atheist because his instinct reacted against

religion, and when instinct demanded religion again he
threw his atheism overboard without even bothering to
find replies to those arguments he had thought so formidable when his instinct had been, on their side.

Yet he was not at all stupid. No one whose brain
was not a strong instrument could have taught himself
Latin on a ship with nothing to help him but a copy of
Horace, and anything he took up, whether navigating or
preaching or writing, he did well. But over and above
all this, he had imagination. It is this quality that dif-
ferentiates his narrative from those truthful fictions of
Defoe which it so much resembles in its outward incidents
—adventures, escapes and sudden vicissitudes. No one
could be less like the businesslike heroes of Defoe, with
their matter-of-fact love affairs, their unshakable nerve,
and the British common sense with which they confronted
the most unlikely situations, than this passionate, superstitious creature who was guided in the most momentous
decisions by omens and prophetic dreams; who trembled
before the baleful influence of the African moon; and
was upheld through the blackest misfortunes, and prevented from committing appalling crimes, by the memory
of a girl of sixteen whom he was convinced he would
never see again. He was extraordinarily sensitive to the
influence of Nature; he found in later life that only from
country solitudes could his soul soar easily to heights of
spiritual ecstasy. His letters, too, crude and absurd as
they are, are full of flights of naïve fancy, touches of
beauty, humor and intimacy, only possible to a man
of imagination.

Nor was this out of keeping with his character.
The imagination is a thing of instinct rather than of
reason, and often men of action have more of it than
men of thought. Hobbes had less imagination than

Cromwell, Luther more than Erasmus. Newton, indeed, had more in common with these heroes of the Reformation than with his own contemporaries. Like theirs, his character was heroic and unsymmetrical, freaked with a Gothic quaintness, misted with a Gothic sublimity. He had their faults, too. He was narrow and uncouth; he was not molded of fine clay. He could hardly have survived such a life if he had been; and in so far as he was not like Luther, he was the eighteenth-century sailor he looked, clumsy, careless and insensitive. His kindness was generally tactless, and his piety sometimes profane.

But all these qualities, good and bad, remarkable or commonplace, were subservient to the single one of fanaticism. His whole life was a succession of slaveries to successive single ideas. Now he was convinced that his own particular brand of religion was the best thing for any one, anywhere, in any circumstances. His every word, whether serious or cheerful, trivial or important, whether it was connected with people or politics or gardening, was made to refer to religion. His very jokes were Evangelical. This exclusive devotion was bound up with the strongest sides of his character—his will, his passion, his imagination, his faith. He would have given his life for his beliefs, without a thought. But exclusiveness is also responsible for his defects. He carried out the precepts of his creed so literally as to be at times both indecent and ridiculous. "Good news indeed," he remarked, with conscientious joviality, on hearing of his favorite niece's translation to another world. It might sound heartless, but it was Evangelical, and therefore must be right. Again, whatever could not be by any means forced into connection with his religion must necessarily be of the devil. "If there is any practice in the land sinful," he exclaimed, "then attendance at the theatre is so." And all he could see in the graceful symbolism of Venice's *Marriage to the Sea* was "a lying, antiquated Popish Bull."

It is difficult to talk long about one subject without becoming boring. And Newton often did. He would have given his life to save your soul; but nothing could persuade him not to thrust his views down your throat. He tended to become arrogant. There was only one God, and John Newton was His prophet. So that though he was always repeating that he was sinful, he never admitted he was wrong. It was impossible to argue with him. If any one asked Newton to explain a contradiction in his argument, he merely looked at him with the dreadful, glassy good-nature of the fanatic, forgave him for his error, and went on with his exhortation.

With such a man as his spiritual director, it was not odd that Cowper had little time to himself. Newton had made Olney a whirlwind of Evangelical activity. When he was not preaching—and he was sometimes in the pulpit for six hours a day—he was visiting the sick, or giving Bible lessons to the children, or holding a joint service with the Dissenters, or leading an extempore prayer-meeting in the Great House, a large empty barrack of a place, opposite the Vicarage. Into the midst of this whirlwind Cowper was caught up. He had to leave his monastery and come forth into the world, a preaching missionary friar. No more of those placid walks after tea with Mrs. Unwin. Dinner was at one and tea at four, and after that sermon or lecture till bed. Cowper did not object to the change in his life. His spirit was irresistibly drawn to Newton's buoyant vitality, as it had been to the calm certainty of Mrs. Unwin. He spent eight hours of every day in Newton's company; prayed with him; with him attended the bedside of the sick and dying; rode or walked by his side through the lanes, when he went to preach at a neighboring village. Newton gave him some work of his own to do. He visited the poor and he taught in Sunday-school.

Such work was easy to him. His kindly nature had always gone out to children; and he had a simple and diffident sympathy which made all the people he visited love him. It was a very different thing when Newton asked him to lead in prayer. His conversion had not cured him of that morbid horror of making a public exhibition of himself which had occasioned his first madness. When he first went to Huntingdon he had thought of becoming a clergyman, and then given it up because he could not face the publicity it would entail. And when, after Mr. Unwin's death, he had been asked to lead the day's prayer for the family and their two servants, he had almost broken down. "I was so troubled at the apprehension of it," he wrote, "and so dreadfully concerned at the conflict I sustained on this occasion that my health was not a little affected thereby." But this new task was far harder. In front of a number of people whom he did not know and who might not be in sympathy with him at all, he was required to lay bare all that was most sacred and most painful in his existence, and to speak as he was used only to speak in his bedroom alone. His whole being recoiled from the thought. However, Newton would not listen to such morbid hesitations for a moment. And, indeed, Cowper himself thought it only another sign of his uncontrollable weakness and vanity. Was he, just because it embarrassed him to do so, to withhold from others, less fortunate than himself, the encouragement they might gain from the glorious testimony of his conversion? With set face he nerved himself to the task.

For four or five hours before service began he would sit shaking with nerves. Then, in that barrack-like room, with the lines of decent cottage people composed in respectful attention before him, and the summer dusk falling on the fields outside, he would begin to speak. The first sentences came toneless and halting; but he gathered strength as he went on. And soon he had forgotten his fears, forgotten his audience, forgotten everything, save that he was trying, wretched, helpless creature as he was, to convey something of his gratitude to the compassionate Savior who raised him from the depths of hell, to tell Him how exclusively, how desperately, he put his trust in Him. The worn sensitive features grew tense with an unearthly enthusiasm, an uncontrollable emotion began to throb in the quiet educated voice. It seemed to the people sitting round as if they were listening unseen to some inconceivably holy, inconceivably intimate conversation, as if Cowper really saw his Lord in the room with him, and saw no one else. And they were moved as they had never been moved by the glib emotionalism of the professional Evangelical preacher. "I have heard many men preach," said an old villager years later, "but I have never heard anyone preach like Mr. Cowper."

Outside his religious activities his days pursued the same unvaried course they had at Huntingdon. It was a sensational event, for instance, when he and Mrs. Unwin had to cross the street to spend a few weeks at "The Bull" because one of their servants was ill with smallpox. One can not well imagine a sleepier little country inn than The Bull; but to Olney it represented the very epitome of worldly rush and frivolity. "What can you both do at the Bull," wrote Newton, "surrounded with noise and nonsense every night? But," he added with pious jocularity, "may the Lord preserve and comfort you in the midst of bulls and bears."

Life was also varied by the stream of Evangelical men and visitors who were always coming and going at the Vicarage. Mr. Venn came, and Mr. Berridge and Lord Dartmouth; and on one occasion, formidable thought, thirteen Baptist ministers at once. Cowper's heart leapt up when he saw them all seated round Newton's dining-room table. "It was a comfortable sight," he exclaims, "to see thirteen Gospel ministers together." On another evening he sat watching the candlelight playing on the austere countenance and glittering regimentals of Captain Scott, "the pious captain," who had come over to spend the night with Newton in order to avoid the races at Northampton.

But most of the glimpses of Cowper's life which we get at this period reveal him occupied in the recurring avocations of every week, picking his way to early service by the light of a lantern in the chill murk of a November morning, while Mrs. Unwin clattered on pattens at his side; or at even-song, in the Augustan gallery lately fitted on to the Gothic columns of the church in order to accommodate more worshipers, listening to Newton praying with ardor for "my maid Molly, who is troubled on the point of election."

Newton's servants were not the only ones whose spiritual condition gave cause for anxiety. Cowper and Mrs. Unwin had a great deal of trouble in that way. When they had first arrived at Olney their household had consisted of a man and a maid, both, as they thought, in a happy state of grace. But the maid early began to show signs of backsliding, and before long behaved in such a dreadful manner that they began to doubt whether she had ever really been converted at all. She left in a hurry. Her successor was respectable, but grossly incompetent, and after Mrs. Unwin had given her some "pious advice" she went too. Finally they fell back on a young woman from Olney, who, though religious, suffered from very poor health. Cowper could only hope that "as the Lord had designed her to the work He would give her strength equal to it."

So passed 1767, 1768, 1769. But though the outward circumstances of his life were so calm, Cowper's mind was once again the scene of a terrible crisis. Gradually, relentlessly, with gathering speed and momentum, that faith which had signalized his first recovery from madness, and upon which he had rested the whole structure of his subsequent life, was slipping away from him. The spell was breaking; the bridge was ceasing to bear; the single flame of his life's happiness was flickering to extinction. Indeed, it was a wonder that it lingered so long, for the method by which he attempted to keep it alive was radically defective; his ideal of religious life was a practical impossibility. Mortality is the first law of man's existence on this planet. Nor is his ecstasy exempt from its tragic jurisdiction. A breath of the Divine Spirit induced by love or art or prayer, suddenly it blows upon him; for a brief space of time he is swept up and borne along by the wind of its going; then he flags and falls back exhausted. It is beyond the power of his earth-bound spirit to sustain such an ethereal intensity of emotion for more than a moment: and such moments visit the most inspired of mankind only once or twice in a lifetime. Any system of life, therefore, which aims at constantly maintaining them must necessarily fail; but most of all one like Cowper's, which tries to do so by deliberately refusing to allow the mind to dwell on anything else. An emotion can not be induced by an intellectual effort; and, besides, the same emotion can not be roused often by the same stimulus. The mind is numbed by familiarity. One soon becomes used to the coloring of a room, however striking; the change of key that sent a thrill down the spine like a douche of cold water on first hearing becomes a mere insignificant noise if it is often repeated. So the unvarying round of Cowper's existence, instead of maintaining the emotional state, hastened its departure. The regular sequence of prayer and meditation ceased to stir him just because it was regular. He was trying to do an impossible thing, and he was trying to do it in the way that of all others would fail the soonest.

Of course, it was partly the fault of the Evangelical creed, which, as we have seen, made an emotional condition into a moral virtue. But its average adherents did not in practise carry this doctrine to a logical conclusion: the pressure of ordinary life was too strong to allow them to think about their souls all the time. So their emotions were often refreshed by new stimuli. It only shows the strength of the original experience, that, concentrating exclusively on it, Cowper should have felt its effect for as long as he did. But it could not last for ever; and already before he left Huntingdon a change in his feelings had appeared.

He began to notice periods of spiritual stagnation within himself, during which the things that had most moved him in the days of his conversion stirred no response at all. He could not keep his attention on the passages of the Bible he loved best; prayers that he had once not been able to say with a steady voice, so exactly did they express the most poignant and intimate experiences of his life, hymns in which he had been used to pour forth his whole soul in thanksgiving, now slipped from his lips almost without his realizing what he was doing. The great phrases of Evangelicalism, Election, Reprobation, Final Perseverance, the very sound of which had been enough two years before to thrill him like the sound of a trumpet, were now so dulled by repetition as hardly to convey any idea at all. "Oh, that I retained my first love," he said sadly to Mrs. Madan, "that it was with me as when I first came forth from the furnace, when the name of Jesus was like honey and milk upon my tongue and the very sound of it was sufficient to sustain and comfort me."

These periods of lethargy did not last long. But they were distressing while they lasted; and he had never known them before. What could be the cause of them? Perhaps God wished to save him from the danger of being over-confident; or perhaps He was trying his faith. All the saints had trials. He hoped this was the cause, not any fault of his own, and that he would be able to stand the test. If he did, perhaps the periods of lethargy would stop. But though he made every effort, they went on. He welcomed the change to Olney with enthusiasm. A new home under the personal supervision of one of the burning and shining lights of the Gospel, might prove just what was needed to make his troubles disappear.

For a few months his hopes were fulfilled. The change of scene and life was a stimulus. His new work gave him too much to do and too much to think about to allow him to worry about himself; while his whole spirit was revived by the impact of Newton's personality. He became confident, hopeful; at moments he knew again the religious ecstasy of two years before. But it was not quite the same ecstasy; he had become self-conscious about it. No longer did it flood his mind, compelling and unbidden, carrying him away whether he would or no. He watched for the least sign of it, tended it, savored it to the last drop, and when it was gone lingered over its memory—sole witness in a drab world to the living reality of his salvation. Nor was it induced, as before, regularly by the regular incidents of his religious life; but capriciously, by some chance accident—a detail in a service, a phrase in a book hitherto unnoticed, which brought the truth home to him afresh by suddenly presenting it from a new angle.

"The Lord has dealt graciously with me since I came, and I trust I have in two instances had much delightful communication with Him. Yet this opportunity of access was intimated to me in such a way as to teach me at the same time His great care that I might not turn it to my prejudice. I expected that in some sermon or exposition I should find Him, that the lips of His excellent minister would be the instrument by which the Lord would work upon and soften my obdurate heart, but He saw my proneness to praise the creature more than the Creator, and though therefore He gave me the thing I hoped for: yet He conveyed it to me in a way which I did not look to. On the last Sabbath morning, at a prayer meeting before service, while the poor folks were singing a hymn and my vile thoughts were rambling to the ends of the earth, a single sentence—'And is there no pity in Jesus' breast?'—seized my attention at once, and my heart within me seemed to return answer, 'Yes, or I had never been there.' The sweetness of this visit lasted almost through the day, and I was once more enabled to weep under a sense of the mercy of God in Jesus. On Thursday morning I attended a meeting of children, and found that passage 'Out of the mouth of babes and sucklings,' hast thou ordained praise, verified

in a sense I little thought of, for at almost every word
they spoke in answer to the several questions proposed
to them my heart burned within me and melted into tears
of gratitude and love."

In these moments all the old confidence returned, and
he upbraided himself for his inability to endure the
smallest trial with unfaltering heart. But he could not
feel this confidence long. It was induced by change of
scene and society, and when he got accustomed to this
change it went. The fact was that he was "through"
with Evangelicalism. Its appeal to him had been a purely emotional one, and his emotion had ceased to respond
to that kind of appeal. As we have seen, the quickening
of the spirit that had attended his first arrival at Olney
was never able to reawaken his response to those expressions of his religion which he was already bored with.
It could only stir him to respond to some aspect of it
he had not noticed before. And this response was pale,
flickering, premeditated, compared with the soul-shak-
ing thrill of his first vision. Within a few months of his
arrival at Olney all the old disquieting symptoms began
to reappear. When he tried to say his prayers he could
not keep his mind on what he was doing; after a few
moments he would suddenly recollect himself, and then,
in a second revulsion of feeling, he would upbraid himself for his lack of trust in God's mercy. He had loved
to meditate on his solitary walks—the sights and scenes
of the country, which were what he thought most lovely
in the world of sense, combined with the thought of
that Gospel which was what he thought most lovely in
the world of spirit, to soothe his soul in a celestial harmony. Now he could not concentrate on the Gospel at
all, except to think how little gratitude he felt for it.
How he had loved, in the old days at Doctor Cotton's,

with lighted eye and flushed face, to detail the story of
his conversion to any one who could be brought to listen!
Now, the moment religion was mentioned in conversation he found his attention begin to wander; and if
Newton asked him to tell his story to hearten up some
fellow Christian, he felt nothing but a dull nausea at
having to say it all over again.  Writing about it became as bad as talking.  Minutes would pass as he sat,
the ink drying on his pen, trying in vain to work himself
up into the state of mind in which he could deliver a
comfortable religious homily to Mrs. Cowper or Mrs.
Madan.  And then he would suddenly remember how,
two years ago, his pen would have been too slow to keep
pace with the flowing tide of his thought; once more a
sense of guilt would strike him, and he would lay his
letter aside.  He could not bear to fall below the standard he had set himself then—to do so would be equiva-
lent to a confession of his own decline—so he gradually
ceased to write at all.

Sunday, too, became intolerable to him.  In the old
days he used to look forward to it as the climax of the
week's devotion, the day in which, undistracted by worldly care, he could give himself up to thoughts of God.
Now he felt it as the climax of nothing but his own in-
adequacy, a day in which nothing was allowed to distract
him from realizing what a failure his religious life was.
The twenty-four hours passed like twenty-four days. The
time spent in church was the most unendurable.  When
he first came to Olney Newton's influence had revived his
enjoyment of it; but soon it was as little comfort as anything else.  He knelt, and bowed, and sang, and responded, as the service demanded, but the words had no
more significance to him than if they had been in Sanskrit.
His eye roved listlessly round the congregation, all, as he

thought, uplifted in an ecstasy of devotion. But no longer, as on that first Sunday at Huntingdon, did his spirit rise with theirs. Indeed, the contrast between their feeling and his own only made his depression worse. Not only was his spiritual life a failure—it was a far greater failure than that of any one else.

Prayer, meditation, conversation, correspondence, church, one by one the doors through which the light of salvation had penetrated to his heart were shut against him. But it was not without a struggle. Desperately, assiduously, with every art and energy of which his nature was capable, he did battle with his fears and his boredom, tried to find reassuring relief for his dark moments, cried shame upon himself for succumbing to them so easily, adjured himself to take heart once more. Perhaps, he would still comfort himself, his faith was being put to the test; he was required by an all-wise Providence "to walk through a romantic scene with mountains, deep and dark valleys, caves and dens." Or perhaps he was guilty of some secret sin and was now suffering its punishment. Could it be that he had been spiritually proud, convinced that he was immune from temptation? Or had he not trusted wholly in God, but relied on his own good works to save him? If he really examined himself, unburdened himself of his sins, his troubles would probably disappear. And he must always remember that his own troubles were trivial compared with those that Christ had undergone for his sake. He set to work diligently to examine his smallest action and thought for a sign of worldliness or vanity, cut himself off more rigorously than before from any interests that might turn his mind from the narrow path. He spent hours on his knees, striving to get his soul into a proper state of contrition.

It was in vain; his depression did not disappear. His mind was so dazed with self-analysis and self-torment that he hardly knew if he was contrite or not. He hoped God did. Not for a moment could he revive the faintest glimmer of his old ecstasy, not for the briefest instant did his heart glow with the old love, burn with the old faith. He could only pray to God for help. But the help did not come. He began to wonder if it was ever coming at all. He had done all he could, and to what purpose? Push, coax, wedge as he might, one by one the doors creaked on their hinges, swung to, shut. Without confidence, he resigned himself to God's mercy. He was His own interpreter, and He must make it plain.

Now an event happened which removed his last resistance.

Cowper had not seen much of his brother during the last few years. They had long ago agreed not to argue about religion; but as William did not really care to talk about anything else, such an agreement prevented them from taking much pleasure in each other's society. Since he had been at Olney he had actually been over to Cambridge only once, when John was ill. And then, terrible to relate, he had found his counterpane littered with plays. John came more regularly to Olney; but his visits were far from being an unmixed pleasure. William felt he ought not to let them interfere with his Evangelical duties, but it embarrassed him to perform them if he felt John was sitting by disapproving. Besides, since John was a clergyman it might hurt his feelings if he were not asked to take family prayers. And yet, since he was not converted, this was impossible. It was all very upsetting. John, for his part, carefully conformed to the habits of the house, and avoided all controversial topics. But one trembles to think what his decorous academic mind must have thought of a household whose time was divided between irregular piety and unre-strained philanthropy; where masters and servants alike were liable at any time to burst out with intimate rev-elations about the state of their souls; and in which every detail of daily life was directed by a fanatical sea-captain, with a passion for asking personal questions, and without a degree. Altogether he felt it a great relief when the time came for him to climb into the coach and drive back to the peace and the port of Cambridge.

But Fate had decreed that, before he died, he too was to be uprooted from the placid seclusion in which he had loitered away his life, and pass through the fires of Heaven and hell. In March, 1770, William was for the second time summoned to Cambridge by the news of his brother's illness. When he arrived the doctor told him he was dying. Under the shock all William's dying faith flared up once more. Loss of faith and lethargy of spirits were alike forgotten. He only remembered that his brother was dying, and that unless he died in grace he was damned. He was not yet in grace, but Providence had clearly brought William there to save him.

And now began a strange drama. Day after day, night after night, cut off from the world in that quiet college room, alone he wrestled for the soul of the dying man, implored God to soften his heart, himself with breaking voice urged his brother to hearken to the divine message. At first his efforts were vain. Daily John grew weaker; soon it would be too late. William's sus-pense grew unbearable. Three times in a night he would start up thinking he heard a cry. Was it John's dying groans, or the exultant yell of fiends come to carry off his soul? Or was it some celestial intimation for his own

ear? Holding his breath, he listened; and then rushed
to the bedside, and once more implored John to believe;
once more in vain. Could it be that God meant him to
fail? But within the depths of John's own spirit forces
were working on his side.

John Cowper's life had followed a calmer course than
his brother's. But his nature was very similar—a bundle
of nerves, a prey to superstitious fears, afraid of life.
And, faced for the first time with a real crisis, in the
shape of a dangerous illness, his true self came to the
surface. It is said that already, before he fell ill, his
composure had been ruffled by a strange incident. Years
ago, when he was a schoolboy, a vagrant gipsy in a tattered red military coat had told his fortune. He fore-
told various events of youth, but had said that he could
see nothing for him after the age of thirty. John had
not paid much attention to his words; but a short time
before his illness, as he was sauntering in the college
garden, his eye was caught by a red coat. Looking up,
he saw, as he thought, the very gipsy, peering at him
through the gate. Before he had time to say a word,
the man had disappeared. The sight of him brought the
whole incident back into his mind. With a thrill of fear,
he realized that every prediction hitherto had been fulfilled. What then could it mean, that the predictions
stopped at thirty? Could it be there were no more to
make, that what he thought was the gipsy had been an
apparition come to forewarn him of his end?

Any fears he may have had were increased by his illness, and as he lay in bed he began to review his past in
the light of approaching death. It was a discouraging
spectacle. All the things he had cared for seemed equally
valueless. He felt that his whole view of life must have
been wrong. Perhaps William's view was the right one.

But he had had no experience that could enable him to feel as William felt. A drab melancholy invaded his spirit.

And then one evening as he lay there, suddenly, in the span of a second, the Heavens opened and the Divine Light irradiated his soul. He gave a cry which brought William to his bedside; he clasped his hand in silence, and after a little he said, "Oh, brother, I am full of what I could say to you." The nurse asked him if he needed any lavender or hartshorn. He replied, "None of these things will serve my purpose." William said, "But I know what would, my dear, don't I?" He answered, "You do, brother." At last he had seen what William had seen. And, like William, he had believed.

For six days more he lingered in a still unearthly ecstasy. Only on one occasion did he reveal a trace of his old unconverted self. It was roused by the thought of Newton. "I shall rejoice in a conversation with him hereafter," he confessed to William, "but I could not bear it now." On the eighth day he sank into a torpor; on the tenth he died.

William's prayers had been answered. He returned to Olney in tremulous exultation and listened with rapture to Newton expatiating from the pulpit on John's holy death. But the strain which his nervous system had sustained was to prove disastrous to him. Alone in a strange town, he, who had never moved a step from home for three years, had watched his only brother die, himself for half the time in an agony lest he should be going to eternal perdition. He had not even been supported by comfort from Olney. Mrs. Unwin, for reasons unknown, had hardly written; and this was an added worry to Cowper, who began to think he had offended her. While Newton only wrote to tell Cowper, with his usual plain-spoken trenchancy, not to deceive himself into thinking good works could save his brother; unless he was in grace he would certainly go to hell. The consequence was that whatever was left of Cowper's nervous resistance was destroyed. Within a few weeks of getting back to Olney the fitful flame of religious emotion which had flickered up for the last time by John's bedside was extinguished; and he found himself incapable of making the slightest effort to recover himself. With mechanical lips he continued to repeat the words of his belief, but they no longer meant anything to him. Evangelicalism had finally and absolutely ceased to stir his emotions. He had drained it to its last drop. He was not going to get any happiness from it ever any more.

It was not only his religious happiness that left him. With it went all other pleasures too. According to his belief, religion was the only source of genuine happiness, so that if he found he had been made happy by anything not specifically religious he was logically forced to connect it in some way with religion, to look on it as a channel of the Divine Grace. The pleasant domestic life with the Unwins was the prototype of the corporate unity of Christians living together in faith and charity. Natural beauty was the expression of the Divine perfection in things sensible. As long as he still cared about his religion this way of looking at things accentuated his enjoyment; for it suffused the most trivial moment of pleasure with a glow of transcendental emotion. Every quiet evening by the fire, every cowslip by the roadside, whispered to Cowper's spirit intimations of a blessed immortality. But when he lost his pleasure in religion he lost his happiness in these things as well. It was not only that his conscience would not allow him to be happy if his spiritual condition was not such as to deserve it;

he could not feel pleasure in doing anything without remembering that in former days such a pleasure would
inevitably have culminated in a moment of religious rapture; and the fact that it did not do so any more took
away such enjoyment as he felt. He paid the proverbial
penalty of one who puts all his eggs into one basket.
When the basket broke, all the eggs were broken too.

The outward ordering of his life did not alter with
the change in his inner man. He taught in Sunday-school,
visited, attended sermons, even said his prayers just as
he had when he first came to Olney. But the motive that
had guided his life into such a course was dead. He
went on automatically because he did not know what
else to do. His mind alternated between a leaden lethargy and a yet more leaden gloom. Hardly for a minute
did he forget his bonds and quicken into feeling once
more. Only sometimes, as he wandered amid the wood-
land solitudes, which lately had brought such happiness
to his heart, but now no longer, his response to the
beauty around him would mingle with his memories and
his sense of present misery to well up and flow away in a
gush of lyrical emotion,

> O happy shades! to me unblest,
>   Friendly to peace, but not to me,
> How ill the scene that offers rest,
>   And heart that cannot rest, agree!
>
> This glassy stream, that spreading pine,
>   Those alders quiv'ring to the breeze,
> Might soothe a soul less hurt than mine,
>   And please, if anything could please.
>
> But fixed unalterable care,
>   Foregoes not what she feels within,

Shows the same sadness everywhere,
And slights the season and the scene.

For all that pleased in wood or lawn,
    While peace possessed these silent bowers,
Her animating smile withdrawn,
    Has lost its beauties and its powers.

The saint or moralist can tread
    These moss-grown alleys, musing slow;
They seek, like me, the secret shade,
    But not like me, to nourish woe.

Me fruitful scenes and prospects waste,
    Alike admonish not to roam;
These tell me of enjoyments past,
    And those of sorrows yet to come.

By a paradox, his frustration became for a moment its own fulfilment, and his sorrow sighed itself away in song.

But though these sudden gloryings in affliction might relieve his feelings, they did not make him happy. For to be happy one must believe in the solid stability of what one holds valuable. And the only thing Cowper held valuable, the pearl of great price to obtain which he had sold all that he possessed, had melted into air within his hand.

Such an event would have been dangerous to Cowper's nervous system at any time; for it might always cause the despondency and self-depreciation bred in him in childhood to resume their sway over him. But it was far more dangerous now than it would have been when he was twenty-four. For the faith he had now lost was the only thing that stood between him and definite madness. John Cowper and Doctor Cotton had been wrong in thinking Cowper's religion a sign of mania. But

they were quite right in thinking that Cowper himself
was not normal. The delusions of 1763 had never
wholly left him. He would be haunted for days together by a strange dream. Sometimes, as when he was
agitated whether he should go and live with the Unwins,
his mind would be obsessed by some phrase or sentence,
which he took to be a message from God. Lying in
bed in the early morning—always a bad time for neu-
rotics—these phrases intruded themselves so insistently
on him that he thought they were spoken by a voice.
But his faith had given him control over these spiritual
disturbances. It taught him to welcome them if he
judged them to be of God, to despise them if he judged
them to be of the devil; at any rate not to pay much
attention to them, since his salvation was already decided.
But now that the light of his faith was extinguished, his
inflamed fancy could make him its slave whenever it
chose. The truth was that the fundamental cause of his
madness had never been rooted out of his mind. His
conversion had neutralized the effect of his sense that
he was singled out from the rest of mankind by the
curse of God, but it had done nothing to make him
realize that it was the figment of his imagination. So
that when he lost his faith he was as open to its attack
as he had been in 1763.

Indeed, his state of mind in 1772 was that of 1763
over again. His nervous resistance had been sapped by
the strain of bereavement; he was the victim of visionary
fears; he was disgusted with his own spiritual condition.
And he had lost all living sense of the value of anything. For the second time the foundations of his sanity were undermined. Within eighteen months he was
mad for the second time.

But as he descends to his inferno, once more the

smoldering clouds rise and hide him from our sight. Such scanty records as we possess can not enable us to follow the steps of his journey.  Now and again the clouds lift, and we catch a glimpse of his face, but it is distorted beyond recognition by the flames of misery and madness that leap around it.  The actual form of his insanity arose, ironically enough, from that very doctrine of salvation which he had been confident would remove all fears from him for ever.  The soul was apprised of its salvation, he held, by a sudden feeling of religion—felt itself to be in grace.  He had known the feeling once. But he knew it no longer; and he was convinced that, in spite of any efforts, he never would again.  Could it therefore mean that he had fallen from grace, that he had forfeited his salvation?  Hastily, in horror, he brushed the idea aside.   But, do what he would, it returned and began to eat into his mind, till he could think of nothing else.  For the second time in his life Cowper was possessed by the fear of his own damnation.

It was inconsistent of him, since it was one of the first articles of his faith that no one could fall from grace. But Cowper's fear was the result not of logical process, but of mental disease, so that its inconsistency made no difference to him.  Like all mad people, he thought himself different from any one else in the world, and therefore that no analogy from the life of any one else could apply to his.  Even if it was God's usual law that no human soul should fall from grace, yet, for some divine purpose of His own, God had designed his, Cowper's, to be of all souls ever created the one exception.  It was only too easy for him to believe this.  Did it not agree exactly with that sense that he had been marked out from his fellows by the curse of God which had tormented him ever since childhood?

His lethargy turned to anguish; and daily his anguish grew blacker. Fits of despair would sweep over him, when he would not speak or even look up; almost every night his sleep was broken by awful dreams. And as always when he was agitated, he began to hear voices. Newton and Mrs. Unwin watched him with dismay, and did their best to help him. It was odd that Newton did, for his enthusiasm for religion led him in general so far as even to look favorably on religious mania. Once he had sent a girl into fits by his preaching, and had refused to express any concern, on the ground that fits might be the means ordained by Heaven to lead her to grace. However, he did realize that Cowper's delusions were due to disease; and he threw himself into the task of curing him with the same ardor with which he threw himself into everything else.

Unfortunately, neither nature nor circumstance had qualified him for the rôle of mental alienist. He knew Cowper liked writing verses, so, in order to distract his thoughts to more pleasant fields, he proposed that they should collaborate in writing some hymns "for the use of plain people, with the imagery and colouring of poetry, if admitted at all, only in a sparing form." Cowper dutifully carried out his part of this bleak task. Hymns are, however, of necessity all about the Christian's desire for salvation and fear of damnation, and so they only made him worry more than ever about his soul. Newton also tried taking Cowper over to his house to divert his mind by a bright cheering talk, but there again he was incapable of talking about any subject except religion, and Cowper's mind remained undiverted. Impassioned adjuration did no good either. Newton used to hold forth for hours about the mercy of God as they paced up and down the leaf-strewn garden paths of the

Vicarage. For the time Cowper would be convinced, but in a few hours he was as bad again as before. Newton began to despair. "Dear Sir Cowper was as much in the depths as ever," he wrote to his sister. "He led me to speak last night from Hebrews xi:10. I do not think he was the better for it." When Hebrews xi:10 failed, what was one to do?

Mrs. Unwin's placid firmness was far better suited than Newton's apostolic zeal to deal with Cowper's difficulties. And, indeed, when he was feeling really miserable, her presence was the only thing that gave him the slightest comfort. Yet even she could only soothe him temporarily. She did not know enough about mental diseases in general, or Cowper's in particular, to do him any lasting good. Actually, poor lady, she was, through no fault of her own, the cause of an event that may finally have sent him off his head. For some time past the little household at Orchard Side had been dwindling. Two years before William Unwin had left to take up a living at Stock; and now Miss Unwin became engaged to be married to a Mr. Powley. It was a most desirable match, for not only was he a clergyman, but he had actually been sent down from Oxford for holding Evangelical prayer-meetings. Nor could Cowper much regret the departure of Miss Unwin, whose early shyness of him had hardened into suspicion. But propriety would not permit him to go on living with Mrs. Unwin alone. To part was unthinkable to either; and so, in the autumn of 1772, they agreed to marry. Can it be that the prospect of so momentous, so intimate a change in his life, the basic horrors of his existence, the thought of his mental disease, and perhaps his physical imperfections, swept back into his mind and thrust his tottering reason finally from its throne? It does not seem unlikely.

At any rate, from this time events moved rapidly to their catastrophe.  On January 24, 1773, Newton was awakened at five in the morning by a messenger from Mrs. Unwin asking him to come over to Orchard Side at once.  He hurried through the raw darkness to find Cowper in a fit of raving madness brought on by some peculiarly horrible dream.  After some hours the fit passed, but it recurred.  And from this time on he was treated as an invalid.  He was moved to the Vicarage, where, he had a fancy, he felt more at ease.  Doctors were sent for, and Mrs. Unwin never left him.

But not yet was he quite defeated.  In his more lucid intervals he still clung with a feeble, unconquerable pertinacity to the Lord who saved him.  In an awed wonder Newton listened to him as he lay half dead on his bed, after some frightful bout of mania, whispering with the last painful breath of his spent forces that he welcomed his sufferings, and that if he could get rid of them by stretching out his hand he would not do so without God's approval.  For he knew God was good and he trusted in Him.  But he could not hold out for ever.  Another shock, the few frail strands of faith to which he still clung were torn from his bleeding fingers and he fell headlong into the abyss.  On the night of February twenty-fourth he had a dream.  What it precisely was no one knows; but in it, amid circumstances of unspeakable horror, he heard from the lips of God Himself the certain and irrevocable sentence of his damnation.  The next morning the last vestiges of sanity had left him.  He did not know where he was or who was speaking to him.  Cowering back on his bed in that pleasant Vicarage room, he saw only the distorted faces of the demons, heard only the roaring of the flames of hell open to receive him.

# Faith and Mr. Newton 165

Once again the powers of darkness had beaten him. Risen in the storms of madness, in the storms of madness the short strange day of his faith had sunk to its setting. And it has been a commonplace of subsequent literary history that the madness was brought on by the faith. A commonplace, but not a truth; Cowper's madness finds its origin far deeper in the sufferings of childhood, it may be in inherent physical defect. All his life it was hung over him. And religion, so far from being the cause, was the most considerable of the remedies by which he tried to get rid of it. It failed. And once he realized that it had failed, it is true that the emotional tension encouraged by Evangelicalism, and the personal responsibility for its own state which it placed on the individual soul, did increase Cowper's nervous agitation and so accelerate the advent of his madness. But though it accelerated it, it did not make that advent more sure.

On the contrary it had been far nearer curing him than any other remedy. The life of active interests and cheerful social amusements so naïvely recommended by subsequent historians he had tried without any effect, because such a life did not try to deal with the causes of his malady at all. Of course, Evangelicalism did not go to the root of it, for it had not the necessary scientific knowledge; but it did face its deeper problems. It did seek to fight the enemies of the spirit with spiritual weapons, to expel, not merely to evade them. And the consequence was that 1763 to 1767 was the one happy period of his mature existence. Under the shadow of later years he would look back and ask himself if it had not been part of another life. In wonder he gazed at the world of familiar things transfigured by a golden and unearthly radiance, himself in the midst, free and fearless.

# CHAPTER V

## POETRY AND LADY AUSTEN

THE next two years of Cowper's life are a lurid blackness, spasmodically lit up by flashes of more lurid light. The structure of his nervous system was overturned, the coherence of his thought destroyed, as they had not been even in 1763. It was not only that he had succumbed a second time, and therefore of necessity minded far more than he had the first, but his collapse came as the result of a far severer shock. His first madness had been the culmination of a slow decline of spirits from a happiness at best but partial. This was the sudden and complete failure of a force in whose ability to protect him he had believed implicitly. All his life he had sought such a force; at last he thought he had found it, and he attached himself to it with all the unquestioning trust he had never been able to give to anything else. Then it collapsed. And in proportion as it had made him happy, its collapse made him wretched. It was as if he had been foully betrayed by an old and beloved friend. The bottom was knocked out of his universe. His whole scheme of things had been turned upside down; and obscurely he felt that all his other values were turned upside down with it. The one supreme good had proved false; how should lesser goods prove more genuine? The only coherent thought in the inchoate quagmire of agony in which he writhed was a

166

dim obsession that he must not trust to any one or anything. From Newton and Mrs. Newton, at times even
from Mary (Mrs. Unwin) herself, he shrank in wild-
eyed horror. He refused to touch any food they brought
him, for fear it was poisoned. Had he not loved them
next his faith? Then they must be next his faith in
falseness. Doctor Cotton was called in to help him;
but Doctor Cotton was associated in Cowper's mind with
the happiness of his conversion, and he turned away from
him with dull suspicion. Suicide, which had seemed
to him the unforgivable sin, now began to present itself
to him in the strange guise of a Christian obligation. It
struck him that Abraham had reconciled himself to God
by the sacrifice of what he held most dear—his son;
might not he reconcile himself to God by the sacrifice of
what he held most dear—his own life? Once again he
tried to hang himself. Once again he failed.

But this time he had no reaction against it. He only
felt that he had lost the last despairing chance of redeem-
ing himself, and he sank into a dumb lethargy of despair.
He came down to meals and went for walks and worked
in the garden, with bent brows and tense fixed stare, oblivious of all around him. Only when he was asleep did
he forget his troubles. Mrs. Unwin, tiptoeing into his
room with shaded candle to see how he was resting,
would wonder to see the lined brow smooth, the worn
face relaxed in a childlike smile, while at intervals he
murmured in a drowsy happiness fragments of those
hymns and prayers in which of old he had been wont
to express his unsullied trust in God. When morning
came he would be as bad as ever. He knew the normal
world only in dreams; awake he lived in a nightmare.

It seemed impossible that he should ever rise a second
time from such an abyss, but he did. For all his hyper-

sensitiveness Cowper was not without vitality. Indeed, his very sensitiveness, his quick-silver responsiveness to circumstances and suggestion, could only have belonged to a nature in whom the pulse of life beat high. You must be very much alive to feel as much as that. His spirit, so fragile, so dejected, so palpitatingly naked to pain, yet bore within it a small, welling fountain of vitality that, unless completely destroyed, could never long be kept from flowing. Cramped by physical disability, clogged by nervous inhibition, shut in by external circumstances, it yet within a short time began to gush forth and force a passage for itself to the daylight. Nothing happened to alter his conviction that he was damned; but slowly, gradually, impelled by nothing but the sheer impulse to live behind them, his torn nerves began to mend, his spirits to resume their equilibrium.

All the same they could not have done it alone. Cowper could never have endured through his period of chaotic despair long enough to let the mysterious forces of life within him begin to work unless he had had something or some one to support him. In a word, he would never have recovered if it had not been for Mrs. Unwin.

From the moment he became ill she gave herself up body and soul to his service as calmly and unobtrusively and decisively as she did everything else. It was not a light task. At first, Cowper as often as not was a moaning, gibbering maniac, later sunk in a stupor. Sometimes he shrank away from her in suspicious horror, more often sat for whole days together without showing a sign of pleasure at her presence. Yet he could not bear her to be away from him for a moment. Every minute of every day she watched with unrelaxed attention for the first signs of one of his fits of mania, that she might soothe it before it grew uncontrollable.  Often she never left him even at night; when she did she never knew if she might not be waked up to stop him killing himself.  The days lengthened to summer, contracted to winter, lengthened to summer again.  And still the crisis was not passed, and still her task went on.  It was a terrible strain.  Her health was impaired for ever.

She had other annoyances to put up with.  The parishioners of Olney thought her connection with Cowper an odd one, and they said so.  But Mrs. Unwin was unconventional, as only the simple-minded can be.  She had always been accustomed to do what she thought right regardless of difficulty.  And she never thought about what other people would think of her, because she never thought about herself at all.  Nor was she encouraged to do so by her religion.  Her Evangelicalism was not the religion of respectability.  It had the virtues as well as the defects of its exclusiveness.  If it taught her to shun the pleasures of the world as wicked, it also taught her to scorn its censures as trivial.  It shone out, the sole and heavenly light by which she should guide herself in a dark world.  It was the fanaticism of her faith that enabled Mrs. Unwin to go through what she did.  Nor did its narrowness matter.  Depth, not breadth, was what she needed.  Against the surrounding blackness her plain determined figure assumes the heroic proportions of an Antigone.

She saved Cowper; the mere consciousness of a tangible human relationship gave him a solid foothold on existence when all the rest of the ground seemed collapsing beneath him.  The feeling that some one loved him, and some one sane and good, made him want to cling to life when he was far too distracted to be affected by a more abstract motive.  He held on to Mrs. Unwin's hand like a child in the dark, and after two years a few faint streaks of light began to appear. He grew calmer, began to take an interest in things around him; in 1774 he was well enough to go back to Orchard Side.

Newton could not pretend he was sorry to see him go. Not that his Evangelicalism had been any less practical than Mrs. Unwin's. He had put up Cowper in his house for a year. He had put up Mrs. Unwin too, in face of the outraged public opinion of his parish. And he had refused to let either of them pay a penny for their keep, because he thought a Christian minister ought not to take money for doing good. But he had found it a strain. It was no joke to have a lunatic living in one's small house for a year, especially such a gloomy lunatic. "Yesterday, as he was feeding the chickens," he writes with a certain pathos, "some incident made him smile. I am pretty sure it is the first smile that has been seen on his face for sixteen months."

Such a guest certainly detracted from those amenities that the most Evangelical of clergymen had a right to expect of family life. And there seemed no reason why Cowper should ever go. By 1775 he was physically quite well, and there was his own house waiting for him, just across the garden. But when Mary suggested they should return there, he only burst into tears. The robust-minded Newton found it indeed hard to sympathize with such an attitude, especially as Cowper was putting him to considerable expense. Try as he might, as week succeeded week and month succeeded month he could not help remembering this. "Upon the whole, I have not been weary of my cross," he reflected when at last they had gone, "yet sometimes my heart has been importunate and rebellious."

For the second time Cowper had begun to emerge

from the black cloud of madness. But this second recovery was of a very different kind from the first. That
had broken over him in a great wave of joy that had
washed all the horrors of madness clean out of his mind,
and quickened him to an intensity of spirit he had never
known before. But his second madness had inflicted a
deeper wound on his nervous system—far too deep, in
fact, to disappear in a moment. And now he felt no
sudden change in his spirits. He still believed he was
damned. So little hold had he on reality that for years
after this he could never be sure if the Newton he saw
was really Newton or some phantom masquerading in his
shape. Only his vitality was so strong that in spite of
injuries it had begun in time to force him toward recovery. Even if he was to be damned in the next world
he found some enjoyment in things in this; and he began
to feel he had better take his pleasure as he could and
while he could. Resolutely averting his eyes from the
painful subject of his soul, therefore, he began to concentrate on the interests and happenings of every day.

First he could only do this sporadically. His whole
being had been so shattered by his illness that he was
incapable of apprehending happiness except in snatches,
and those far too seldom for him to string together
on them any scheme of existence. Most of the time he
lay like a man rescued from drowning, in a sort of twilit
coma, neither sad nor happy, only relieved to be free from
the struggling agony of the moment before. A chance
phrase or thought would as often as not recall his
spiritual condition to him; the world would grow dark
around him, and he would bury his face in his hands. But
now and again the sight of some natural beauty would
breathe a whiff of happiness into his heart; his eyes would
brighten, and he would look around. Or his wasted

lips would part in involuntary laughter at some prank of cat or dog playing in the garden. All his moments of enjoyment came from Nature or animals; the keenest pleasures of his childhood had been connected with them. And now, at this his second rebirth into the world of sense, it was the pleasures of childhood that first stirred a response within him.

One day, a little time after they had come back to Orchard Side, a neighbor arrived with a tame hare he thought Cowper might like to keep as a pet. He was delighted with it. For hours every day he would watch its antics and try to train it. The good people of Olney, delighted that something had at last given pleasure to the poor gentleman at Orchard Side, all began to give him hares. This was too much of a good thing. Cowper thanked them all with his usual politeness, but kept only three of their presents.

For the next few years these hares—Bess, Puss and Tiny—were a dominating interest in his life. His sympathy had always enabled him to enter into the lives of those he saw around him. And with the hares he had entered into a life from which all the painful problems of human existence were necessarily absent. In their company he escaped for a moment from hell—not into Heaven, but into Eden before the Fall; into a life physical and sylvan, innocent of the knowledge of good and evil; a remote Hans Andersen garden world, where a blade of grass was as big as a bush and the greatest enemy was a hornet and the garden wall was the end of the cosmos. The hares—bold Bess, timid affectionate Puss, who pulled at his coat with his teeth to make him go out, and surly Tiny, who gamboled with an expression of dignified disgust on his whiskered features—grew as individual and entertaining to him as his friends; only they were without that disturbing human attribute, the soul, the very name of which made him feel depressed. He never tired of observing their habits: noticing how Bess liked to spend the morning asleep among the cucumbers, and Tiny always frisked most wildly when the sky grew dark before a storm.

He had work to do for them too: to get their food, bread and lettuce in the summer, and bread and shredded carrot in the winter; to shake out their straw beds; to shut them up for the night. He made them each a little wooden hutch, and devised a little entrance into the drawing-room through which they could run in and out of the garden on summer evenings.

All this was a great step forward. For the first time since his illness he had found happiness, not in capricious moments of emotion, but in a regular interest outside himself. The daily tasks imposed something of order on his life without regard for his moods; while the light manual labor of carpentering and cleaning diverted his attention, without tiring his brain. From now on he took a steady turn for the better. The hares had so intensified his love of animals that be began to keep more pets. Goldfish, guinea-pigs, birds, a cat and a dog—Mungo—successively made their way into the house, till poor Mary must have felt she was living in a menagerie rather than a human dwelling. Then Cowper took to gardening again. There was not much garden at Orchard Side. But he sowed and weeded and watered every inch of what there was; was always out if the weather allowed, sweeping the paths or planting the neat rows of mignonette and lavender, whose scent was to blow so deliciously in at the window when the summer did come.

At first all his garden was outdoors. Then some one

gave him some pineapple seeds; he got a frame for them
and finally a little greenhouse. Besides the pineapples,
he grew geraniums in it and orange blossom, and even
a New Zealand flower called the broallia, which both he
and Mary thought "the most elegant flower they had
ever seen." Lord Dartmouth, who came over one day to
see it with Newton, thought so too, so they felt they must
be right.

Cowper threw himself into gardening and keeping
hares with the same passion with which he had thrown
himself into Latin-verse writing when he was fifteen, and
religious exercises when he was thirty-two. But they
could not occupy his whole attention, and as he got better
he began to look about for occupation that would take
up more of his time. Carpentering was his first choice.
He used to do odd jobs about the house, mending cracked
windows and rickety table legs, and he made a stool and
a chair as a present for Mary. He enjoyed the work
very much, but it hurt his eyes, so he had to give it up.

Drawing attracted him next; by its help he felt he
would be able on the rawest winter day to dwell for a
little amid those summer scenes that had such power to
soothe his soul. He had a master at hand in a Mr.
Andrews, who lived near by. Olney was no center of the
visual arts, and most of this poor gentleman's time was
spent in carving scythes and draped urns for tombstones.
But he also taught people to draw. Cowper gave himself up to his new pursuit with his wonted enthusiasm, sat
all day before his easel drawing dabchicks and mountains,
and by the end of a few months had become sufficiently
proficient to present Mr. and Mrs. Newton with two
sketches for their parlor wall. But, as he might have
expected, the work began to hurt his eyes, as much as
carpentering had done, and he was forced to give it up
too.

And now what was he to do? Idleness left him vitally
open to nervous attack, yet there seemed nothing he could
do that would occupy his time. Suddenly he thought of
literature. Ever since he was a child he had amused
himself by writing occasional verses. Why should he
not attempt something more ambitious? The idea took
hold of him as no other had done. Not only would composition occupy his mind, but he might by means of it
teach valuable moral lessons. For even in his present
condition of mind, when the whole subject of religion
looked black in his eyes, his conscience was worried by
the thought that he was not in some way trying to further
the cause of God. Once more he took up a new task
with tremendous energy, and within a few months he had
finished two long poems. He worked so hard, in fact,
that Mary thought he was making himself ill, and begged
him to stop. He submitted; but the lack of occupation
brought on such an alarming fit of depression that she
very soon besought him to take up his pen again. He
was never to lay it aside till his last illness. Thus, as
a chance diversion of convalescence, did Cowper begin
that work which alone has kept his name clear from
those mists of oblivion which enshroud most of his contemporaries. At the age of forty-nine, unintentionally,
he entered on the career of a famous poet.

The effect of his new work on his life was immediate.
At last he had found an occupation which really filled
his time. Gardening, carpentering, drawing, had at best
been able only to occupy him while he was actually working at them, and as he got more accustomed to doing so
they had not been able to hold him even then. While
his careful fingers worked, his mind wandered, wandered
irresistibly as Fatima to the forbidden door of his
spiritual condition. But he could not write without think-

ing about it all the time he did it. And he would go on thinking about it when he was not writing at all. His life was therefore no longer a darkness lit up by spasmodic and capricious flashes. It had structure and purpose, and though there were dark moments in it, they did not break up this structure and purpose. Besides, writing gave him a means of self-expression, an outlet for his rising energy, a satisfaction for his starved vitality, which accelerated his nervous recovery seven-fold. Soon he felt strong enough to turn his attention to the world of human beings. He began to write regularly to Hill and Unwin again, to take an interest in the life of Olney. By 1780 he had managed to weld the shattered, scattered fragments of his life and thought into some sort of permanent pattern. The mists of madness have parted on a new phase of Cowper's existence.

It was not at all like the one on which they closed. The unearthly light and unearthlier darkness have vanished, and we are back into the plain daylight of the eighteenth century, the busy, sequestered, domestic world of Berkhamstead and Southampton Row. On Cowper himself neither his Evangelicalism nor his madness had left much outward trace. Long absence from society had, indeed, given his manners a shy, old-fashioned cere-moniousness. But this only added an individual and delightful flavor to the irony and sweetness which they enshrined: and to women especially his anxious courtesy was charming. He was grown a little fat and a little bald. Was he not nearly fifty! But there had always been a sober foppishness about him which had made him take care of his appearance. Even at his most religious, he would always write to William Unwin to get him a "smartish" stock-buckle or a new-fashioned cocked hat. And now, dressed for the afternoon in blue coat and green satin waistcoat, with his scanty hair reinforced by some from the barber and done in a bag with a black ribbon, and carrying a snuff-box in his hand, he looked, as he said, "a very smart youth for his years."

Nor did the outward ordering of his life offend against the conventional standards of his neighbors. The holy singularity of which he had been so proud at Huntingdon was gone. Instead of vigils and meditations and prayer-meetings, his time was taken up by the thousand trivial necessary avocations of house and garden that occupied the people around him. His life was still very regular, its unvarying round modified only by the seasons. In winter, when the greater part of his work was done, it was spent mostly in one room—the little wainscoted parlor of Orchard Side, thirteen feet square, with its spindle-legged chairs and its view of the street and its print of Cowper's old friend, Thurlow, over the chimney-piece. It was here, at the civilized hour of ten, in his dressing-gown and cap, that he had his breakfast, and Mary poured out his morning cup of steaming, scented bohea for him. He used to sit on for a little after breakfast, reading while she sewed. If something struck him in his book he would read it aloud to her; then they relapsed into a placid silence. Next he must see after the greenhouse and the hares and the birds and the cat. And now he must sit down to the two or three hours' writing which made up his very reasonable working day. His writing-table was an old card-table; but of course it had never been used as such since it had come into the possession of this godly household. It was not very good for writing on, as it was so low. Cowper had painfully to heave an atlas on to it every time he wanted to work. He and Mary ate off it too; but it was no better for that than for writing. It had little shallow hollows round the edge, originally meant for counters, and Cowper and Mary always forgot about these when they were covered up by the table-cloth, and put their glasses down on them. So that they were always spilled, and often broken. Still, it was the only table in the house that was the right size, and they made the best of it.

A walk followed, then dinner; and then possibly another walk, sharp, through the frozen or muddy lanes, with the sear leaves rustling round Cowper's feet, and Mungo leaping before him. Nobody in those days was so silly as to go out if the weather was really bad. Indeed their clothes did not permit it. And during the bad weather of 1781 Cowper and Mary hardly stirred from their tiny house and tinier garden from November to February. But Cowper was far too regular in his habits to forego his daily exercise, and on bad days he used to swing dumb-bells or skip or play a decorous game of battledore and shuttlecock with Mary. As the short winter's day faded to a close, once more he heaved the atlas on to the table, and sat down to read or write.

Sometimes as he sat there in the gathering dusk, where the fire-light set the room astir with shadows, the paper would drop from his hand and he would sink into a drowsy reverie. Idly he fancied castles and forests in the crumbling coals, discerned portents in the fantastic filaments of soot that formed and fell on the bars of the grate. And then his attention would wander, and he would sit gazing with fixed, absent eyes, lost for a short moment perhaps in some country of his desire—green blossoming woods of spring, or by the glittering sea. Suddenly a noise would penetrate his consciousness— the wind rattling the window, or the maid coming in with the tea. Blinking his eyes in the unaccustomed brightness of the candle-light, he would shift his position and return to earth.

And now began that moment of the day that Cowper liked best—tea-time on a winter's evening. He liked tea better than any other drink—it gave him just the mild stimulus that his nerves required. And the little meal in the cozy, candle-lit room, alone with his best friend, and the winter's night shut out by curtains, was the very incarnation of that innocent security which all his life had been his idea of perfect happiness. The rain might drum on the window, the wind whistle along the deserted street; it only emphasized the warmth and comfort inside, where the kettle hummed, and the cat lapped up its milk, and Cowper and Mary laughed over the day's happenings. They were interrupted by the twang of a horn and the hollow sound of the galloping of hoofs outside. It was the post arriving at the Bull Inn. And a few minutes later a rush of cold air would blow into the house as the door opened to admit letters and newspaper—that newspaper that brought to Olney the news of Mr. Fox's last speech, and the Duke of Devonshire's last rout, and Mr. Wilkes's last enormity. After tea, the little door in the wall was unlatched, and for a short time the room was alive with the scampering of the hares. Then Cowper and Mary settled down to a quiet evening. She always worked, either knitting his socks or embroidering.

> The well-depicted flower,

as Cowper put it,

> Wrought patiently into the snowy lawn
> Unfolds its bosom. . . .

Sometimes he read aloud, sometimes copied out what he had written in the morning, sometimes, if he was

tired, just wound her wool for her.  But whatever either
of them was doing, it generally ended in conversation—
long delicious conversations, now gay, now serious; and
now their voices would soften in tender reminiscence,
now hush into a silence more intimate than speech.  A
country supper of eggs and radishes, enlivened by a
modest glass of wine, rounded off their evening; and
then, candle in hand, they said good night.  Summer
days passed in much the same occupations as winter.  But
they were spent for the most part outdoors, reading or
working in the garden; and Mary and Cowper often
took a walk before supper.

They were not confined exclusively to each other's
society.  The "County," indeed, they did not see much
of.  To do so entailed keeping a carriage; and, anyway,
Cowper had very little in common with the card-playing,
ball-going County ladies, and still less with the red-faced,
two-bottle, fox-hunting Squire Westerns who were their
husbands and brothers.  His pets had given him a hatred
of all forms of sport.  He attacked cruelty to animals
unceasingly both in prose and verse—not always his best
verse:

> I would not number in my list of friends
> (Though graced with polished manners and fine sense
> Yet wanting sensibility) the man
> Who needlessly sets foot upon a worm.
> An inadvertent step may crush the snail
> That crawls at evening on the public path,
> But he that has humanity, forewarned,
> Will tread aside and let the reptile live.

But to find friends Cowper did not need to fly high
or far.  Newton, indeed, was with him no longer.  He
had not been so successful at Olney as he had intended.

After the first shock of surprise had worn off, the people had ceased to pay much heed to his vehement ministrations; and in spite, possibly because of, the fact that he redoubled his efforts, they came in time actually to dislike him.  His unpopularity reached its climax when he announced from his pulpit one autumn Sunday that he hoped no one would illuminate their houses or make a bonfire on the approaching fifth of November.  Not only did many people stick candles in their windows who had never thought of doing such a thing before, but a large crowd of infuriated revelers marched down to attack the Vicarage.

Newton was for defying these Sons of Belial like the prophets of old; but the prayers of his panic-stricken wife persuaded him to take the more pacific course of paying them to go away.  His pride was doubly wounded.  And when in 1779 he was offered the Parish of St. Mary Woolnoth in London he accepted it.  His resilient spirits soon recovered themselves at the prospect of the greater scope for his talents and enterprise afforded by a London parish.  "I am about to form a connection for life with one Mary Woolnoth, a reputed London Saint in Lombard Street," he remarked humorously.

His departure did not mean as much to Cowper as it would have done ten years before.  Since his illness each of them felt the other's company a slight strain.  Cowper could not bear to mention the subject of religion; and he knew Newton cared to talk of nothing else.  So that, though he was still very fond of him, he felt awkward in his presence; and even when he wrote to him, as he did regularly after he had left, it was in an embarrassed, self-depreciatory tone, as if apologizing for his inability to provide what Newton had a right to demand.  Newton, for his part, had not lost his affection for Cowper.

But his dominating nature resented the feeling that any one has escaped, however unwillingly, from the orbit of his influence; and temperamentally he had no sympathy with defeatism. He could not help thinking Cowper would be all right if he would only make an effort: and he told him so. This in its turn irritated Cowper, who felt Newton was not making the slightest attempt to understand him.

All the same, when the moment of departure actually arrived, all Cowper's other feelings were overwhelmed in a gush of regretful emotion. His timid, constant nature, fearful of the future, tenacious of the past, felt any change a painful wrench. And, besides, Newton and Mrs. Newton and the whole Newton household were bound up in his mind with that period of his life which, however tragic its termination, was yet its only period of joy and of hope. "The Vicarage looks a melancholy object," he wrote to Mrs. Newton. "As I walked in the garden I saw the smoke issuing from the study chimney, and said to myself, 'That used to be a sign that Mr. Newton was there, but it is so no longer.' The walls of the house know nothing of the change that has taken place. The bolt of the chamber door sounds just as it used to do; and when Mr. Page goes upstairs, for aught I know the fall of his foot could hardly be distinguished from that of Mr. Newton. But Mr. Newton's foot will never be heard upon that staircase again. . . . Though in many respects I have no more sensibility left in me than there is in brick and mortar, yet I am not permitted to be quite unfeeling on this subject."

Even when Newton was gone, however, Cowper was not deprived of clerical society. Fashionable or fox-hunting parsons were even more dreadful in his eyes than fashionable or fox-hunting squires; but Newton had managed to make Olney a little center of "faithful" ministers. Mr. Scott, the curate of Weston, was an example of the extraordinary force of his personality. Till middle life he had lived the respectable, unimpassioned life of the orthodox Church of England clergyman. Then, going into a cottage one day by chance, he found Newton praying by a dying man. The faith that glowed in his eyes, the ardor that rang through every modulation of his voice, so affected Scott that from that very day he became a strong Evangelical. Cowper saw a certain amount of him. He was a scholar, and used to drop in to ask advice on a point of style in some commentary he was writing. And once a fortnight at least the little parlor at Orchard Side was filled with the huge form and exuberant personality of Mr. Bull, the non-conformist minister from Newport Pagnell.

The Reverend William Bull was one of those strong, independent, eccentric characters that England, and rural England especially, seems to produce at all times as frequently and effortlessly as those writhen and sturdy oak trees which they so closely resemble. He was the son of a yeoman; and a strong religious experience when he was a child had decided him to enter the Independent ministry. He had taught himself Hebrew, been ordained, and had spent the rest of his life at Newport Pagnell, where he divided his time between ministering to his flock and working in his study.

This lonely and self-dependent course of life, in which all his natural idiosyncrasies had been allowed to develop unmodified by conventional influence, had streaked every aspect of his character and habits with a kind of quaintness. He had a rich, fiery, winning personality, and imagination and humor and learning as well. But his imagination ran riot in fantastic flights; his humor was extravagant and uncouth; and his learning was a lumber-room of curious information and ideas—valuable and worthless indiscriminately heaped together—more like that of some seventeenth-century savant, Browne or Burton, than the regulated classicism of eighteenth-century scholarship. His amusements were eccentric, too. He had a niche cut in his garden wall, where he would sit and contemplate, almost completely surrounded with brickwork within three or four inches of his nose. And he measured the circumference of his small plot of garden, and then took exercise by walking doggedly round it every day, marking each round by moving a bit of shot along a groove in the wall till he had walked five miles.

His life revolved round religion; but his religion, like his learning, seemed to belong less to the eighteenth than to the seventeenth century. It was mystical and dis-ordered, given to expressing itself in wild vagaries of the imagination, even in jokes. He was an eloquent preacher in a style of his own, full of homely metaphors and allusions, and so much in earnest that the very mention of the Passion was enough to fill his eyes with tears. But in the midst of the most emotional passage, perhaps on the Passion, he would stop to bawl objurgations at some one trying to slip away from church before the sermon was over. He was naïve, too. Once he was persuaded to visit Scotland. He enjoyed himself, but was very much concerned not to be ensnared by the worldly splendors he saw there. Cardinal Beaton's palace he said was fine, but not so fine as Heaven; he was at pains that people should realize he could not think of comparing it to Heaven.

But in spite of his peculiarities he was by far the most interesting person living near Olney. After all, it was something to find some one with humor and imagination and learning, however eccentric his habits. Cowper met him with Newton, and took to him immediately. He had that infectious vitality that always attracted him; and soon it was a recognized thing that Bull should dine at Orchard Side once a fortnight. His idiosyncrasies appeared even in his personal relationships. Sometimes he would be robustly mirthful, at others subdued, melancholy and confiding; but Cowper liked him all the better for this. To be made a partner of another's mood gave him just that assurance of intimacy without which friendship was no pleasure to him. He was more put off by Bull's smoking, a habit which, as a symbol of exclusively male society, he had always detested; but he grew even to like it, so much did it seem part of those happy evenings when dear "Taureau," as he affectionately called Bull, sat puffing away beside him in the garden of Orchard Side, or, more rarely, in the dusky, casemented library of his own house at Newport Pagnell.

But the great of Olney—clergymen and school-masters—were not the only people in whom Cowper took an interest. From the sash-window of the parlor, year after year, he used to watch the sleepy, desultory life of the country street, and note with unfailing, amused interest its distinctive figures: Palmer, the draper, standing in the doorway of his shop; Wilson, the barber, strolling along, a wig box on his arm, such a strict Sabbatarian that he refused to dress even the hair of a lady of title on Sunday, so that she (poor thing!) had to have it done the evening before, and sit up all night for fear of disarranging it; Nathan Sample, the maltster, who, though less regularly religious, was always ready to declaim against the Papists. Every morning, just as Cowper was cleaning his teeth, he would see old Geary Ball shambling past the window—Geary Ball, once a burning and shining light of the Gospel, but now only regular in his attendance at the bar of the "Fox and Grapes." And after him, perhaps, might strut a pursy figure, with thumb on hip and blasé expression on his face—a lace-maker whose name Cowper never knew, but whom he called the "Olney misanthrope," because in all the years he had seen him he had never observed him speaking to any one.

Nor did he merely look on at Olney life. He took part in it as well. It had got about that he had been a lawyer, and the front door of Orchard Side often opened and shut to admit some shopkeeper anxious to learn some point of law, but less anxious to pay a professional lawyer to tell him. "They cannot be persuaded," said Cowper ruefully, "that a head once covered by a legal periwig can be deficient in those natural endowments that it is supposed to cover."

Then he took part in charitable work. It was he who, when the Olney lace-makers were starving, wrote to Mr. Smith, the rich Nottingham banker, for help; and when Mr. Smith very generously sent fifty pounds, it was Cowper who distributed it. Again, he was one of the prime movers in establishing the Sunday-school in 1785. Indeed, it was high time, for in spite of poor Newton's efforts, the children of Olney, even those of seven years old, were profane; Cowper and Mary had often hastily to turn aside when they met a party of them lest their sensitive ears might be offended by the frightful language they might hear.

Indeed, life at Olney was not without its incidents. Out of the window one day Cowper saw a scene of Hogarthian farce. The beadle was flogging a man for stealing, the magistrate beating the beadle for not hitting hard enough, and an angry virago beating the magistrate for beating the beadle. On another night one of the hares ran away; a terrible excitement! Half the town was out after it. It ran two miles, and a man caught it in a back yard, and Cowper rewarded him with the large sum of six shillings. In 1784 came the election, and the candidate—"a most loving, kissing, kind-hearted gentleman"—came to solicit Cowper's interest, and surprised them all in the middle of tea, and kissed Mrs. Unwin and the cook.

The monotony of the daily round was also varied now and again by visitors. William Unwin came, which was pleasant, and Mrs. Powley, which was less so. Cowper noticed that she never laughed at any of his jokes; he concluded she had no sense of humor. Actually she believed him to have robbed her mother of eighteen hundred pounds; so perhaps she was throughout the visit in a state of scarcely suppressed indignation. Newton came to stay once or twice too. His company, we know, Cowper felt to be rather a strain. But he enjoyed having Mrs. Newton, and still more Miss Catlett, Newton's niece, whom he had adopted, a cheerful child of thirteen or fourteen. "Euphrosyne, the laughing lady," Cowper called her, and "Oh, Miss Catlett," he would say, looking across the table with a gentle twinkle in his eye, "oh, Miss Catlett, will you have a cutlet?"

Other visitors came to Olney besides those who came to Orchard Side. Once, in 1778, a menagerie arrived, with a real live lion. The keeper would have put his head in its mouth, only Cowper besought him not to unless he had another to spare. And in the April of 1784 Lord Houghton's regiment was billeted in Olney, and the band gave a concert one morning just outside Orchard Side. Bright glinted the sun on red coats and pipe-clayed breeches; shrill and sweet came the sound of bugle and fife on the chill spring air. Regardless of the cold, Cowper hung out of the window, striving to catch every note.

He wondered if he was wrong to enjoy it so much. In the days of his conversion he would certainly have thought so; but his life was so starved of esthetic experience, that the little regimental band filled him with a rapture not to be resisted.

Starved, did I say? I was wrong. For though the achievements of conscious art did not come his way, their place in his emotional life was more than supplied by the works of Nature. He had always loved natural beauty, but never with such an exclusive intensity as now. It was to it he had turned first of all when he began to recover, and as his energy increased he only turned to it the more. Cut off as he was from the satisfactions of mysticism on the one hand and those of active life on the other, all the capacity for joy inherent in his highly strung nature had to pour itself down this one narrow channel. The fact that it was narrow only made it flow the stronger. "Oh, I could spend whole days and moonlight nights," he exclaimed, "in feeding upon a lovely prospect! Mine eyes drink the rivers as they flow."

His was not the visionary Wordsworthian feeling that loves the visible world as the incarnation of a divine eternal Spirit. Even the religious tinge with which it had been invested in the days of his conversion had now vanished, though he still prefaced any expression of his feeling by an acknowledgment to God. But in reality a great deal of Cowper's pleasure arose from the fact that natural beauty belonged, like his hares, to that part of life into which the dismal problems of the soul did not enter, which had no need of a remoter charm ungathered from the eye and asked for its appreciation only the immediate instinctive pleasure that it stimulated. Indeed his enjoyment gained an exquisite, intolerable poignancy from his conviction that it had no significance in that world of spiritual values which, in his view, was the only reality, that all this tangible, palpable, ravishing beauty he saw around him was really but the shadow of a shade, which within a few brief years would be lost to him for ever.

And if he did not love Nature in the way Wordsworth did, neither did he, like Keats, love it because it fed his imagination, because he could use those aspects of it he thought the loveliest to create the land of his dream. He loved it with an objective, self-effacing love, for what it was; and every aspect of it was beautiful to him. There was no sound in Nature that was not harmonious outdoors, he said, after sitting out one sunny morning in the garden. Bees, dogs, even geese, he loved them all—except perhaps a donkey; and even the donkey he disliked because it had been braying close to him just when he was trying to work. And what he felt of natural sounds he felt of sights and smells as well.

Actually the country of his preference, humdrum, overgrown Buckinghamshire, was not very pretty. But it was the country he knew best, and therefore he liked it best. With all its intensity, Cowper's love of Nature was of a piece with the rest of his feelings, an affection rather than a passion. He loved it as he loved Mrs. Unwin, quietly, patiently, tenaciously, without moods or explosions, with a strength that grew with the passage of years, cemented by habit, hallowed by a thousand tender recollections.

And he knew the object of his love as one can only know an old friend. It presented no detail so tiny that he did not remark it, no fleeting alteration that escaped him. With the delicate accuracy of a microscope, he would note how already, in September, the sycamore showed red against the varying green of the surrounding trees; how the cock waded with altered, hampered gait through the winter snow; the curious, sweet, amber smell the earth gave forth in hot weather; the squirrel's winter nest of wool and leaves hidden in the recesses of the hollow elm.  Cowper had walked so long and so often in the woods that the animals did not mind him.  The rabbits did not cease to gambol as he passed, and the ring-doves cooed at his approach.

His preoccupation with detail was increased by the fact that the range of his observation was so limited. It was confined, indeed, to the garden and his daily walks, and the walks he could go were few.  There was a sequestered field he liked, especially on the hot summer days, where he lingered listening to the blackbirds beneath the flickering shade of a group of poplars which reflected themselves in the waters of the Ouse, winding between them.  One melancholy day he arrived to find the grass and a few stumps naked to the sunshine.  The trees had been cut down:

> The poplars are felled [sang Cowper], and farewell to the shade,
> And the whispering sound of the cool colonnade.

After this his walks were almost entirely limited to the Wilderness of Weston Park—a country house about a mile from Olney.  It belonged to a Mr. Throckmorton, who gave Cowper the keys.  It was one of those civilized wildernesses that Capability Brown devised to satisfy the longings of a society weary at times of play and masquerade, but shrinking from the grossness of rustic reality: elegant Arcadias in a style of conscious irregularity, a discreet English version of the baroque pastorals of Trianon and Bayreuth; deliberately winding walks

THE TEMPLE IN THE WILDERNESS
After an engraving by J. Greig, published in
*Cowper Illustrated by a Series of Views, etc.*
London, 1810

that opened as by chance on lovely calculated vistas; smooth-swept swards where an eighteenth-century lady might commune with Nature and not soil her silken skirts; artfully disposed groves "sacred to retirement," where the Gibbonian philosopher might meditate in comfort on the pleasures of rural solitude.

Weston Wilderness is a small example of the style; but it is none the less charming for that. The artificial always looks best in miniature. It is a feathery plantation only about half a mile square, but it is divided up into a network of narrow walks thickly planted on each side, to make it seem three times its real size. And there is a Gothic temple in it, and an avenue; and now and again one comes on a little sculptured urn with an inscription on it to the memory of one of the Throckmortons' dogs. It is a forlorn place now. The paths are piled with leaves; the grass waves knee-high; the carving on the urns is blurred with moss. But it still retains a charming flavor of the past. Amid a prosaic agricultural landscape, it stands like a fragment of the eighteenth century strayed by some strange accident of time and space into an age not its own; and as one passes between the classical piers that form its entrance into the green twilight of its walks one seems to be stepping back into 1780, and half expects to meet Cowper's lanky figure, flecked by shifting gleams of sunshine, pacing the turf toward one. Perhaps his ghost does walk there— with a spectral Mungo barking soundlessly at his heels; certainly the whole place is instinct with his spirit.

He had always liked Nature best slightly tamed, and there was no moment of the year when the Wilderness was not beautiful to him. It was lovely on a sunny, breezy May morning, when the trees were in early leaf, gray willow and silvery poplar and glossy maple, with

guelder-rose and laburnum and bending lilac flowering
beneath them, and violet and mezereon at their root;
and the birds sang and the squirrels chattered and
scampered

In anger insignificantly fierce;

or at the late end of a summer's day, when all was indistinct in the warm dusk, and the scents of evening
were fresh in the air. Exquisite summer evenings, when
Cowper and Mary loitered home to supper contentedly
weary, their arms full of honeysuckle, and the young
moon going up the sky before them. But the Wilderness was lovely in winter too: on calm, crystal mornings
after snow, when Cowper's figure slanted, blue and
grotesquely long, across the glaring whiteness, and
Mungo leaped and rolled and buried his nose in the
powdery cold, and beneath the thick branches of the central avenue the moss was still green, and it was so quiet
that you could hear the bells of Clifton Church, now
loud, now soft, away the other side of the valley; or
on winter afternoons, when already at a quarter to four
Cowper would gaze between the leafless boughs across
the furrowed fields, sparkling with frost, to where on the
horizon blazed the tremendous conflagration of sunset.

He enjoyed the walk back from the Wilderness as
much as the Wilderness itself; through the gate and
past the fountain, and down the narrow path, ankle deep
in thyme, to the rustic bridge. Then came the shrub-
bery, with its moss-house and alders, and then up to the
cliff, where he would stop to get his breath. It was not
really a cliff, but a ridge overlooking the valley of the
Ouse. Cowper would stand, with the wind blowing the
hair about his face, staring across the glittering loops of

the river, far away into the hazy distance toward Steventon; and his eye would rove round, pausing for a moment, maybe, where the smoke rose from a thatched roof
solitary in the middle of an elm wood.

The "Peasants' Nest," as he called it, had always
caught his imagination. He liked to fancy himself living
there—a rustic hermit, alone with birds, animals and
trees. With pensive eyes he gazed; then with a half-
smile he would remind himself that he had once visited
the cottage and found it extremely uncomfortable, with
no water supply. It was the healthy side of Cowper's
self-distrust that it never allowed his imagination to become self-indulgent or self-deceptive, as the romantic
imagination was so often tempted to be. With modest
amusement he would prick the bubble of his day-dream,
and turn toward home.

He spent even more time in the garden than in walking. It was not just when he was gardening—he liked
to sit there as well. At first this was a little difficult.
The narrow strip of ground, closed in as it was by high
walls, was insufferably hot if it was sunny, and if it was
not sunny it was cold. But it was intolerable to be
forced to spend a lovely morning in the stuffy parlor,
distracted by the street noises. No wonder he hankered
after the seclusion of the Peasants' Nest. Then one day
in 1780 he conceived the idea of taking the plants out
of the greenhouse and sitting there. He hung the wall
with mats, put down a carpet, a table and a comfortable
chair, and arranged a little row of myrtles in pots at the
entrance to serve as a sunblind. Thenceforth he sat
there morning, afternoon and evening, from May to the
end of September. These summer days in the greenhouse were the pleasantest in the whole year to him.
Whenever he speaks of them the sentences begin to lilt

and dance as to some sylvan orchestra of piping birds and rustling leaves.

"We have not envied you," he writes to Bull away on a visit. "Why should we envy any man? Is not our greenhouse a cabinet of perfumes? It is at this moment fronted with carnations and balsams, mignonette and roses, jessamine and woodbine, and wants nothing but your pipe to make it truly Arabian, a wilderness of sweets." And again, "Our severest winter, commonly called the spring, is now over, and I find myself sitting in my favourite recess—the greenhouse. In such a situation, so silent, so shady, where no human foot is heard, and where only my myrtles presume to peep in at the window, you may suppose I have no interruption to complain of, and that my thoughts are perfectly at my command. But the beauties of the spot are themselves an interruption, my attention being called upon by those very myrtles, by a row of grass pinks just beginning to blossom, and by a bed of beans already in bloom; and you are to consider it, if you please, as no small proof of my regard, that though you have so many powerful rivals, I disengage myself from them all and devote this hour entirely to you."

It was not odd that he liked it so much. It combined the two things to which he now looked for happiness— domestic life and natural beauty. The garden was only a few feet away from the noise and sordid bustle of Silver End, but Cowper heard nothing but birds and bees, saw nothing but flowers and waving treetops. For all his senses could tell him, he might have been in the depths of the country. Indeed, it was like a bit of the country—a plot of remote, leafy silence, set as if by enchantment at his very door, where he could escape from the harsh hurry of the world, and where, as he sat through the placid hours, all the troubles of his jangled nerves would dwindle to a green thought in a green shade.

And yet there was none of the roughness of the really wild about it. However fiercely the sun might beat down, it was cool in the greenhouse; if a summer storm came up the sky, all Cowper knew of it was a few claps of thunder and a sudden sharp patter of rain on the roof above his head. And the whole atmosphere of the neat, old-fashioned garden, tended by his own hand, and the neater little outdoor room, with its well-worn, well-kept, well-remembered bits of furniture, and dear Mary within easy call, breathed cozy, cheerful, civilized security. The different elements that go to give its character to this phase of Cowper's existence sum themselves up in his garden life. If he rises before our mental eye, it is in the greenhouse on some golden September afternoon; a tranquil figure writing at his desk, with his linnets twittering in a cage above his head, and the dog slumbering at his feet; while outside the air is sweet with mignonette, and the sunlight filters greenly in through the myrtle leaves, and patterns itself on the carpeted floor.

It was a life before all things sequestered—a refuge, a sanctuary, an escape. It is true that with his recovery his interest in the great world and its doings had returned. With what delighted expectation did he open the rustling folds of the newspaper! With what zest he read its contents and expounded them with appropriate comments to Mary! The American war, the Gordon Riots, the controversy over George III and his Parliament—he had his views on them all.

His point of view was the typically respectable one of the period. He was a Whig, nurtured in the tradition of 1688, convinced that the Constitution was the culminating achievement of an all-wise Creator; and George III's attempt to tamper with it struck him as so much sacrilege. On the other hand, he could not wholly approve of Fox and the Opposition; not only were they most unevangelical in their private lives, but they had an unnatural tendency to take up the cause of foreigners.

For Cowper gloried in the name of Briton. The Americans in his eyes were simply rebels against the cause of God. As for the French, they were to him, as to most of his contemporaries, the despicable swarm of grinning, posturing frogs, as we see in Hogarth's picture of Calais Gate, three of whom any Englishman ought to overcome single-handed. If they defeated England in the war it could only be through treachery; and their typical representative was Vestris, the professional dancer, Vestris, whose unmanly prancings had roused all Paris to frenzies of enthusiasm. For such people Cowper could only feel contempt. This jaunty chauvinism sits oddly on his nervous, complex character.

Yet for all his outward excitement, he was not deeply interested in politics. His attitude was that of the spectator seeking diversion rather than that of the interested actor. As he said to Newton, "You will suppose me a politician, but in reality I am nothing less. These are the thoughts that occur to me when I read the newspaper, and when I have laid it down I feel more interested in the success of my early cucumbers than in any part of this great and important subject. If I see them droop a little I forget we have been many years at war."

His interest in books was similarly limited. He read a great deal, both to himself and aloud to Mary—on summer afternoons in the greenhouse, and by the crackling winter fire. But he would not read anything philosophical—it demanded too serious an attention—or poetry—it competed with his serious work. No, what he liked was something picturesque and full of incident— Clarendon's *History of the Rebellion* or, still better, *Captain Cook's Voyages.* "My imagination," he remarks of the last, "is so captivated that I seem to partake with the navigators in all the dangers they encountered. I loose my anchor, my mainsail is rent into shreds, I kill a shark, I converse with a Patagonian; and all this without moving from the fireside."

The truth was he had never so far recovered his mental health as to lose that horror of the world that had originally inspired him to leave it. Even if Olney had no very pleasant associations for him, it was yet a haven; and the very idea of being sent back into the whirlpool of active life made him shudder. Only now and again, by way of varying the monotony of his daily round, he liked to take a look, as in a magic mirror hanging in the recesses of his sanctuary, at the pageant of the great world, past and present, moving now bright, now dark, before him. When he had seen enough, he covered it up and returned to the comfortable reality of the garden and the hares and Mary.

But the dangers that his mode of life was primarily designed to avoid were those that came not from the crowd, but from solitude. He wished to escape the pressure of this world, it is true, but, far more imperatively, the pressure of the next. Not that he had ceased to be an Evangelical. Every idea or event or practise he heard or read of was weighed in the "experiential" scale—weighed and generally found wanting. Public schools, foreign travel, rouge, ballooning—did they further the cause of God? On the whole, he thought not.

Ballooning was, he admitted, a difficult question. There was nothing morally wrong about it, but he could not believe that God, who had given man two legs to walk with and had created the earth to use them on, could really approve of his neglecting these endowments to career about the sky in a machine of his own invention. The question of rouge presented no such difficulties. It could only be used from two motives—to deceive or to attract the male, and either, though perhaps pardonable in a wretched unenlightened Frenchwoman, must be reprehended in an English lady.

But indeed England was now wallowing in a slough of vice and luxury. It was an additional reason for retirement if one was needed. The way the Sabbath was broken—and by the most distinguished people in the land, the Duke of York and the Duchess of Devonshire—made him shudder. But even their shortcomings did not rouse him to such angry eloquence as did the growing prevalence of sacred music. He had it for a fact that a London clergyman gave concerts in his church on Sunday afternoons—concerts without words. "I believe that wine itself, though a man be guilty of habitual intoxication, does not more debauch or befool the natural understanding than music, always music; music in season and out of season, weakens and destroys the spiritual discernment, if it is not done in an unfeigned reverence to the worship of God and with a design to assist the soul in the performance of it, which cannot be when it is the only occupation—it degenerates into a sensual delight."

And he had heard, too, that a lady, anxious to dissuade her daughter from indulging in the dangerous delight of walking in Ranelagh, called in this very clergyman to support her, and he had actually said in front of the daughter that he saw no harm in it. Such were the

alarming results of promoting Sunday concerts! As for
the Handel Festival at Westminster Abbey, Cowper did
not know whether it made him laugh or cry. That a
number of people, all in danger of eternal damnation,
should collect together and sing about it, that they should
do it in honor of a music-monger, a fellow sinner like
themselves, and that they should do it in a church, was
beyond any folly that he could have dreamed of. Newton sought to recall these people to a sense of their true
situation by preaching a course of sermons on the words
of "The Messiah." Cowper applauded his intention;
but he could not expect it would do much good.

Clearly the American war was a judgment inflicted on
England for her wickedness. But was it a sufficient
punishment? When he thought of the sacred concerts
and the Handel Festival, Cowper began to doubt it.
Only final perdition seemed adequate to such offenses.
And indeed, in the summer of 1785 he thought there
were great signs that it was not long to be delayed. The
weather was unnaturally stuffy, he saw several shooting
stars, and the moon shone dull and small like a red-hot
brick. Such phenomena could not be without significance.
Altogether, he felt he would not be surprised if the world
came to an end before the year was out.

But though he still judged mankind by Evangelical
standards and envisaged his future in the light of Evangelical ideas, the religious conceptions which under-
lay these ideas he tried as far as possible to forget.
His Evangelicalism was ethical; it consisted wholly of
ethical judgments on men and events; it expressed itself
in an easy, conversational style, altogether different from
the Biblical phraseology, the fiery emphasis, that had
characterized his utterances in the days of his conversion.
The purely religious aspects of his creed ever since his

illness he had striven, with the pertinacity of desperation, to put out of his head.  He would not go to church or attend family prayers; and when others stood with bowed heads during grace, he sat down, knife and fork in hand, deliberately averting his mind from the subject.  Newton wanted him to write a book about religion, but Cowper told him that though he did not mind making short references to the subject in verse, he simply could not let his mind dwell on it for as long as would be needed for a prose work.  And if people tried to talk about it to him, or argue about it in his presence, he first tried to change the subject, and if that failed, left the room.

For of course there was a reverse side to the homely monotony of his life—a reverse side of blackest horror. Within the center of his consciousness remained unaltered the conviction that he was damned, that every day that passed brought him a day nearer to an eternity of torment; and he had fixed his eyes exclusively on such things as could still give him pleasure, had laboriously devised from them the whole elaborate scheme of occupation and habit and amusement which was his mode of life, in order to distract himself from the frightful fate that awaited him.  But the certainty of that fate remained like a dark pit in the grassy garden world of his every day.

He looked at it as little as possible, but sometimes he could not help it.  One day, for example, when he was in the garden, he heard an old breeches-maker who lived in a neighboring cottage, singing at his work.

> Oh, for a closer walk with God,
> A pure and heavenly frame,

he sang in aged, quavering tones,

A light to shine upon the road
That leads me to the Lamb.

It was one of Cowper's own hymns; and as he listened he recalled with an anguished twinge of regret how trusting and hopeful he had been when he wrote it. Now he trusted and hoped no longer, and never would again. Others might take comfort from the words; they only made their author more sadly conscious of his own despair.

He had other moments of more sensational depression, in winter especially when he sat for weeks together, cooped up in that dark poky house, with the rain drumming on the panes outside and nothing to keep his mind from brooding on itself. January was the worst month, January, that included the anniversary of the awful dream that had finally shut him out from hope. His sick, suspicious nerves fancied that there was something fatal to them in the month; and for weeks before his heart would be beating in an agony of apprehension. Would he go mad again in January? When he thought about it rationally such a fear seemed nonsensical; but he could not stop it from worrying him. Until February was safely begun he was in a fever.

In these moments of discouragement Cowper turned once more to Mary. Calmly and unobtrusively as ever, she bore his burden, and in time it passed. But he was never so far recovered as to face his fears and have them out and examine them in the light of reason. He would not listen to argument. Mary, Newton, Bull—all his friends—reasoned with him and reasoned again, in vain. In 1782, Newton, optimistic as usual, sought to see if the force of example would have more success, and wrote Cowper a letter describing the strange case of Simon

Browne.  This was a non-conformist preacher residing in London during the earlier years of the century, who, like Cowper, had, for no sensible reason, become convinced he was damned.  He made every effort to escape his fate, even going so far as to write to Queen Caroline asking her to intercede with God on his behalf, as he felt that a person of her exalted rank would have more chance than a nobody like himself of engaging the attention of an overworked Creator.  Whether the Queen granted his request we do not know.  It would have been a great favor on her part if she had, as she was more than half an atheist.  At any rate, the prayer was not granted, and poor Mr. Browne died without hope.

Newton thought that the patent absurdity of his story would lead Cowper to realize the equal absurdity of his own.  However, Cowper only replied with polite acrimony that the cases were different.  "I could point out to you," he said, "some essential differences between his state of mind and mine which would prove mine to be by far the most deplorable.  I suppose no man would despair if he did not apprehend something singular in the circumstances of his own story, something that discriminates it from that of every other man."  This was always the burden of his case: he was unique.  As he says on another occasion: "My friends expect I shall see again.  I admit the validity of this reasoning in every case but my own."  The truth was that about this particular subject he was still mad, the victim of an obsession —an obsession which blinded him to reason or common sense.  The pit remained dark in the middle of the garden, and he still walked round it with averted eyes.

His condition of mind reflects itself in his letters and poems.  The letters are the best things he every wrote, the finest achievement of one who had cultivated to the highest point of perfection a natural genius for intimacy. They are unpretentious—he hated consciously well-written letters, and even thought that a letter should be destroyed after the recipient had read it—but they are not in the least like notes dashed off in the intervals of a busy life. They are composed in a lucid, unforced, graceful English—the very perfection of the plain style, by no means to be attained in a hurry. Every corner is rounded: there are no abrupt transitions: the briefest note begins and ends with a charming, easy turn of phrase. They are beautifully differentiated, to suit the temperament of his correspondent: serious to Newton, sensible to Hill, playful and confiding to Unwin. They do not tell much news, for there was little to tell, but rather follow whatever whims and thoughts happened to chase one another across Cowper's mind as he sat in the garden, or by the candle-lit table on a winter's evening. No letters show such variety of mood. The stream of sparkling, limpid sentences flows on, now in sunshine, now in shadow, and now it dimples in humor, now lingers somber under the shade of melancholy boughs.

The poems are not so good as the letters, but they reveal other things about Cowper. One realizes from them that he was an amateur who wrote as a distraction. Only very rarely do his verses attain that complete felicity of expression, that indissoluble marriage of word and thought that characterizes the work of those to whom their art is the undisputed center and fulfilment of existence. But when he speaks about any subject he cares about the authentic accents of poetry come into his voice; and as his peculiar mode of life had given him tastes not common among poets, he had a real vein of his own.

His is almost the only domestic poetry; "I sing the

sofa," begins his most considerable poem, and the line might stand advertisement to one whole aspect of his achievement. He sang the sofa, of the respectable country home of his day, and the tea-table by the sofa, and the chest of drawers opposite the sofa, and, leaning against the sofa, the chessboard with its carven armies, and the gay needlework on the sofa cushions and the woolly lap-dog that leaped up from them to bark at an intruder. The animals he loved play a large part in his poetry. He writes fables about them—*The Dog and the Water-lily, The Retired Cat*—fables which are made to point a neat moral, but which vividly portray the peculiar tricks and idiosyncrasies of their furred or feathered protagonists. Turning to human beings, he is still domestic; writes lively occasional verses to Mary, on a nosegay he had picked for her, or to Newton, on his return from Ramsgate; celebrates in mock ballad style the misadventures of a muddy walk. With gentle, penetrating satire he painted the bores who come to call—the emphatic speaker who "dearly loves to oppose, in contact inconvenient, nose to nose." Or the wearisome tellers of anecdote:

> 'Tis the most asinine employ on earth
> To hear them tell of parentage and birth
> And echo conversations dull and dry
> Embellish with *"he said"* and *"so said I."*
> At every interview their route the same,
> The repetition makes attention lame:
> We bustle up with unsuccessful speed,
> And at the saddest part cry—Droll indeed!

Or sometimes, his voice changing to a tender tone, he will sing for a while the simple affections and sorrows of family life. Such writing may never glow with the

white-hot temperature of the greatest poetry; but its
author has caught an aspect of life not often touched on
by poets and crystallizes it into art.

Cowper writes beautifully of Nature too. With exquisite precision he isolates the characteristic features of
the landscape:

> The clouds that flit or slowly float away . . .
> Hypericum all blooms, so thick a swarm
> Of flowers like flies clothing her slender rods.

The streams that

> . . . chiming as they fall
> Upon loose pebbles, lose themselves at length
> In matted grass that with a livelier green
> Betrays the secret of their silent course.

Or the robin in winter

> . . . flitting light
> From spray to spray. Where'er he rests he shakes
> From many a twig the pendant drops of ice,
> That tinkle in the withered leaves below.

No other writer has "caught" the character of the landscape of southern England so exactly. And yet Cowper
is never consciously English, as some later writers have
been. He describes England because he wants to describe the country, and it is the only country he knows.
He does not even bother about an appropriately rustic
style but employs the formal Miltonic diction he had
been brought up to think correct for serious poetry. Yet
this seems to make his descriptions all the more genuine,
as the water-colors of his contemporaries, Girtin and

Cozens, for all their conventionalized style of drawing, their faded classical graces, communicate the spirit of the English countryside as the lifelike snapshots of later impressionists never do. It is the visitor who notices local terms and typical "bits"; the inhabitant knows the place too well to be conscious of such external features.

Cowper writes well, too, when he gives rein to the ebullience of his florid eighteenth-century patriotism, the gallant stirrings of emotion roused in him by some heroic event or personage:

> Weigh the vessel up
> Once dreaded by our foes
> And mingle with your cup
> The tears that England owes.
>
> Her timbers set aside
> That she may float again
> Full charged with England's thunder,
> And plough the distant main.
>
> But Kempenfelt has gone,
> His victories are o'er;
> And he and his eight hundred
> Must plough the waves no more.

Is there not a fine martial clang about that?

But now and again, misled by conscience, a most unreliable guide in esthetic matters, Cowper adopts a tone of religious reprobation, girds against the wickedness of the world and summons people to throw themselves upon the mercy of God. Immediately all the light fades from the page, and it becomes pompous, wordy and uninspired. For Cowper had left the realm of his real feelings. Though he still thinks Christianity true, he has

ceased to feel anything for it; he does not care a pin if
the world is wicked or good. As for the mercy of God,
as far as he himself is concerned he profoundly disbe-
lieves in it. He may tell people they ought to think of
such subjects, but they are the subjects that he spends his
whole life trying to forget.

This he does with growing success. The ordered life
of Olney was so unvaried, each day so exactly like the
last, that often it seemed to him that time was standing
still. But in reality it hurried all the faster. A year
there passed as quickly as a week of more diverse existence. "My days steal away silently," he said, "and
march on as poor mad King Lear would have made his
soldiers march, as if they were shod with felt." And
with time came change. Beneath the level, uniform surface went on a steady, persistent process of alteration.
Cowper was regaining his mental health. Not that he
was getting more amenable to reason; if you argued
with him he listened as little as ever; but other forces
than reason were working for his recovery. Gradually,
stealthily, the movement begun in 1776 was advancing,
his natural vitality was reasserting itself with a growing
force. He felt no sudden change of mind or conviction;
he simply began to think more and more about the outside world and less and less about his own internal
problems. The pit remained unillumined, but it was
diminishing in area, and grass and trees were encroaching
on its slopes.

In 1779 his predominant condition had been one of
dull despair varied by fits of anguish and rarer snatches
of enjoyment; by 1780 these moments recurred often
enough for him to construct a relatively normal system
of life around them, and he had glimpses of an altogether
more light-hearted condition of mind. "I wonder that

a sportive thought should ever knock at the doors of my intellect, much less gain admittance," he remarks to Unwin. "It is as if Harlequin should intrude himself into the gloomy chamber where a corpse is deposited in state. His antic gesticulations would be unseasonable at any rate, but especially so if they should distort the features of the mournful attendants into laughter. But the mind long wearied with the sorrow of a dull, dreary prospect will gladly fix its eyes on anything that will raise a little variety in its contemplation, though it were but a kitten playing with its tail."

By 1781 happiness had become the rule rather than the exception. His fits of actual anguish were few, and in between whiles their memory cast only a faint shadow over his life. He was further taken out of himself by the publication of his first book. Cowper always denied he was ambitious, said he only wrote for pleasure and did not care what the critics said. Indeed, how should he care, seeing that he was only too painfully aware that all the glories of the world were vanity? But in fact when his book was accepted by a publisher he could not contain his pleasure; and when it first appeared before the public, he was in an agony of apprehension as to how it would be received. Of course he had really a large fund of natural ambition which he had always repressed, partly in consequence of bad health, but still more because he was convinced he was born to be a failure. He said he did not care for honors, because he feared he was never going to get them. Actually, though his first book made no great stir, it was decidedly no failure; and his growing interest and pleasure in life were so far encouraged.

However, before the book was out another force had come into his life that was to affect him more profoundly.

One afternoon in July, 1781, Cowper was staring idly out of the parlor window when his attention was caught by the sight of two ladies emerging from the bulging, bow-windowed little draper's shop opposite. One he knew; she was Mrs. Jones, wife of the clergyman of the neighboring village of Clifton. Her companion was unknown to him, but there was something about her appearance by which he was immediately and strangely attracted. Moved by an impulse foreign to his usual retiring character, he besought Mrs. Unwin to find out who the lady was, and ask them both in to tea. She complied; the invitation was accepted; and the unknown proved to be Mrs. Jones' sister, a Lady Austen, widow of a baronet called Sir Robert Austen. Now that the object of his interest was actually in the house Cowper's mood underwent a strong reaction. He became even shyer than usual, lingered for several minutes outside the parlor door trying to screw up enough courage to go in; and when at length he did so, was so overcome with confusion that he could barely stammer out the first formal words of greeting. A few minutes' talk with Lady Austen, however, and all his embarrassment had vanished. She had an easy, intimate manner, and a vivid, responsive personality. Her dark eyes sparkled with laughter at the least hint of humor, softened with concern at a suggestion of sorrow. And her own contributions to the conversation were alive with shrewdness, wit and infectious gaiety. She seemed to take to Cowper at once; when she rose to go it was with many protestations of hope that they would meet again. Cowper was only too willing. Not only was she far and away the most dazzling figure that had appeared at Olney for years, but he felt her peculiarly sympathetic to himself. And the very next day he and Mary were trudging along the water meadows, thick with yellow irises, toward Clifton.

Their visit led to a return visit to Olney; and soon the rigid ritual of Cowper's existence, unvaried for twelve years, was broken up in favor of a succession of engagements to walk and dine and drink tea in the company of the ladies of Clifton Rectory. They even had a picnic. It was a decorous kind of picnic. At midday the ladies and Cowper started off to walk about a mile to a spinney, where, suitably waited on by their servants, they had dinner in a summer-house. But a masked ball could hardly have been a more sensational variation to Cowper's usual course of life. He enjoyed himself immensely. "Lady Austen's lackey and a lad that waits on me in the garden drove a wheelbarrow full of eatables and drinkables to the scene of our *fête champetre*. A board laid over the wheelbarrow served us for a table; our dining-room was a root house lined with moss and ivy. At five o'clock the servants dined under a great elm on the grass at a little distance, boiled the kettle, and the said wheelbarrow served us for a tea-table. We then took a walk into the wilderness about half a mile off, and arrived home again a little after eight. We had spent the day together from noon to evening without one cross occurrence or the least weariness of one another—a happiness few parties of pleasure can boast of." In the pleasant warmth of such gentle gaieties Cowper's and Lady Austen's early liking for each other ripened into a close friendship; and by the end of the summer she was talking of selling her house in London and coming to live with Mary and Cowper at Olney.

Throughout the whole affair she had been the active party. One can not, indeed, imagine her passive in anything. She was all quick-silver and electricity, a live, high-strung, compelling personality, with an intense desire to please and considerable powers of doing so.

Though she was not at all uncultivated, people were the principal interest of her life. She was quick to sum up character, to detect foibles, to appreciate charm and originality, to get into the key of another's mood, to say the things that pleased, to avoid the things that jarred. And her feelings were as responsive as her mind. She could not be in company without her spirits rising in a bubbling fount of vivacity; the smallest service would fill her eyes with tears of gratitude. When she took a fancy to some one it was immediately and enthusiastically. She had the defects of her qualities. She was over-excitable, indulged her emotions, liked to dramatize her life, to see herself as the heroine of a situation. And like most people whose charm is an important factor in their lives, she was an egoist; demonstrative herself, she exacted demonstrations from her friends; and though she forgave easily she was easily hurt. She had been married and widowed young, and since then had divided her time between London and France. And she had all the polish and experience that come from so varied an existence. But at the time she appears in Cowper's story she was in strong reaction against the great world. "She had seen much of the world and accounted it a great simpleton," said Cowper. For the time being at any rate, she was in love with the pleasures of retirement; and it was in pursuit of them she professed to have come to stay with her sister and brother-in-law. But she was too young, too energetic, and too exclusively interested in people, to be satisfied for long with a life of self-sufficient seclusion; and the truth was that she had come to the country because she was restless. She had no settled position and no responsibilities and nothing to do. She was ready to throw herself into the first friendship that came her way. Cowper, too, was the very man to attract her. He had always had great charm for women, and Lady Austen was far too quick to be put off by his stiff provincial manner. Indeed in her present mood it only added to the attraction she felt. Cowper incarnated for her the happiness of country solitude, so preferable to the bustling, strident vanity of the world she had left. Her inflammable fancy caught fire the moment she met him; and she devoted all her arts and energies to cementing the connection.

He seconded her willingly. The romantic glow which had haloed her figure when he first caught sight of it out of the window had not faded on closer acquaintance. He was by temperament peculiarly susceptible to the subtle sweetness, the intimacy, the feminine shimmer, of an accomplished, charming woman; and this susceptibility had been sharpened by the fact that for many years he had seen so little of them. Lady Austen was a lot of other things he liked as well—vital, spontaneous, humorous and tender-hearted. Nor, with all her arts and experience, did he feel her to belong to a different and more worldly existence than he did. If he talked of serious subjects she immediately became admirably serious herself; and he was pleased to find that she disapproved of Sunday concerts as much as he did. It is possible that her views became stricter when she was with Cowper.

But at moments he felt a little nervous, a little self-conscious, about his relationship to her. It was certainly delightful, but very unlike any that he had ever had with any one before; and he was not at all sure what it might lead to, or what other people might think of it. With a comic anxiety he assures and reassures his correspondents that she is quite as much Mrs. Unwin's friend as his own, that he likes her in great part because she is so fond of Mrs. Unwin. What Mrs. Unwin herself felt is not so clear. The summer had been certainly more amusing than usual, and Lady Austen, charming to every one, was especially charming to her; she was not likely to be anything else to Cowper's closest friend.  But Mary must have felt that the character of their lives, of their time-honored tête-à-tête, would be enormously changed by the addition of a third, especially such a lively third.  It is hard to believe that she regarded the idea with unmixed feelings.

Certainly William Unwin, to whom the whole affair was communicated, was dubious.  He wrote to say that he had heard Lady Austen's financial position was uncertain, and that they ought most emphatically to find out about it before engaging themselves to her, anyway. Cowper wrote back a vehement letter assuring him that her financial position was impeccable, and added that he was in favor of her coming to live in Olney chiefly because it would be so much pleasanter for Mrs. Unwin to have a woman friend near at hand.  Anyway, he wound up, Lady Austen would not be able to come for nearly two years, so that there was no need to get excited about it.  Indeed for the moment the whole affair remained vague; and in October Lady Austen went back to London.

Before she left she proposed that Cowper and she should open a regular correspondence.  It was to be with him rather than with Mary, he carefully explained to William Unwin, "because writing does not agree with your mother."  Lady Austen also suggested that they should address each other as brother and sister.  Cowper was quite willing; it seemed to place their relationship on an admirably safe and sensible basis, encouraging to intimacy, discouraging to dangerous sentimentality.  Alas, he was wrong!  It is one thing when a woman asks a man to look on her as a sister after he has made love to her.

It is quite another when she does it before. In the present instance it was nothing less than the thin end of the wedge of love. Any vague apprehensions that Cowper may have felt at the beginning of his connection with Lady Austen were to be justified. Week after week he wrote and she replied; and gradually, to his horror a more impassioned note began to creep into her style.

One can not blame her. Cowper's position in regard to such matters was so queer. Passion had always been foreign to him; and now mental troubles and his association with Mary together put any idea of a love-affair quite out of the question. On the other hand, the only relationship he cared to cultivate with any one was an intimate and tender friendship; and it is almost impossible for an unattached man and woman to live in intimate and tender friendship without one of the two beginning to look on it as a dawning love-affair. The very fact that Cowper was so little open to passion made this more likely, for he was careless how far he pressed the intimacy. He felt no danger himself, and so could not remember that she might not feel the same. For all his shy good-breeding, his manner toward women was remarked on for its "tender gallantry." He had the kind of temperament that always prefers tête-à-tête to a general conversation. He singled out the object of his interest by a thousand small personal attentions, small personal solicitudes, small personal confidences. He loved to laugh with her at some joke private to themselves, to recall with sentiment some memory they shared together.

All this was bound to make a difficulty in any friendship he had with a woman; but the circumstances of his connection with Lady Austen made these difficulties peculiarly acute. He saw her as a glittering goddess who had suddenly descended from a sky-borne chariot to illuminate his drab life, and this made him feel his relationship to be different not in degree but in kind from any other he had known.   This feeling appeared in every word he said to her.

"Dear Anna," he writes to her in December:

> Dear Anna, between friend and friend
> Prose answers every common end,
> Serves, in a plain and homely way,
> T' express th' occurrence of the day—
> Our health, the weather, and the news,
> What walks we take, what books we choose,
> And all the floating thoughts we find
> Upon the surface of the mind.
>
> But when a Poet takes the pen,
> Far more alive than other men,
> He feels a gentle tingling come
> Down to his finger and his thumb,
> Deriv'd from Nature's noblest part.
> The centre of a glowing heart!
> And this is what the world, who knows
> No flights above the pitch of prose,
> His more sublime vagaries slighting,
> Denominates an itch for writing.
> No wonder, I, who scribble rhyme
> To catch the triflers of the time
> And tell them truths divine and clear
> Which couch'd in prose, they will not hear,
>
> .    .    .    .    .    .
>
> Should feel that itching and that tingling
> With all my purpose intermingling,
> To your intrinsic merit true,
> When called t' address myself to you.

This is not quite a love poem, but it is very near to one. And it expresses exactly the state of Cowper's feelings. In a respectable, rarified sort of way, he was a flirt. He did not wish, as we know, a declared love-affair; indeed, he avoided it. But he preferred a personal relationship that involved a slightly raised emotional tension, that moved in an atmosphere tinged with half-hidden, half-hinted romantic sentiment.

Lady Austen's ardent temperament understood no such half-shades. She did not actually make a confession of her love to him; indeed, she may not actually have confessed it to herself. But she answered his hints of sentimental regard with open protestations of affection; and finally, early in January, he got a letter from her in which, after expatiating his virtues in a strain of lyrical rhapsody, she ended by prophesying their friendship would attain a culmination of unique and supreme felicity in the near future. Poor Cowper became very agitated. Clearly he would have to do something at once to damp this rising flame. But it was an embarrassing task. She was so touchy. Only a few weeks before, she had taken violent offense at some slighting reflection she professed to have found in one of his letters; and he had been forced to write an elaborate apology and explanation before she was pacified. He hardly dared to think what her feelings would be if he ventured openly to rebuke her.

However, her wrath was a less disturbing alternative than her love, and, sighing, he sat down at his table and composed a letter. It was in a lofty vein. Solemnly, he bade her remember that he was an erring mortal; that by exaggerating his perfections she was in danger of falling into the sin of idolatry; and, starting off with such false hopes, a closer acquaintance with him would certainly fill her with disappointment. It is to be doubted whether a strain of apocalyptic exhortation is that best fitted to deal with the fragile affairs of the heart. Mary, it is true, thought Cowper's letter admirable; but she may have had her own reasons for approving of it.

Not so Lady Austen; nor did she. She was even angrier than Cowper had feared. Within a few days he got a letter back from her, of such a violent kind that he could only suppose she had made up her mind to sever their connection for ever. He stifled a few involuntary pangs of regret and resigned himself to the inevitable. After all, there was a brighter side to the affair. It might have been a great strain to have her always in the house. She was so very vivacious. He remembered that, in some ways, it had been quite a relief when she went away in October. He and Mary had felt exhausted at having to maintain a level of conversation so persistently sparkling.

Meanwhile, however, Lady Austen's volatile feelings had suffered a revulsion. Her wrath had died down as quickly as it had flared up. And now she could only remember how much she liked Cowper, and seek about for some means of making it up with him. She had been working three pairs of ruffles for him, and by way of opening negotiations she sent them to him by the hand of her brother-in-law. Cowper could not restrain his pleasure at this sign of good-will. He did not thank her directly, but he asked Mr. Jones to do so, and to show that, for his part, he bore her no malice, he sent her in return a long-promised copy of his first book. But his cooler temperament could not so soon forget the past; his peaceful disposition was nervous of reopening a connection liable to such storms. This diffidence was increased by the next news he heard of Lady Austen.

"She is to spend the summer in our neighborhood," he

wrote. "Lady Peterborough and Miss Mordaunt are to be of the party: the former a dissipated woman of fashion, and the latter a haughty beauty. Retirement is our passion and our delight. It is in still life alone that we look for that measure of happiness we can rationally expect below. What have we, therefore, to do with characters like these? Shall we go to the dancing school again? Shall we cast off the simplicity of our plain and artless demeanor to learn—and not in a youthful day either—the manners of those whose manners at the best are their only recommendation, and yet can in reality recommend them to none but the people like themselves?"

It was very sad. Enchanting creature though Anna might be, it was clear from the company she kept that, contrary to his first impression, her background was too different from his for their friendship ever to rest on a firm basis. Essentially he feared she belonged to another world, even if she did disapprove of Sunday concerts.

Still, there were signs that he had not completely resigned himself to her loss. William Unwin had taken advantage of the formal reconciliation to go and inspect her for himself, under cover of a call of courtesy. It is significant that he was disappointed in her, and told Cowper that she was strange and stiff in her manner toward him. Immediately, Cowper blazed up in her defense. There must have been some misunderstanding, he wrote; she was ordinarily most forthcoming. It was no good; he could not conceal the fact that he liked her, that he longed for her friendship again.

His longings were satisfied. There was no more talk of Miss Mordaunt and Lady Peterborough—baleful priestesses of the Moloch of fashionable life. In the summer Lady Austen came back to Clifton alone; and within a few days of her arrival she had hurried over to Orchard Side, rushed into the house, and flung herself with a torrent of smiles and tears into Mary's arms. She had come determined on peace. She explained, she apologized, she forgave, she captivated; and Mary herself admitted that there was no resisting her. Before the visit was over they were once more, officially at least, on the terms of the previous summer. Cowper and Mary did, indeed, feel a little awkward, but Lady Austen did not; and after a few weeks' constant intercourse they did not either. The quarrel was as forgotten as if it had never taken place.

There was no doubt it was more amusing when she was there. Once again the monotony of their daily round was brightened by a ceaseless course of gentle diversion. Actually they were prevented by the weather from enjoying so many of the delightful outdoor schemes, walks, expeditions and picnics as they did last summer; there had not been such a bad summer for years. During weeks together the meadows between Olney and Clifton were in flood. However, Lady Austen was not the woman to be daunted by a trifle like that. She got hold of a donkey, and day after day, mounted on its back, she splashed through the water to come and discuss and joke and tell tales with her dear "brother." Even when the weather made it impossible for them to meet, she managed to brighten his life. She wrote to him, and got him a small printing press, so that he could while away the time in clumsily stamping out, in blurred, uncertain type, a letter or a copy of verses for her.

The summer was not without its more sensational incidents. One evening when Cowper was sitting peacefully in the parlor he was startled by a knock at the door; and he rushed out to find Lady Austen being supported up the steps, apparently in great pain. She had come to Olney Church for the afternoon service, and had suddenly been taken ill there. She was put to bed, and a doctor was sent for, who reported her to be suffering from "bilious colic." Any one of a bilious habit should be thankful that they do not live in the eighteenth century, for colics then seem to have been formidable affairs. Twenty-four hours later, after an afternoon in which Lady Austen had appeared her usual lively self, Cowper was called into her room, to find her in a violent fit of convulsive hysterics. However, this may not have been due to the sort of illness so much as to her highly strung temperament, which could not but show itself, even in her ailments. It would be fanciful as well as ungallant to suggest that she was influenced by a desire that Cowper should come in and comfort her. Anyway, two days later she was well enough to ride back to Clifton on her donkey.

So passed the summer; and now the autumn was here. And Lady Austen determined not to leave her "brother" again. But where was she to live? There was no room for her in Orchard Side. However, as usual, she had a plan. One evening, as they were sitting calmly at Clifton, she suddenly suggested that they should all set up house in the deserted Clifton Manor House. Cowper looked at her with mingled fear and delight. That he and Mary should break up the twenty-year-old order of their existence and start life in a new house at a month's notice— only Anna could have conceived of so fantastically bold an idea. Still, he could not help being attracted by its very boldness; and in his next letter he mentioned it to William Unwin, in an airy, half-laughing way, as if he were nervous that he might not like it. However William Unwin was less suspicious of Lady Austen than formerly. She had tactfully told Cowper that she thought Mr. Unwin was the most elegant figure she had ever seen; and Cowper had passed the information on; which perhaps accounts for the modification of William's views. The scheme proved impracticable; but it was settled, instead, that Lady Austen should take the Vicarage, which was, of course, quite near Orchard Side, and which the Vicar—a man of large family and small means—was only too willing to let. In October she moved in, and for the next eighteen months it was her home.

She had got what she came for. Cowper and she hardly spent a moment of the day apart. A door was cut in the wall between the two gardens, and immediately after breakfast he walked across to "pay his respects" to her. Later she nearly always accompanied him and Mary on their walk; and sometimes, when Mary was tired, Lady Austen and Cowper went alone. During the week they had dinner together alternately at Orchard Side and the Vicarage; they were still sufficiently Evangelical to deny themselves such a dissipation on Sunday. From dinner on they were together till bedtime.

Cowper enjoyed the change in his life. "Lady Austen," he told a correspondent, "was the cleverest and most entertaining woman in the country." Her wit and vitality doubled the amusement he got out of his ordinary relaxations—talking and walking and reading aloud. And besides, she could play deliciously on the harpsichord. His letters begin to sparkle with gentle gaiety. "How different is the complexion of your evenings and mine!" he said to Joseph Hill. "Yours spent amid a ceaseless hum that proceeds from the inside of fifty noisy and busy periwigs; mine by a domestic fireside, in a retreat as silent as retirement can make it, where no noise is made but what we make for our own amusement.  For instance, here are two rustics and your humble servant in company. One of the ladies has been playing on the harpsichord, while I, with the other, have been playing at battledore and shuttlecock.  A little dog, in the meantime, howling under the chair of the former, performed in the vocal way to admiration.  This entertainment over, I began my letter and, having nothing more important to communicate, have given you an account of it.  I know you love dearly to be idle, when you can find the opportunity to be so; but as such opportunities are rare with you, I thought it possible that a short description of the idleness I enjoy might give you pleasure.  The happiness we cannot call our own, we yet seem to possess, while we sympathize with our friends who can."

In a word, his life was still as secluded from the rush of the outside world as he could desire.  But Lady Austen's presence gave it a liveliness and a color that made him ten times stronger to resist his spiritual enemies. For these had not ceased their attacks.  Indeed, in the autumn of 1782, Mary was in terror lest he might go mad again.  Not only was the winter-time coming on— always a dangerous time—but it was just ten years since his second attack; exactly the same length of time as had elapsed between that second attack and the first one. This was just the sort of fact, as Mary, with her long experience of Cowper, well knew, to send him mad.  His mind was such an inchoate mass of superstition and fear that if he thought it was time for him to go mad again, he would do so.

Sure enough, as the autumn went on, Cowper was seized with fits of gloom.  In the middle of a conversation he would suddenly fall silent; his jaw would drop, and an expression of anguish would overcast his features.

With impotent dismay Mary watched him. Her patient, tenacious, self-denying character, so wonderfully able to give support in a tragic crisis, had not the resource to forestall such a crisis by diverting Cowper's mind from the dangerous slopes it was descending. However, Lady Austen had.

One evening, when he was particularly downcast, she offered to tell a story which, she said, had amused her as a girl. Mary begged her to; but Cowper only preserved a stony silence. Undaunted she began, and with all the spirit and humor she could muster, recounted the sad adventures that befell a linen-draper of London in his efforts to celebrate the anniversary of his wedding. Cowper listened to the first incidents with his face still fixed in an expression of dejection. But Lady Austen was nothing if not high-hearted. She went on; within a few minutes a smile began to steal across Cowper's face; and by the end of the story he was in peals of laughter, all the heartier from the fact that they came as a reaction from profound depression. He was so amused, in fact, that he could not sleep, but lay awake putting the story into verse. Next morning he read the verses aloud; this time it was the ladies' turn to laugh. He retired to the greenhouse—it was still early in October—and set to work to finish the poem. As he polished off each passage he gleefully sent it across the way to provoke the laughter of his friend, Wilson, the barber. When the whole thing was finished it was sent away and published in a broadsheet; and within a few days all London was laughing over the story of John Gilpin.

Cowper was delighted at its reception; but it gave him a slight qualm too. He, who had hoped to shine through the world as a light of the Gospel, had only succeeded in becoming famous as the author of a comic poem. He

was still more distressed to learn that his rivals for the
chief share of the public interest were the antics of a
performing pig and the unedifying confessions of the
notorious Mrs. Bellamy. "Alas!" he said ruefully,
"what is an author's popularity worth in a world which
can suffer a prostitute on one side, and a pig on the
other, to eclipse his brightest glories?" All the same,
he had reason to be grateful to John Gilpin, for he had
saved him from going mad. Owing to Lady Austen's
tact, winter passed and spring, and he was safely back in
summer, without his spirits having passed through anything worse than a mild melancholy.

She stimulated him to write other things besides. She
often wanted words for music; and Cowper would em-
ploy a dull morning in composing a copy of verses to be
sung to the tune of *The Lass of Pattie's Mill,* or *The
March in Scipio.* She believed strongly in his powers,
and thought he could attempt something more ambitious.
One day he was declaiming against Pope's translation of
Homer; it was a favorite theme with him.

"Why don't you write a translation yourself?" she
said.

The idea sank into his mind and later bore fruit. Another day she urged him to write something in blank
verse.

"I have no subject," he said.

"Write about anything," she returned impetuously.
"Write about the sofa."

He took her at her word. And a few days later, began a poem which started, as required, about the sofa,
but gradually blossomed into something bigger; in fact,
into the biggest work he ever wrote: *The Task,* a long
meditative poem of several thousand lines, into which he
poured more or less at random the chief conclusions and

reflections and observations that remained to him from fifty-five years of troubled life. His genius had always been meditative, and the subject absorbed him as no other had. He grew happier every day—happier, indeed, than he had been since his last illness. He felt all the sense of well-being and self-satisfaction that comes through regular, hard, congenial work; and all the time he was not working he spent delightfully talking and walking, reading and eating and laughing with Lady Austen. He hardly had time to write a letter. "Yours, more than I have time to tell you," he scribbles off to a correspondent. "The ladies are in the greenhouse, and tea waits."

It was a delightful life; but it did not, it could not last. The circumstances that had made his relationship with Lady Austen impossible fifteen months before remained unchanged. It was no easier than it had been then for a man and a woman to spend almost every hour of every day together for months without danger to the deeper feelings of either. And while still avoiding the boiling point of passion, Cowper still liked to keep the emotional temperature decidedly warmer than that of mere friendship. Indeed, since he had safeguarded his position by declaring it openly to her, he sailed nearer the wind of a love-affair than ever. He had carefully explained to her that she should look on him as an unromantic and imperfect fellow mortal. He had carefully explained to everybody else that she was more Mary's friend than his. Surely, therefore, he need not fear any misunderstanding. But his tender and gallant manner was just as tender and gallant as before. Indeed, more so. He gave her a lock of his hair, and she had it set in a diamond brooch; and he wrote some lines to celebrate the occasion:

The star that beams on Anna's breast
  Conceals her William's hair,
'Twas lately severed from the rest
  To be promoted there.
The heart that beats beneath the breast
  Is William's well, I know;
Another prize and richer far
  Than India could bestow.
She thus his favoured lock prefers
  To make her William shine;
The ornament indeed is hers,
  But all the honour mine.

Such language might well have kindled hope in the most discreet of women—and Lady Austen was very far from being that. Her character had not changed, any more than Cowper's. She was still susceptible, still uncontrolled, and still peculiarly open to Cowper's kind of charm. The long winter of 1783, when she spent whole days indoors, with nothing to distract her from thinking about Cowper, was enough to revive the still-glowing embers of her passion. By the New Year Cowper was beginning to feel the atmosphere uncomfortably hot. Apart from anything else, her interest in him was so inconvenient from the practical point of view. He could only work in the morning; but in the morning she liked him to come and see her. Now that he was fairly started on a long piece of work, he wanted to give up these visits; but she was dreadfully wounded if he even suggested not coming. The situation was getting very difficult; he would soon be compelled to bring matters to a crisis.

Before he could force himself to the fearful task, however, he was forestalled by some one else. No man in the world can live permanently in the same house with two strong-willed women, both violently in love with him.

Indeed, only a man of supreme tact and dexterity in personal matters could have done it as long as Cowper did. Mary had submitted to Lady Austen's presence as long as she felt it held no danger for her, for she was glad of anything that amused Cowper. But in time she did begin to suspect danger, and then the very same qualities that made her Cowper's slave in most matters made her his master in this. Her love was intense, self-sacrificing and exclusive. She would die for him, but she would never share him. When she thought there was a possibility that she might have to, she took action at once.

What actually happened we do not know; but in the spring of 1784 it was made clear to Cowper that he must choose between Mary and Anna, and also that he must choose Mary. Not, indeed, that he would have hesitated to do so. Constancy, gratitude, the claims of old friendship, these had always been far and away the strongest motive powers in his life. And to Mary he was bound by every tie that gratitude and affection could form. Had she not seen him through the brief strange summer and bitter winter of his days? Was it not by her help that he had lived to see the sun shine once more? She had dedicated her life to him; for him she had risked the sacrifice of her small fortune and her good name. If he were to spend the rest of his life in her service he would hardly recompense her for what she had done for him. Anna, on the other hand—ravishing creature though she might be—had only known him for two years, and he was not bound to her by any bond of gratitude. From the point of view of the highest principle, there was no question what he ought to do. And anyway, with all her charms, Anna could be very tiresome. He made his decision quickly. Sitting down once more at his table, once more he wrote her a letter.

Of all the pages torn by an undiscriminating fate from the records of Cowper's life this letter is the most tantalizing. He was very proud of it himself. He said that it made it unmistakably clear that they must separate; but that it did so in a tone both "tender and resolute." Lady Austen herself, in later years, admitted that it was an admirable letter. Not at the time, however. Yet once more her hasty passion blazed up; she threw the letter into the grate; and within a few days had left for Bristol. In a flurry of dust her coach rattled away out of Olney, and out of this history.

For it was the end. This time there was no reconciliation. Within the next five years she came twice to stay at Clifton; but she never saw, or spoke or wrote to Cowper again. A few years later she married a Monsieur de Tardiff, and went to live in France. Did her love for Cowper linger for long after they parted? Did she ever, amid the hard glitter of Napoleonic Paris and the lawful embraces of Monsieur de Tardiff, cast a wistful eye back to her brief Arcadian yearnings, and the peaceful evenings of Olney? So the historian wonders and conjectures; and is ignorant. Lady Austen's exit from the stage of Cowper's life on that May morning was as abrupt and complete as had been her entrance.

Cowper did not waste time in fruitless regret. For all their similarity of taste, for all her exquisite sympathy with his moods, at the bottom of his heart he had never lost the feeling that she was different from him, a brilliant, exotic bird of paradise who had alighted, by chance, in his quiet country garden. It had been pleasant for a few dazzling moments to watch her preen her feathers and flutter her wings; but he had always known that in the end she would fly away. So that when she actually did so, he remained cheerful. Her departure was a pity, but it was to be expected.

Lady Austen, had she seen him, would certainly have upbraided him for heartlessness. But in reality she had no cause to repine. She had affected his life profoundly. And it is the measure of this effect that he could face life with much equanimity when she was gone. Four years ago such a loss would have depressed him, however certainly he had expected it, for his spirits then were too weak to stand the loss of any support. But his connection with her had increased his power of resistance ten times over. Apart from anything else, the fact of having two delightful women in love with him must have added to his self-confidence. And the complications arising out of their rivalry, tiresome though they might seem at the time, diverted his mind from morbidly brooding on itself. But Lady Austen had exercised a more direct and individual influence on his recovery. Her mere presence revived his interest in life; she was so flamingly excited about everything that happened that any one who was with her could not help catching fire too. The books Cowper read, the subjects he talked about, the poems he wrote, all seemed more absorbing when she was there. It was on his work, above all, that her influence was so important. Cowper had always worked better under direction. He was hard-working and enthusiastic once he had got something to do; but timid and unenterprising about getting it. Lady Austen's sympathetic imagination supplied him with subjects; her confidence in his powers gave him the impetus to take them up. Before she came, the locomotive of his genius had never properly started; by the time she had left it was running at full speed. And Cowper was too occupied in guiding its course to vouchsafe her more than a passing glance of farewell.

# CHAPTER VI

## FAME

THERE was nothing now to distract Cowper from his work. He was able to spend a large part of every day in writing. He had found a refuge even more secluded than the greenhouse: a summer-house at the extreme end of the garden. It was an extraordinary little erection of lath and plaster and red tiles; as Cowper truly said, just like a sedan chair, with barely room in it for himself and a table. On one side, the door opened on to the roses and honeysuckle of the garden; on the other, he could gaze through a window at the gray-lichened trunks of the fruit trees in a neighboring orchard. Cowper loved the summer-house. "It is a place in which I fabricate all my verse in summer-time," he wrote. "The grass under my window is all bespangled with dewdrops, and the birds are singing in the apple trees, among the blossoms. Never poet had more commodious oratory in which to invoke his muse."

However, summer came to an end, and he had to write indoors. But still he worked on through murky morning and candle-lit evening, and still, as he worked, his spirits steadily rose; still, the return of nervous health, begun so haltingly fifteen years before, got faster and more irresistible. By May, 1785, when *The Task* was just at the point of completion, it achieved such a speed and momentum as never before. Hard work had proved the very best thing for him. One of the strongest forces against Cowper's recovery had been his fatalistic submission to evil; and this had been encouraged by his habit of life. For years his whole existence had perforce been one of inert and idle submission to circumstances. But during the last fifteen months he had been working; and working not just to pass the time, but to achieve a desired object. This could not fail to put him in a more active frame of mind, to make action, rather than submission, his first involuntary response to events; and the action that inevitably presented itself to him was struggle against his nervous enemies.

Besides, he could embark on his struggle with more hope of success than of old. No one can bring a long, ambitious work to a successful conclusion without gaining confidence in his own powers. And over and above all this the sheer excitement of creation had keyed up his spirits to a pitch at which they could not but be hopeful.

The black pit of his fears shrank to the size of a pinpoint. He could not understand it, still less could he account for it, but he felt more cheerful every day. Unexplained, unexpected movements of delight began to stir in his consciousness, and for the first time there stole into his heart the thought that all his fears might come to an end, that he might be saved. On he worked; ever tenser grew his emotional excitement. And then, actually, the incredible happened. He woke up one morning in May, 1785, to find that the burden of fear which had been the central fact of his existence for thirteen years had rolled away. He felt he could believe what Mary and Newton had always said. God loved him, as He loved other created beings; and, all being well, He would save him in the end. He felt no dazzling ecstasy as in 1763; the sky was not yet clear of clouds. But that gray pall, now dark, now faint, which since his illness had overcast every inch of its surface, was rent apart at last.  And he saw the sun.

For three dreamlike days, days ever to be remembered, the mood lasted.  And then once more the clouds covered the sky.  Facts fell back into their former proportion; the old fears resumed their power; the old convictions recovered their force.  The truth is, that if the mind runs on one line of thought over a number of years, it makes a sort of rut for itself; and though it may be lifted out of that rut by a violent emotional excitement, after this excitement passes it tends to fall back into it. Cowper's mind had, as we have seen, been dominated by his conviction of damnation ever since 1775.  The organization both of his outward and his inward existence, his interests, his occupation, his general habit of mind. had grown up in the light of this conviction; and except when he was swept away by a great gush of creative energy, it was very difficult to live according to the forms of such an existence without unconsciously accepting the views on which it was based.

Reason, no doubt, should have told him that if he had been able to reject these views for three days, he should be able to reject them always.  Nothing had happened at the end of three days to make them more probable. But reason, as usual, weighed little with him, for his belief was the result, not of a logical process, but of disease.  After all, his nerves had been so injured, it had been so long before they had even begun to mend, that the process of their recovery was necessarily irregular. He might have moments of relief, but at first he must expect a relapse to follow them.

Such a relapse was disappointing.  "The heavens," he said, "only opened to shut again."  But, oddly enough, he did not feel deeply discouraged. Perhaps in his heart of hearts he had never expected happiness to last. Anyway, any other feeling was far outweighed by his pleasure in the realization that he could even for a moment be hopeful. He had taken his damnation for granted so long that any more sanguine mood, however short-lived, was a bright sign. He wondered if happiness might not come again, and come to stay.

Certainly, his general condition of mind continued to improve; even if he did not feel as he had during the three days, he felt better than he had before them. It is true that he still became irritable if any one suggested that he was better; indeed, his spirits still went through dark periods. But they were gray rather than black. And his mind was far too absorbed by his work to succumb to their influence, as he had been used to do. Whatever his conviction about his damnation, he thought about it less, and about other things more. In every way he was more normal.

He was so much more independent than he used to be. *The Task* was finished by October, 1787, and he had to arrange for its publication. Newton had been his intermediary with his publisher for the first book; but for some reason Cowper now thought that he would prefer to do it through Unwin; and he did not even tell Newton he had written a book until it was just coming out. Newton was extremely hurt. He had never been able to bear the thought that Cowper was escaping from his influence, and this seemed to point unmistakably to the fact that he was. He wrote to him in that tone of Christian forbearance which is only employed by those seriously out of temper, and demanded an explanation. Ten years before such a letter would have shaken Cowper to the earth. That he, the despised and rejected of

God and man, should have so provoked one of the paladins of the celestial army would have been intolerable even to think of. However, now he only wrote back a calm note, giving his reasons for his action, but offering no apology. Newton replied, less Christian and more censorious. And now it was Cowper's turn to lose his temper. Really, Newton was too interfering. He had half a mind to tell him frankly what he thought of him. On second thoughts he refrained. But he did not give way; and in the end it was Newton who made the first overtures for peace. Cowper in an attitude of dignified defiance is a comic thought. Still, the fact that he should be able to take up one was a healthy sign.

His old interest in the classics, too, had returned—returned after an absence of twenty years. In the days of his conversion he had looked upon them as pagan vanities; and since then, except for an occasional glance at an old Virgil, he had never had the heart to take them up again. Now he wrote off to Unwin to ask him to send him a Homer. He enjoyed reading it enormously. But he did not merely read it. He was at a loose end after *The Task* was finished; and, as always, when he had nothing to do his spirits began to sink. Suddenly he remembered Lady Austen's suggestion that he should translate Homer. He took up the *Iliad,* and started on one book as an experiment. It was so successful that he went on. For the rest of the winter he was completely absorbed in this work. For the second time Anna had saved him from a bad winter. Poor Anna! Let us hope that Cowper had the grace to miss her a little!

Perhaps he did not, though. Already new friends had sprung up to take her place. One evening when he was sitting in his room, a Mr. Bagot was announced to see him. It turned out to be a Bagot who had been a friend of his at Westminster. There had been several brothers, and one was now a bishop; one of the very few bishops, as it happened, of whom Cowper conscientiously could approve. His caller, William Bagot, had become a clergyman too. Cowper was delighted to see him. He loved to recall with tenderness the happy days of the past, and he liked a friend ten times better if he had known him a long time. Besides, Mr. Bagot was a scholar. There was no one in Olney with whom Cowper could discuss the niceties of Homeric scholarship, and he now poured forth a flood of opinions and questions. Bagot did not live in the neighborhood; he had merely been staying with one of his brothers, who did. But the connection was not allowed to drop when he went away. Whenever he visited his brother he used to come over to see Cowper; and between whiles they corresponded about Homer.

Cowper had also got to know the Throckmortons, the owners of Weston Park. The present owner was not the same as he who had originally given Cowper the key of Weston Wilderness. He had died lately, and had been succeeded by his son, John. To him Cowper wrote, asking if he still might keep the key of the Park. And he received an answer which not only granted his request, but invited him and Mrs. Unwin to come and see a balloon sent up in the park a few days later. In spite of Cowper's doubts as to the morality of ballooning, he accepted the invitation.

The balloon, however, failed to go up; but Cowper and Mary enjoyed themselves as much as if it had. Both Mr. Throckmorton and his wife were very kind. Singling them out from all their other guests, they led them into the house to drink chocolate, asked them to use the garden as well as the Park to walk in, and repeated over and over again their wish to see more of them. Cowper liked the idea. He thought both Mr. and Mrs. Throckmorton charming. It was true that they were Roman Catholics, born of the breed of that Scarlet Woman who preached that works were worth as much as faith. But it is the measure of how much Cowper's Evangelicalism had modified that this fact, which twenty years ago would have made him shudder, now made no difference to him at all.

All the same, he felt shy. After all, the Throckmortons lived in such very grand style. It would be pleasant to go and see them once in a while; but anything like a common social life seemed impossible. So, though he was cordial, he made no decided movement toward cultivating a friendship with them. Mr. Throckmorton was also shy; and for a year or two the acquaintance remained at a standstill. In the summer of 1785, however, for one reason and another, they met more often than usual. And now Cowper was in a much more active condition of mind—willing, nay anxious, to follow up the acquaintance.

These new additions to his list of friends did their part in accelerating his recovery. He was living more like an ordinary man than before, and he became more like an ordinary man. And now an important event happened. *The Task* came out. It was a quiet time in the literary world, and it had a huge and immediate success. At one swoop Cowper soared to the top of the tree of contemporary poetry. Preachers, politicians, literary pundits united to praise him. Olney became a famous place, the summer-house and the greenhouse celebrated objects. Mrs. Throckmorton brought over a party of fashionable ladies down from London to see them. Cowper feared they would be very disappointed when they did. Things seem much more attractive when described in poetry than they are in reality. But he showed them everything, with gratified care, made them each a neat bunch of myrtle, and took the opportunity to repay a small part of Mrs. Throckmorton's hospitality by giving her some cuttings of a special kind of canary lavender for her own garden.

Nor was she the only one of his friends to congratulate him. One morning he was excited to receive a letter in a familiar hand. He tore it open, to be faced with the demonstrative, opinionated, entertaining, helter-skelter style, the heavily underlined writing of Harriet Hesketh. She had read his poems; she thought them perfectly delightful; she had felt she must get into communication with him again. Cowper was overjoyed. If Bagot's visit had unsealed the fountains of tender recollection, how much more did this! Harriet was associated with some of the pleasantest days of his life: the drawing-room of Southampton Row; the walks to Ranelagh; that summer in Hampshire—all the forgotten beloved scenes of the past crowded in a glowing haze of memory before his mind's eye. He hurried from the table and wrote off an enthusiastic letter of thanks. Harriet was now a widow, comfortably living in London, with nothing much to do, and she talked of Cowper and his poems to all her friends. Soon her letter was followed by others, from other members of Cowper's family. And the letters were followed by gifts. A silver snuff-box and several bottles of Madeira from Harriet, and a beautiful desk, inlaid with ivory and silver, from an anonymous donor. Harriet asked him about his financial position. He admitted he was pinched. She wrote round to her relations, and soon his income was increased by a hundred a year.

This was very pleasant; he had disliked feeling that he was indebted to Mary. But his renewed friendship with Lady Hesketh was still pleasanter. It engaged his attention as no personal relationship had done since his first meeting with Lady Austen five years before. He neglected all his other correspondence in order to write to her. She took as intense an interest in him as he did in her. When he sent her a chicken as a present she was in an agony lest such a present might have involved a sacrifice on his part. He reassured her. And with growing enthusiasm and more and more adjectives and exclamations and endearments, the correspondence continued.

At last, Lady Hesketh suggested coming to stay, in June. Cowper's excitement knew no bounds. His letters became lyrical with joy. "I have nothing to do but wish for June; and June, my cousin, was never so wished for since June was made. I shall have a thousand things to hear, and a thousand things to say, and they will all rush into my mind together, till it will be so crowded with things impatient to be said that for some time I shall say nothing. . . . After so long a separation, a separation that of late years seemed likely to last for life, we shall meet each other as alive from the dead." And again, "I shall see you again. I shall hear your voice. We shall take walks together . . . you shall sit with a bed of mignonette at your side and a hedge of honeysuckle, roses and jasmine; and I will make you a bouquet of myrtle every day."

But as the time of her visit drew near, one difficulty after another sprang up to prevent it. First, there was the question of the house. She refused to come to Orchard Side, as she wanted to spare Cowper's income; but it was difficult to find lodgings with enough rooms for the three servants without whom Lady Hesketh could not think of traveling. The linen-draper had rooms to let, with a charming sitting-room, but they contained no bedroom for Lady Hesketh's woman. A lace-buyer near the church had good bedrooms, but no sitting-room for the cook and footman. The Vicarage alone was big enough to hold her retinue comfortably, but it was completely unfurnished. However, after a little discussion a Quaker of the neighborhood offered to supply furniture for five months for the very moderate sum of five guineas, including two large armchairs and a "superb bed" adorned with a bedspread of linen with a picture of Phaethon kneeling before Apollo printed on it.

The little household at Orchard Side gave itself up to busy, delighted, excited preparation for the coming visit. Mary began fattening up her chickens, Cowper got ready a fine passion tree in a tub to fill up the unused fireplace of the Vicarage parlor. The weeks passed, and then, only a fortnight before she should arrive, Lady Hesketh wrote to say that her coach was broken down and she must wait for it to be mended. Cowper nearly burst into tears. For the whole day he sulked and complained, deaf to Mary's consolations. It was the last delay, however. The coach was soon put right; Lady Hesketh wrote a last letter imploring them to make no grand preparations to entertain her; and on the twentieth of June, 1786, amid peals of bells from the church tower, she drove into Olney.

As might have been expected, when he knew she was actually on the road Cowper had been seized with a fit of nerves. He was so excited at the thought of meeting her that he wondered if it might not prove too much for him. A thousand fears began to stir in his troubled brain. Even if it did not make him ill, the meeting might prove a disappointment. He had acquired few lasting convictions in his melancholy fifty-four years of life; but one of them was that anticipated joys generally proved disappointments. When she arrived it seemed for a moment as if it was going to be justified. A cloud descended on him, and during the whole afternoon he sat, glum and stiff, his eyes fixed on the ground, barely opening his mouth. For once, however, his fears were not realized. Within a few hours he had got his spirits back. Lady Hesketh was just the same as she used to be, just as lively and warm-hearted and managing and enthusiastic and respectable, just as full of jokes and advice and demonstrations of affection and orthodox opinions. Even her brilliant complexion had not altered.

Her presence made a lot of difference to Cowper. It was not the same sort of difference as Lady Austen had made. In his relation with Lady Hesketh there was no hint of romance. She was his cousin, and he felt for her that comfortable, friendly regard, founded on a common origin, cemented by common memories, that one feels for a relation. They understood each other by instinct. They had the same prejudices, the same conventions, the same jokes. Lady Hesketh was always throwing Cowper into fits of laughter, especially when she told him "the story about the Gloucestershire Attorneys." He saw a great deal of her. Unlike Lady Austen, again, she did not interfere with his work. During the morning he was left completely alone, but the afternoon they spent together, walking, or driving in her carriage. If they walked, Lady Hesketh used to carry a velvet bag full of pennies with her and scatter them to the village children—a homely charity, after Cowper's own heart. They dined together and spent the rest of the day in each other's company. If it was fine, they sat in the garden, if wet, indoors, "comfortably round one dining-table, without stirring, till after supper," says Lady Hesketh. "Our friend delights in a large table and a large chair. There are two of the latter comforts in my parlour. I am sorry to say that he and I always spread ourselves out in them, leaving poor Mrs. Unwin to find all the comfort she can in a small one, half as high again as ours, and considerably harder than marble. However, she protests it is what she likes; but I hope she is sincere. Her constant employment is knitting stockings. . . . Our cousin has not, for many years, worn any other than those of her manufacture. She sits, knitting, on one side of the table, in her spectacles, and he on the other, reading to her, in his." Lady Hesketh used to listen while he read aloud. If he wrote, she copied out the manuscript of his translation.

But she did not merely enhance his life as it was. Her practical, feminine nature, anxious to do good to her fellows, and sure she knew how to do it, thought Cowper needed society. His nervous attacks were, to her common-sense eye, due to his abnormally solitary life with these queer, religious people. So, day after day, the wheels of her chariot rolled out of Olney, bearing her and Cowper and Mary to pay a visit at Weston or Gayhurst.

Cowper was very well able to make himself agreeable, and he enjoyed these visits. Mary, too, strongly approved of these excursions. Her patient, loving observation had long ago told her that Cowper was the better for variety. Was it not this knowledge that had made her put up with Lady Austen for so long? When it came through Lady Hesketh, she welcomed it. It was a great comfort that she liked Lady Hesketh so much.

From the first she had been pleased by the tone of her letters. "Please tell Lady Hesketh that I truly respect and love her," she had said to Cowper. Lady Hesketh sent her a silver snuff-box. When they met the favorable impression produced on both sides by these amenities had been confirmed. After all, Mary had no reason to be jealous of Lady Hesketh.

William Unwin liked her too. He had paid a formal call on her in order to form his own impressions, as he had before on Lady Austen, and, as before, he had been dubious. Lady Hesketh's complexion was so very brilliant for a woman of her age. Could it be real? Cowper earnestly assured him that it was. He had seen it come and go. William came to stay during Lady Hesketh's visit, and was completely won over to her. Never indeed had four people got on so famously. "Now we want Mr. Unwin," said Lady Hesketh, the day after he left. "Her reason for saying so," explained Cowper to Unwin, "was that we had spent nearly half an hour together without laughing, an interval of gravity that does not often occur when you are present."

One of Cowper's friends, however, was not so pleased at the new developments in his life. Since the disagreement over the publication of *The Task,* Newton had watched Cowper's career with growing suspicion. He had been disagreeably surprised to learn that Cowper was spending his time in translating the writings of the heathen. Cowper, fearful that he might not like it, had made as little of it as he could, merely referring in a casual way to the fact that, by way of passing the winter days, he was making an English version of the old Asiatic tale of Homer. Newton felt not altogether satisfied. He said to a friend that in the days of his conversion Cowper would no more have thought of doing such a thing than of putting the tale of Jack the Giantkiller into Greek. Nor were the Throckmortons, a Roman Catholic family of social habits, the friends he would have expected or approved for a sincere Evangelical. In 1786 he began asking questions about them. Cowper assured him that they were charming people and that he was certain the acquaintance was blessed by Providence. For a second time Newton felt not altogether satisfied. And now, as the summer advanced, what should he hear but that Cowper was off every afternoon on some party of pleasure in the Babylon of Bedfordshire County society. He wrote off hurriedly, demanding an immediate explanation. Cowper was not so concerned to please the susceptibilities of Newton as of old. He told him what he had done, and defied him to see any harm in it. Actually, as he was careful to point out, his conviction of his own damnation had not altered. Newton need not worry. He was still fundamentally miserable, and Mrs. Unwin still spent hours praying for him. This was reassuring news; but Newton's fears were not completely removed. He had heard for a fact that Cowper had been seen in a green coat and had even taken part in an archery competition. In face of such facts no amount of plausible explanation could set his mind at rest.

Cowper might say he was miserable, but, in fact, his recovery progressed daily. It was not only what Lady Hesketh did which raised his spirits. It was the fact that she did it. She returned to Cowper's life, a figure from his dead youth, that blissful period before he had gone mad; and in her company he unconsciously tended to fall back into the habit of mind of those days. Old jokes, old names, were ever on his lips, and old thoughts began to creep back into his mind. Harriet, especially, had been a cheering influence, even in the past.

Was it not she who had brought him back to happiness at Southampton? And in her company his outlook steadily brightened.

It had brightened before: but now for the first time improvement of spirits began to show itself in outward form. He spoke of himself in his letters, except those to Newton, not as one surely damned, but as one who, though not yet admitted to salvation, cherished a constant hope that one day he would be. In response to Lady Hesketh's request, he even began to say grace at table.

Shortly before she came, Mr. Throckmorton had told Cowper that Weston Lodge, a house of his in the village, had fallen vacant, and he wondered if Cowper would like to take it. For himself he had rejected the idea as too revolutionary, but he told Lady Hesketh about it in case she might like to take it herself. In her turn, she rejected the proposal, but she took up the idea of Cowper living there with passion. She thought that his depression arose in great part from his living at Olney in a gloomy little house, associated with, and inseparable in his mind from some of the gloomiest experiences of his life. If he could live somewhere else, and somewhere like Weston, where he would be near pleasant and only mildly religious friends, she thought it probable that his morbidities would vanish away.

It remained to be seen, however, if the house was a suitable one. One afternoon they all drove over to see it. Even in its vacant state it compared very favorably with Orchard Side. It was certainly a most incongruous setting for spiritual disorder, a neat, square, sunny house, in a style at once unpretentious and well-bred, with window-seats and low white-paneled rooms and a shallow, charming staircase. And its situation was in keeping with its appearance.  The front, unlike that of Orchard Side, looked forth over the open fields, and the back on to its own walled garden that rambled up the hill, half useful, half ornamental, with currant bushes and damask roses mixed, till it was bounded by the treetops of Weston Park.  So that it was quiet.  But it was not lonely.  If one walked a few yards down the road on one side, one came to the classic gates of Weston Park, and on the other to the straggling end of the village of Weston, with its thatched cottages and gardens gay with hollyhocks: the perfect English village of idyllic imagination, where red-coated huntsmen jingle gallantly to the meet on a soft autumn morning, or, on a glowing evening in summer the cumbrous hay-carts creak home with sun-bonneted children perched atop.

Lady Hesketh was determined Cowper should have the house.  And though he could not have made up his mind on such a change by himself, he was really very glad when she made it up for him.  There was a little difficulty finding the money.  But Lady Hesketh helped them; and early in October they moved.

When the actual moment for going arrived, Cowper minded as much as he had always minded a change.  He had lived at Olney for twenty-five years, and he was bound to it by the tentacles of a thousand memories. There, in the distant days of his conversion, he had joyfully prayed and praised; there his second madness had fallen on him; he had recovered there; there played with his hares and written his first book; there met and laughed and quarreled with Anna; there known his first belated taste of fame.  Many of these recollections were sad; but he felt as much bound to the place by sad as by happy recollections.  Change is painful to man because it puts him in mind of his mortality.  "This," he tells himself, "was once the present and now it is vanished; and so will vanish everything else." His sorrows seem among the deepest and most permanent things in his life; and thus, their disappearance strikes him as proportionately telling evidence of the frailty of things mortal. As he drove away from the house, Cowper's eyes were dazed with tears.

He happened to go into Orchard Side again two months later. In the cold light of the winter afternoon the plaster hung from the ceiling and the dust blew up and down the floors. It seemed impossible to believe that only a few weeks before here had been the friendly, warm abode of human beings. The sense of mortality swept over him once more, and with a double force. His mind reverted to the theme of its most somber meditations. "Such and so dismal," he said to himself, "is the condition of a soul deserted by God."

However, his melancholy soon left him when he was back at Weston Lodge. It was so cheerful to do one's work in a newly furnished room, looking south; much more cheerful than in a dingy room looking north. Now and again he would pause for a moment and look out of the window, and his eye would light, not on a dull row of houses, but on green foreground and blue distance. Then his view would be blocked perhaps by the head and shoulders of Mr. Throckmorton, turning in at the gate to pay a morning call. Cowper's life was full of mild social events. He dined with the Throckmortons several times a week, and in the afternoon Mrs. Throckmorton would sometimes call, and her husband, or the chaplain used to meet him in his rambles in the Wilderness, now only a few easy steps from the door. There was no doubt the change was a success. "I think every day of those lines of Milton," he writes, "when congratulating

myself on having obtained, before I am quite superan-
nuated, what he seems not to have hoped for sooner:

> '. . . And may at length my weary age,
> Find out a peaceful hermitage.'

For, if it is not a hermitage, it is a much better thing;
and you must always understand, my dear, that when
poets talk of cottages and hermitages, and such-like
things, they mean a house with six sashes in front, two
comfortable parlours, a smart staircase and three bed-
chambers of comfortable dimensions—in short, such a
house as this." Could it be that Harriet was right: that
his melancholy had been but a temporary illness, from
which he had now recovered? And that such moments
of depression as he had lately experienced were fancies
called up by the gloomy memories associated with his old
dwelling? Could it be that the storms and breaking seas
of his life's day were behind him, and that now, as evening drew on, his battered bark was to be permitted to
rock to rest, softly in a sunlit harbor?

# CHAPTER VII

## GATHERING SHADOWS

ALAS! Cowper's hopes were vain. In the middle of November news came to Weston that William Unwin had been taken suddenly ill at Winchester. A week later he was dead. A lifetime of patient resignation to evil, and the desire not to make things worse for Mary, stopped Cowper from giving way to grief. Bull, who rode over on a visit of condolence, was amazed how calm he managed to appear. But in reality he was suffering under a great shock. It was not only that he had been especially fond of William. He had come to the age when man can ill bear the loss of any one he cares for; for he feels it to be the sign and prologue to his own dissolution. Besides, he can not well spare a friend when he is too old to make new ones and too weak to live a life of solitary independence. The circumstances of Unwin's death, too, were particularly painful to contemplate. He left a young wife and two small children. "I cannot think of it," said Cowper, "without a heartache I do not remember to have felt before." A mood of lassitude and dejection took possession of his spirits. He lost all pleasure in society, would sit for hours at his table, unable to bring himself to work at anything.

So passed December; and now January, fatal January, was here. Sure enough, the old symptoms began to reappear. His sleep was troubled by dreams, his wak-

248

ing hours by accusing voices. In his present condition they were fatal to him. His shaken nerves could muster up no power of resistance. Every day he grew rapidly worse. Melancholy swelled to obsession, obsession to delusion. Finally one terrible night once more in dream he heard the voice of God raised in wrath against him. "I will promise you anything," it declared, and again, "I will promise you anything." To Cowper this could only have one meaning. It was the firm and final declaration of Heaven that any hopes of salvation he had cherished were vain, and any good God might seem to promise him was not to be believed. The foundation of such confidence as he still possessed was swept away, and the whole structure of habit and security which he had managed to erect on the broken remnants of his old life fell to the ground. For the third time in his life Cowper was a raving maniac.

Six weeks had sufficed to destroy the work of thirteen years. At first sight it seems astounding. But the truth was his recovery had been more apparent than real. The seat of his malady had never been touched; the infected area had never been examined, much less cleansed; he had never lost any of his delusions. Only his intense vitality had enabled him to achieve a partial return to mental health in spite of these handicaps. Whatever his delusions, he managed to prevent them dominating his thoughts. But he was like a man breathing through one lung. And, like a man breathing through one lung, he could go on only if he was subjected to no extra strain. In Unwin's death for the first time he sustained a severe shock; and, most unluckily, at that very time of year when he was always at his weakest. The consequence was that he immediately succumbed.

The disease followed its old course. Once again he tried to kill himself. Once again he shrank from all other friends, and clung only to Mary. In one respect it was a worse attack than before, for it came after a period of so much hope and he felt proportionately discouraged by it. On the other hand, this time it lasted much less long than before. There was no period of gradual recovery. One day in July he returned to his right mind; and by September he was working and writing letters and dining out, to outward appearance just the same as he had been before the attack.

It was to outward appearance only. His inner man had in that time undergone a change only less decisive than his original conversion. He had completely and finally lost his capacity for hope. Of course he had despaired many times before: in the throes of madness and when he felt madness coming over him. But now he did so when his health and spirits were improving, in cold blood, and with clear eyes, in the light of a sort of perverted reason. Why should he hope? All the methods to which he had trusted to defend him against the enemies of his spirit—religious, medical, social—all in turn had failed him. He could not face being disappointed again. He had better not hope. Indeed, had he not received a specific warning not to do so? Of course God was omnipotent, and might reverse His decision and save him. But why should He? Everything went to show that his old convictions were right. He was the single created soul predestined to fall from grace. What was God's purpose in so predestining him he could not tell. The only reason he could think of was that He did it to demonstrate His omnipotence, even over His own laws.

Such a view would have been impossible to any one with a living devotional life. No one who still felt God to be the principle of peace and love in His own life could also have believed He could act so unjustly. But it was far too long since Cowper had experienced any spiritual happiness for this to move him. He saw no reason, indeed, to doubt the truth of the Calvinistic doctrinal system. Only now, after his third collapse, he could no longer conceal from himself the fact that to his sinful eyes it did appear inexplicably cruel and unjust.

Nor was it his own sad history alone that brought this home to him. All Evangelical England was at this time ringing with the horrors exposed by the first anti-slavery agitation. Cowper brooded on the fate of these thousands of wretched heathen, created, as it seemed, only that they might be tortured in this world and damned in the next. His creed told him that it was a part of the beneficent plan of an infallible God; but he could not even begin to think how this could be so. If such was the will of God, why should it be unlikely that He should damn the soul of a single worthless sinner like himself? No; reason and observation alike forbade him to hope.

The strange thing was that, in spite of this, he was not sunk in a black despondency. But though he had lost all heavenly comfort, on earth he was not yet comfortless. Mary's devotion during his last illness had added another strand, if another strand was needed, to the strong cord that bound Cowper to her; and now that all hope of divine succor had finally left him, her figure loomed out, the single citadel of support on his horizon. His relationship to her was far and away the most important thing in his life. It alone stirred a movement of happiness in his deeper feelings; it alone promised not merely distraction from sorrow, but was in some degree its antidote. Without Mary, Cowper would have felt too weak to face life at all. With her at his side, his lot could not be for long wholly without alleviation.

Nor had he lost his power of enjoyment. The amazing vitality that had enabled him—shattered, fragile creature as he was—to survive a third attack of violent melancholy madness, still rose within him. He found that he still responded to the world around him with interest, with delight. In a spirit of sad philosophy, therefore, he abandoned himself to the pleasures of the moment. This, too, was not a new attitude for him. He had adopted it after his last attack; but, like his despair, it was for the first time the expression of deliberate and cold-blooded decision. Even if he was going to go mad the next January, he thought to himself, what was the advantage in worrying about it in June?

"The present is a dream," he said, "but one wishes to make it as pleasant as one can."

Two things in particular made it pleasant. One was his work. Translation was an ideal employment for some one in his condition, for it gave him regular occupation without making too severe a demand on his creative energies. And he found it very soothing for a large part of every day to exchange the society of his own stagnant thoughts for that of the active and unintrospective warriors of Troy and Greece.

He had also recovered his enjoyment of the amusements and incidents of ordinary life. There were more of them at Weston than at Olney. The world he lived in there was less of a hermitage: it was more the ordinary world of the English country gentry of the day; the world depicted with so precise an irony by Jane Austen

—distinct from fashionable London society on the one hand, and more sharply from that of rich farmers and families in trade on the other—a small world of rigid conventions and easy labors and mild amusements and regular habits, where all the men were clergymen or squires, and led much the same life whichever they were; and the women copied out extracts and played the harp; a world whose serious occupations were looking after the land and sitting on the Bench and getting married, whose pleasures were sport and cards for low stakes, and small talk all the time, and now and again a ball.

Cowper never went so far as to attend a ball. When Mrs. Throckmorton gave one at Weston Park he excused himself as too old. But he joined her archery club, and wore its green coat and buff waistcoat with ingenuous delight. The Throckmortons were inevitably the center of his social life: Mr. Throckmorton, placid and pink-faced, his wife, sharp-featured and with lively eyes, as they live for us in the elegant chalk of Downman to this day. There was nothing about them of the scandal-mongering, fox-hunting ladies and gentlemen that Cowper detested. They were quiet and well-bred and cultivated. Cowper could not contain his admiration when he saw the drawings of the Pantheon Sir John had made in Rome when he was there on the grand tour. And his library, too, was a model of what a gentleman's should be. He asked Cowper to use it as if it were his own.

There was, indeed, no end to the kindness of the Throckmortons. All through the winter they sent Cowper braces of partridges, and when Mrs. Throckmorton learned that he no longer had a greenhouse, she gave him complete control of hers. As for invitations, they never stopped. Hardly two days went by that one could not see Cowper and Mary picking their way through the few yards of muddy lane that separated them from the Park. The Throckmortons were seldom alone. As Cowper sat down at table his eyes would travel along a whole row of faces: county neighbors over for the day or relations staying in the house—brothers and aunts and red-cheeked children in sprig-muslin frocks or skeleton jackets, nephews or nieces, as the case might be. Cowper enjoyed all this company; he felt he was getting a glimpse, as from a secure window, at the great gay world.

Not that he was a mere spectator. Now that he was a famous poet his every word was received with respectful interest; and in the pleasant warmth of this attention he blossomed into a raconteur. Characteristically his stories were generally against himself—the ludicrous figure he cut when he had been pursued by a bull or torn his trousers in a public place. He told them with an exquisite zest of appreciation. Before the story was well begun, his gentle eyes had begun to twinkle, his thin lips to expand in a smile; and by the time the point was reached he was in a fit of laughter so infectious that no one who heard him could fail to laugh too. And he liked playing with the children. One day they persuaded him to get into a wheeled chair, and then whirled it at a breakneck and terrifying speed from one end of the house to the other. Such are the penalties inevitably consequent on kindness to children.

His intercourse with the Throckmortons was not confined to their house. Now and again Mary and he mustered their resources, made careful preparation, and had the family to dinner. And more often, if her husband was away, Mrs. Throckmorton would come in and share their ordinary simple meal. She had become a

WESTON LODGE
From an engraving by J. Storer after J. Greig, published in
*Cowper Illustrated by a Series of Views, etc.*
London, 1810

great friend. Cowper liked Mr. Throckmorton very much; but, as usual, it was the woman in whose company he took most pleasure. In almost every letter he writes at this time we catch a glimpse of her neat vivacious figure—Mrs. Throckmorton coming in for the afternoon to copy out his translation for him; Mrs. Throckmorton coming back from mushrooming, her sweeping skirts inches deep in mud; Mrs. Throckmorton stopping with some visitor at the garden gate. If Cowper saw her from the window he would hurry out and bring the party in. Ten years before, an unexpected stranger interrupting him at work would have upset him for the day. Now he stood and talked, unconcerned, even if he noticed a visitor stealing a glance at the sheets of manuscript, the ink still gleaming wet upon them, that littered the writing-table. The Throckmortons were away two or three months in the year; and then Cowper wrote long letters to "Mrs. Frog" as he called her, giving the news of village and garden and nursery, telling her how he had had some children still staying on at the Park to tea, or how Mr. George Throckmorton's fiancée, Miss Stapleton, had come and played spillikins with him.

This Miss Stapleton became as close a friend as Mrs. Throckmorton. She sang beautifully; and this to Cowper, so sharply sensitive to esthetic pleasure, and as ever so starved of it, shed an ideal light over her figure. Some of the most exquisite moments of his life at this time were due to her. She sang his own songs; and as he sat in the quiet parlor listening to the familiar words as they floated up on the sweet true voice, a thousand emotions of joy and regret and tenderness stirred in his heart. One summer evening after she had finished he walked out into the garden. All around, under the trees the air was tumultuous with the song of the nightingales.

Miss Stapleton's voice was still echoing in his ears; it was as if the nightingales had taken up the tale of her melody. For a time he listened entranced, then, as the twilight gathered, he turned homeward.

He wrote a little poem about the incident. His friendship with the Throckmortons was always inspiring him to occasional poetry. He constituted himself as a sort of poet laureate to the family—composed epitaphs for their dogs, Fop and Neptune, to be carved on urns in the Wilderness, and wrote verses congratulating Mrs. Throckmorton on her beautiful handwriting, or lamenting the death of her bullfinch.

The Throckmortons were his greatest friends; but they did not make up the limit of his acquaintance. We find him at eight o'clock in the morning uncomfortably arrayed in all the stiffness of full dress and wig, to drive over and spend a day with Bagot's brother at Chichely. And he was always walking over to Olney to see his old friends, Wilson, the barber, or Palmer, the draper. Prone on Palmer's counter he would lie, watching the customers and gossiping. He had made a new friend in Olney, too—the vicar, Mr. Bean. He liked him so well that he even agreed to contemplate a religious subject long enough to write a hymn for the Sunday-school. Perhaps he felt that any thoughts suitable for innocent children would be unlikely to remind him of the spiritual condition of a hardened sinner like himself. The hymn shows his views to have been still uncompromisingly Evangelical:

> Hear, Lord, the song of praise and prayer
>   From Heaven, Thy dwelling-place,
> From infants made the public care
>   And taught to seek Thy Face.

Thanks for Thy Word and for this day,
    And grant us, we implore,
Never to waste in sinful play
    Thy holy Sabbaths more.

We must hope Mr. Bean was satisfied. It can hardly be imagined that the children entered with much heart into these bleak aspirations.

People used to come to see Cowper too, Bagot and Bull, and Mr. Greatheed, the minister of Newport Pagnell, bowling over in his high-wheeled phaeton; and one day young Lord Ferrers rode over with his tutor, and had the condescension to partake of a dish of chocolate. Old friends used to come and stay for several days—Newton, the Powleys, Harriet Hesketh. With Newton, Cowper, to outward appearance, was on as intimate terms as ever. But it was only to appearance. Newton was on the lookout for the least sign of backsliding. He was extremely distressed when Cowper told him he was writing some verses in response to a request from a lady on a pen which she had found on the Prince of Wales's writing-table. The very name of so famous and so flourishing a sinner filled Newton's mind with suspicion; could it be that Cowper was going to mention it in terms of compliment? Cowper assured him that, on the contrary, "there was no character in Europe he held in greater abomination." But Newton was not satisfied.

The truth was that Cowper had touched that weak spot in his character that all his self-discipline had not enabled him to remove, his desire to dominate. Because he could no longer dominate Cowper, he no longer trusted him, and any alteration in his mode of life he took as justifying his mistrust. Sometimes, as he compared the wild whirl of carriage drives and village tea-parties in which Cowper now lived with the missionary meetings and spiritual exercises of twenty years before, he even wondered if Cowper was not right about his soul—that he really had fallen from grace. Christian charity bade him hope not. The claims of old affection prevented him breaking with him. But holding such views, it was not to be expected that their intercourse was any longer much pleasure to either. For a long time they had been receding from each other; now a gulf had opened up between them, and although they might clasp hands over it, neither of them was ever to cross it again.

Any failure on the part of Newton was more than compensated for by Harriet Hesketh. Her friendship was an even greater source of pleasure to him than that of the Throckmortons. He looked forward to her letters, and still more to her visits, with passion; and if either of them was delayed fell into a fever of anxiety. It certainly was a different place when she was there. Her bustling, caressing presence seemed to brighten any room she came into. Cowper basked in its glow. The most humdrum occupations, like unpacking a parcel, were delightful when Harriet sat on the stairs, her voluminous skirts spread around her, and watched and commented. Even to be interrupted by her was a pleasure.

"Should you find many blots and my writing illegible you must pardon me in consideration of the cause. Harriet Hesketh and Mrs. Unwin are both talking as if they designed to make themselves amends for the silence they are enjoined to keep when I sit translating Homer. Mrs. Unwin is preparing the breakfast, and not having seen each other since they parted to go to bed, they have consequently a deal to communicate."

She usually came in the winter, and it made a valuable

difference to his spirits at that trying time of year. She called him Giles Gingerbread and Jeremy Jago, as she used to do in Southampton Row forty years before. With the youthful nicknames some of the light-hearted confidence of youth came back to him.

Harriet's kindness was not confined to visiting him. As its only link with London, she undertook a thousand commissions for the household at Weston, ranging from canvassing subscribers for Homer to buying "a pound of green wax for a spindle." While as for her presents, Cowper's thanks could not keep pace with them. She practically furnished the house, as well as helping to pay for it. As Cowper's eye ranged round the pleasant walls of his study, from carpet to bookshelf, from looking-glass to brass-studded armchair, it lighted on nothing that was not a present from Harriet. The very cap he wore for working in the morning—that strange turban-like cap—was from her; and she used to brighten his simple meals by sending him claret and Madeira. He had a capacity for attracting presents. A serious-minded lady, Mrs. King, in the neighboring town of Pertenhall, read his poetry and then scraped an acquaintance with him on the grounds that she had known his brother. Cowper added her gladly to his list of correspondents. In return she sent him cake and apples and a brilliant counterpane of her own making.

She was not alone in wanting to know him. By an ironical caprice of fortune, Cowper, who had spent a considerable part of his life in search of retirement, who had found the humdrum narrowness of middle-class London insufficiently obscure for his desires, at the age of sixty, unintentionally, had become a public figure: one of that minute band who, in each generation, manage to make their personalities felt outside their immediate surroundings, to be liked and discussed and disliked by people who had never seen them. To pass the time, he had written some verses, and it had happened. Hurdis the poet wrote to him for advice; Romney wanted to paint him; the Dowager Lady Spencer, mother of the magnificent Duchess of Devonshire, asked to be allowed to call on him. Fox himself could spare a moment from the heady, hectic whirl of debate and dice-box in which his life rotated to contemplate with his usual unrestrained enthusiasm the unsophisticated pleasures of life at Olney.

His work gained him more than admirers; it gained him disciples. In the winter of 1786 a young man called at Weston, who said his name was Rose, and that he had come to bring Cowper the compliments of some Scottish professors. It was only a pretext. Samuel Rose, like many of his contemporaries, if we are to believe the verbose mural tablets put up to them by their relations, lived a life "dedicated to the pursuit of virtue." His every act was part of a deliberate and considered scheme of self-improvement. He had worked conscientiously at the university, and now, at the age of twenty, he worked conscientiously at the London Bar. Reflection suggested to him that he would be benefited both morally and intellectually by intercourse with a man of genius who was also a man of virtue. Such a character is notoriously rare, but Rose believed he would find it in Cowper. Unluckily, he had not given that time to the cultivation of the social graces that he devoted to that of solid worth; with the result that his manners were stilted and awkward. And at first it seemed probable that he would go away before any of the desired beneficial intercourse had been achieved. However, in time, Cowper's tact and sympathy broke through his reserve. Poor Rose! He turned out to be a very simple-minded young man, naïve and candid, and he confessed to Cowper in a gush of confidence that he had been shy all his life, even of his own father. He was touchingly grateful for kindness; in a short time had lost his heart to Cowper and everything to do with him. "I here feel no restraint, and none is wished to be inspired," he wrote to his sister on a later visit. . . . "We rise at whatever hour we choose; breakfast at half after nine, take about an hour to satisfy the *sentiment,* not the *appetite,* for we talk—good heavens! how we talk! and enjoy ourselves most wonderfully. Then we separate—Mr. Cowper to Homer, Mr. Rose to transcribing what is translated, Lady Hesketh to work and to books alternately. Mrs. Unwin, who in everything but her face is like a kind angel come from heaven to guard the health of our poet, is busy in domestic concerns. At one, our labours finished, the poet and I walk for two hours. I then drink most plentiful draughts of instruction which flow from his lips, instruction so sweet and goodness so exquisite that one *loves* it for its flavour. At three we return and dress, and the succeeding hour brings dinner upon the table and collects again the smiling countenances of the family to partake of the neat and elegant meal. Conversation continues till tea-time, when an entertaining volume engrosses our thoughts till the last meal is announced. Conversation again, and then rest before twelve to enable us to rise again to the same round of innocent virtuous pleasure." It was delightful to find that anything so improving could be so enjoyable. Cowper for his part liked Rose very much, urged him to struggle against his shyness, to see more of the world, and to go to call on Lady Hesketh in London. Rose agreed. But the thought of bearding, so to speak, a lady of title in her own den was so formidable to him that it was months before he could muster up courage to follow Cowper's advice.

Cowper's other disciple was also shy.  He was a second
cousin on his mother's side, called John Johnson, a
Cambridge undergraduate.  And, inspired with an admiration for Cowper's poetry, he took advantage of the
relationship to propose himself to stay in the January
of 1790.  He had an eager ingenuous face that attracted
Cowper at once; but for the first three days he sat with
bright eyes and blushing cheeks unable to stammer out a
word.  At last, however, Cowper melted his reserve as
he had melted Rose's.  And Johnson was revealed as
a warm-hearted, untidy boy, who threw himself into
whatever he was doing, scribbled poetry, played the
fiddle, chattered, giggled, and tripped up over the furniture with the same charming, clumsy impetuosity.  He
was, indeed, as clumsy as a young colt; and, colt-like,
when he walked in the fields would suddenly break into
a frisk, a skip or a gambol.  Not that there was anything
untamed about him.  His frolics were always gentle and
innocent; if a serious subject was mentioned he became
suitably serious at once; and he was going to be a clergyman.  He had a tender conscience, too.  A few days
after he arrived he asked Cowper's opinion on a poem
which he said had been written by one of his friends.
Cowper gave it, and Johnson confessed with shame that
he had written the poem himself.  As can be imagined,
Cowper did not find much difficulty in forgiving such a
deception, but it continued to worry Johnson, who, after
he had gone back to Cambridge, wrote profuse apologies.
He would have done anything not to annoy Cowper.  By
temperament a hero-worshiper, he met him at the very
age when such a temperament is most susceptible; and
he fell under his sway even more completely than Rose
had done; hung on his every word, counted it his highest
privilege to do him a service.  He offered to take back

all of the Homer that was ready to Cambridge in order
to copy it out. This, however, with a wise distrust of
the discretion of undergraduates, Cowper politely but
earnestly refused.

But he had grown very fond of Johnson. He would
have been disposed to love any one connected with his
mother; and Johnson's spontaneity and gaiety and in-
nocence were just the qualities Cowper had always liked
in people. Besides, he felt him a little like himself as
a young man; it was almost as if he were his son. Cowper
was a born father, and there is a pathos in the way all
his paternal feeling, deprived by an untoward fate of
natural outlet, now flowed on to Johnson. How it pleased
him to guide his tastes, to direct his studies—characteristically, he told him to give up metaphysics and mathe-
matics as sterile intellectual frivolities—to take pleasure
in his successes, to sympathize over his failures, to warn,
to exhort, to spoil him. His friendship grew only second
in importance to that Cowper felt for Harriet. He
longed for them to like each other, and introduced them.
It was a great success. They had the same vivacity, the
same respectability, the same love of innocent jokes. To
Johnson, Harriet appeared lit up by all the reflected glory
of Cowper's affection; while she, for all her fifty years,
had not so far forgotten the triumphs of her youthful
beauty as no longer to take pleasure in the attentions of
an agreeable young man. Of course, she soon had a
nickname for him—Sir John Croydon—and she wrote
him a great many letters, mostly about Cowper, it is true,
but not without a touch of personal archness. Johnson's
correspondence was much increased by his new acquaintance. He wrote to her, he wrote to Cowper; to begin
with, he wrote to Mrs. Unwin. Somehow this dropped,
and Cowper, very anxious that Mary should not feel left

out of it with his new friend, administered a gentle re-
proof—"One letter of hers," he assured Johnson, "from
the point of real utility and value, is worth twenty of
mine."

Both Rose and Johnson came often to stay. It was
an excellent thing for Cowper, apart from his affection
for them, for they could do things his women friends
could not—help with Homer, or take him for long walks.
Cowper's increased social activities had not diminished
his pleasure in Nature. Indeed, it grew stronger every
year. Long association strengthened this feeling, as it
strengthened all his others. There was not a field, a
path, a blade of grass that was not heavy with memories
for him by now. Whenever he caught sight of Olney spire
rising in the distance he thought of Newton and the hours
he had spent there with him; if he passed a stile or a tree
where he had walked with a friend, involuntarily he
would recall what the friend had said to him there.
Even things of the intellect had natural associations for
him. He always read outdoors if possible, because he
knew that should he forget a passage the sight of the
field or the glade where he had read it would bring it
all back to him. The very passing of time he marked by
the way it registered itself on the face of Nature. Lady
Hesketh would come "when the leaves grow yellow,"
a book would be published "before the first roses"; in a
moment of melancholy he beautifully warns a correspondent against hoping too much from his friendship, "for
the robin may whistle on my grave before next summer."
It seemed as if, as his body declined back to the earth
of which it was made, his spirit tended insensibly to
merge itself in the spirit of earth, and see through her
eyes.

Every day of his life, then, at the end of his morning's

work, he would go up-stairs, carefully put on his wig and shoes and brown overcoat, and sally forth. But it was pleasanter when he had some one to go with him. He generally had, what with Rose and Johnson and the Powleys and the Throckmortons. His acquaintance with Johnson had revived his connection with Donne relations, and they came to stay too: Johnson's sister, even shyer than himself; and her aunt, a placid Mrs. Balls; and Cowper's cousin Rose, whom he had not seen since he had dandled her on his knee when he was a boy. Now she was a precise-featured Mrs. Bodham, but very amiable, and in 1791 she and her husband came and stayed ten days—"a parson's week." Indeed, there were people staying at Weston during the greater part of the year. Never since he left London had Cowper's days been so full, so normal.

Alas! it did not mean that he enjoyed them more. Had not hope departed?—and with hope other interests had lost their power to satisfy his mind. Not even when he was enjoying them most did he look on them except as drugs that might for a moment delude him into forgetting his sad fate, but were powerless to save him. And, strong though the dose might be, the drug did not always work. He had his black moments, and they were black indeed. Now that January had twice proved fatal to him it was an almost unsupportable period. And he began to be worried by an even stranger cause of fear. The moon, the full moon, terrified him; he felt it an unholy power, able to make men mad. With a pathetic flicker of humor he tried to laugh himself out of this.

"I'll instant write a most severe lampoon,
Of which the subject shall be yonder moon,"

he said to Lady Hesketh once when they drove home beneath the cold brilliance of a winter's night. But he could maintain this mood of bravado only as long as he was in company. When he was alone in his bedroom, where the moonlight stood in livid pools on the floor and filled the walls with dim huge shadows, an unaccountable panic would steal into his heart, and he would remember his damnation and tremble. Newton had feared the moon, too. In these prosaic-seeming Evangelicals of the eighteenth century there lurked a wild atavistic strain. They were not called "enthusiasts" for nothing. And in their prim parlors Artemis the Destroyer could still strike terror.

Cowper felt his fears, too, more persistently dangerous than before. So precarious did his peace of mind become that he even refused for a time to write anything against slavery, lest it might upset him. And when his days were happiest he could pass a night of torment.

Indeed, the contrasts presented by his life at this time were extraordinary. Never before had the incongruous strains of which it was made up appeared in such startling, such fantastic proximity. At one moment he might be sitting in the cozy, unromantic little parlor at Weston with Mary and Harriet and perhaps Mrs. Frog, drinking tea and joking and mildly gossiping, himself the gentle life and soul of the little gathering, to all appearance completely satisfied to discuss how a fox had been killed at Kilwick Wood or if there was to be a new curate at Olney. Then bedtime would come. With smiling, decorous friendliness Cowper would see Mrs. Frog to the door, and retire to his room. He crossed the threshold into a world of visionary horror, where the comfortable veil of the flesh was torn asunder, where the voice of God Himself could be heard speaking in His wrath, and

the flames of hell leapt at the very window, and in the
corners frightful fiends crouched, ready to spring. After
a few hours of broken sleep came daylight, and then once
more Cowper would dress and come down and enter for
another few weeks, as it seemed with complete peace of
mind, the humdrum world of an eighteenth-century
country village.

There is something terrifying about such a mixture.
Nightmare and madness seem doubly awful concealed
in surroundings outwardly so prosaically calm. If such
a mode of life does not bring peace of mind one feels
none can. Nothing he can do, nowhere he can go, is of
any use to protect man against the invisible onslaught of
his soul.

However, the mixture was all Cowper hoped for now.
Despairing of cure, he devoted all his efforts to keeping
as he was, to maintaining the balance between night and
day; and if he could get no better, at any rate to get no
worse. And for three years vitality and care combined
to enable him to do it. It was for three years only. In
1790 the balance began to dip ever so slightly on the
side of night.

It was partly due to the passage of time. Mere recreation ceases to distract as it grows more familiar;
while misery becomes increasingly hard to bear. But besides this, Cowper was now near sixty; and he could not
forget it could not be long before his death—death!
which had been for him the ultimate horror since he was
a boy, and which, according to his present views, was to
introduce him to an eternity of anguish. In face of such
a prospect he was not likely to be comforted by the
society of a few old friends and by country walks. Both
the one and the other served rather to put him in mind
of the flight of time, a flight that every day seemed

swifter. "A yellow shower of leaves is falling continually from all the trees in the country," he writes. "A few moments only seem to have passed since they were buds, and in a few moments more they will have disappeared. . . . It is impossible for a man conversant with such scenes as surround me not to advert daily to the shortness of his existence here, admonished of it as he must be by ten thousand objects. There was a time when I could contemplate my present state and consider myself as a thing of a day with pleasure, and I remembered seasons as they passed in swift rotation as a schoolboy remembers the days that interpose between the next vacation when he shall see his parents and enjoy his home again. But to make so just an estimate of life as this is no longer in my power. I would live and live always, and am become such another wretch as Mæcenas, who wished for long life, he cared not at what expense of sufferings."

Nor was this the only way in which the passage of years affected his spirits. For some time he had been a semi-invalid. He suffered from lumbago, from astigmatism, from indigestion; while the strain of his spiritual troubles had shattered his nervous system. The smallest hitch in the ordered progress of his day put him in a fever of anxiety. If Lady Hesketh failed to write he immediately came to the conclusion that she was dying; and once, when he was awakened by a party of drunken revelers reeling past the house, he could not sleep for the rest of the night, and even on the following evening was still too much affected to dine with the Throckmortons.

He was very careful of himself, and studied his ailments with that conscientious zeal which people of uneventful life are prone to devote to their own health.

He consulted various doctors. They recommended strange remedies. For several minutes every day Cowper excoriated his naked back with a brush for the good of his lumbago; while at one time he tried to cure his indigestion by taking an emetic every week. He did not like to interrupt his work, so when the strenuous day came round he would sit throughout the morning, basin and manuscript side by side before him, alternately versifying and vomiting. Disagreeable though they were, these remedies did him no good; and now, as with advancing age his power of resistance weakened, his health got worse. He felt feeble and ill all the time; which in its turn made him more liable to depression and less able to throw it off.

Finally, in June, 1791, he finished his Homer, and was left with nothing to do. This had always been bad for him, ever since early days in the Temple, and since 1774 one of the strongest chains that bound him to sanity had been regular work. Now it was taken away when he was already disposed to melancholy by failing health and spirits. The effect was immediate, although it was in the summer. By September his nervous condition was definitely beginning to get worse.

He realized it, and his daily occupations and interests began to lose such attraction as they still possessed for him. Powerless to sustain him in a real crisis, as he had painfully learned in 1771, they now proved themselves incapable in the long run of maintaining a hold on his attention, even in a period of comparative mental peace. What he had been told about them in the days of his conversion had turned out to be perfectly true: they were false gods that seduced a man from following the true, only to fail him in the end. And it was also true that the only people he knew who were happy were those with faith.   Faith—the humble, unquestioning faith **of** a village woman who knew no more of the world than she could spell out from her Bible—was better worth having than all that society and learning and fame could offer one; faith that removes mountains could even give peace to the heart of man.   Now, at the end of his life, after trying to keep it out of his thoughts for twenty years, he sought once more the consolations of religion. He had no new experience which might encourage him to think he would get them, not one spark of his old ecstasy lit up his horizon.   But his vitality was still **too** strong to let him resign himself to despair: he still struggled involuntarily toward any gleam of hope.   And religion was the only source of hope in which he now believed.   In spite of his conviction of his personal damnation, his creed did teach that God's pity was infinite; so that there was a chance he might be saved even if his condemnation had been declared.   Anyway, it was the only chance there was.   But unless he could revive his faith, he knew he would not get it.   Turning in disgust and disappointment from the pleasures and preoccupations of the world, he sought desperately, hopelessly, anywhere, anyhow, for any one who might revive the spark within him.

This search was the origin of a curious episode. Samuel Teedon, the schoolmaster of Olney, was one of those eccentrics who seem to be an unavoidable by-product of a great religious movement.   In himself he was the kind of man who is equally incapable of inspiring respect or dislike; a well-meaning, industrious little creature, but trivial, self-important and silly.   He was a dreadful bore, too.   If he met you he never left you alone; and his conversation was what one might expect of a feeble intellect that had always known more than the people that it lived among.   It consisted of tedious anecdote, diversified by floods of apologetic and irrelevant digression, and couched in a pretentious jargon of his own invention, founded on the view that a long Latin word is always better than a short English one. He called wine "inebriating fluid" and flowers "variegated flora." Nor were his circumstances more prepossessing than his personality. He lived with a handful of squalid relatives; either they or he were always ill, and he was miserably poor. This last added to the horror felt by others for his company. When he was not boring them he was begging from them.

So far there was nothing about him to call for special notice. But he had been converted to Evangelicalism. He was the very last man whom it could do good to. Incapable of the devotion which was its virtue he was only too disposed to that hysteria which was its defect. Nor was the narrow, monotonous life of a country village likely to keep this hysteria within check. So far was it from doing so, in fact, that he became possessed with the idea that he was the especial favorite of God, who communicated with him direct by some spiritual channel unknown. It seems likely that he evolved this view with the subconscious intention of obtaining some compensation for his failure to stand out among his fellows in other ways. But Evangelicalism gave him grounds for it by its insistence that the despised of this world were more acceptable in the eyes of Heaven than the great. His celestial connection certainly did not better his mundane situation, if we are to judge from a diary he left. Neither his own health nor that of his relations improved, though he solicited the especial benediction of Heaven every time either took the smallest remedy. "Very ill at home," he writes, "but through mercy cured by drinking very freely of brandy," and again, "My cousin took some red bark, which I hope the Lord will bless." He remained so poor that whenever he had anything extra to eat he entered it in his diary with pathetic and detailed precision; and his religion, so far from making him less, made him more boring to other people, even to his spiritual directors. "Went in the morn to church and heard Mr. B. from 'spare the rod.' In the noon went to Weston. Mr. B. overtook me, but never spoke, though just by on the other side of the hedge, and seemed fearful by his own velocity of my overtaking him."

Teedon's Evangelicalism had brought him into touch with Cowper and Mary years before, and he was always in and out of the house. Cowper soon found him as much a bore as everybody else did. He was easily embarrassed, and he never knew when Teedon was most embarrassing: when he expatiated with unctuous self-appreciation on his spiritual privileges, when he laboriously pointed out the best passages in *The Task* to Cowper as if afraid he might have overlooked them, or when he thanked him in a strain of pretentious compliment for his kindness. "I have wanted all my life," he declared one evening, "to be connected with a man of genius and ability, and," turning to Cowper, "in this worthy gentleman I have found it." "You may suppose that I felt the sweat gush out on my forehead when I heard the speech," said the sensitive Cowper, "and if you do you will not be at all mistaken." He had not the heart to snub any one so well-intentioned and so stupid. But for twenty years he had avoided Teedon as much as possible.

Now, however, in his desperate effort to retrieve his faith, his attitude toward him underwent a change. Here was a man who had the very faith he longed for, the pearl of great price for which he was ready to sell all that he had. Even if he was tiresome by worldly standards, that ought not to matter. Were not worldly standards those that had proved themselves most hollow and most inadequate? God was no respecter of persons; He spoke through those whom the world esteemed foolish and despicable. Cowper should humble himself before any soul whom God had thought worthy to illustrate with the faith refused to him. And if Teedon claimed that he had special communication with Heaven, who was Cowper to deny it? Should he not rather take advantage of it, and through his mediation learn what the Divine Will had in store for himself, induce even a ray of the Divine Grace to fall on him? As the princesses of ancient Russia prostrated themselves before idiots as the blest of God, so Cowper humbly sought the spiritual direction of Teedon. He asked him for his prayers, took no decision of any moment without asking Teedon to find out what was Heaven's will in the matter. He did his best to make some return for his kindness by giving him countless meals and an allowance of thirty pounds a year. For his part, Teedon took Cowper's interest as a great honor, prayed for him by the hour, and was never too tired to toil over to Weston to retail any spiritual message he might have received. It was not long before he had to deliver one of importance.

In October, 1791, Johnson, Cowper's publisher, wrote to him saying he was contemplating a new and sumptuous edition of Milton to be illustrated by famous artists; and he asked Cowper to edit it. He was not attracted by the proposal, which sounded laborious without being interesting, but still the offer might be providential. He himself had no means by which to penetrate the wishes of Providence, so he asked Teedon if he would make intercession to discover it. Teedon announced that God had directly called him to the work, which He would make a blessed one for him. Cowper still felt an aversion to it; but of course there was now no possibility of hesitation. With the solemnity and deliberation befitting the execution of a divinely appointed mission, he set to work. But before he had got further than the preliminary preparations a sensational event took place, which rent the whole texture of his life from top to bottom.

One afternoon toward the end of December, as he was sitting working with Mary in the parlor, he suddenly heard her cry, "Oh, Mr. Cowper, don't let me fall!" He jumped up just in time to save her from falling to the floor unconscious. A doctor was summoned, who attempted to reassure Cowper's white face and agitated question by telling him she had only had a nervous seizure of an insignificant kind. But when she recovered consciousness she saw everything upside down, and walked and spoke with the greatest difficulty. And Cowper knew perfectly well she had had a stroke.

In face of such a catastrophe, all other plans and considerations vanished from Cowper's mind. It had always been agony to him to watch any one suffer, but how much more when the sufferer was Mary—Mary, his oldest, nearest, dearest friend, with whom he had lived for over twenty-six years, to whom he owed health, sanity, even life itself. Most likely, he felt, with a fearful qualm of conscience, she had made herself ill by working for him. He felt he could never rest, or read, or think on any other subject till she was well again. And he had a more personal reason for wishing her recovery; as he looked at her prostrate form, the thought came unbidden to his head, "Perhaps she is going to die"; perhaps he would have to finish the last steps of his bleak journey alone. The prospect was too terrible to contemplate, even for a moment. He brushed it aside, but he could not wholly forget it; and it gave an added desperation to his struggle. At whatever cost, with whatever difficulty, she must be saved.

He gave up his whole life to the task. The order of his existence was turned upside down. The calls of his own health, his own spirits, were disregarded; Milton itself, the task set him by God, was put aside—not finally, of course, but until a more convenient moment. Such work as he did, such letters as he wrote, were done at odd times when he was not wanted by Mary. He nursed her, he read to her, he helped her in her first feeble attempts to walk. As the weeks passed, it seemed he was to be repaid for his efforts. A first stroke is often not a severe one. By March, Mary, though still weak, was able to walk and work and talk almost as well as before. It seemed likely she would get perfectly well. Cowper's fears began to wane, and his spirits rose. They were further heightened by the entry of a new friend into his life.

In March, 1792, Cowper received a letter from a Mr. William Hayley, who said he was writing the life of Milton, and he thought it would be of advantage to both of them to work together. The letter was written in a rhapsodical style, flowery with compliment, and it concluded with a sonnet of admiration. Cowper, however, felt far too glad of any help with Milton to be critical. A correspondence was opened; and in May Hayley came to Weston for a visit. Before the stranger's arrival, Cowper was, as usual, overcome by nerves. Perhaps he might not like Hayley; supposing he should be put off by his appearance—he judged a great deal by appearance—he would never be able to conceal his feelings for several weeks. However, Hayley's tall military figure, his eyes bright beneath their bushy brows, did not displease him;

and after a few days of his company he had admitted him into the small circle of his great friends.

He was very different from his other friends. Like Newton, indeed, he wrote his memoirs; but there the likeness ends. Hayley's book was a magnificent affair: two stately quarto volumes with a steel-engraved frontispiece, an elaborate dedication to Lord Holland and two thousand or so leisurely spaced, elegantly printed pages. But the magnificence of its dress, and still more the unfaltering grandiloquence of the style in which it was written, only served to throw out in more startling relief the pathetic absurdity of the story it told. This incongruity was the central feature of Hayley's existence. With the loftiest aspirations, and talents above the ordinary, it was his sad fate to be generally unsuccessful and always ridiculous. It was not the fault of his character, which was an excellent one: warm-hearted, disinterested and industrious. But he had a romantic temperament, no sense of humor and, like Marianne Dashwood, he had learned his view of life from the literature of sensibility.

Of all dead-and-gone habits of mind, that expressed in the eighteenth-century novel of sensibility is the hardest to enter into. How could people, even in imagination, take a view of life so flagrantly false to every fact of their experience and observation? It is even more incredible that any one should have looked at his own life in such a way. But Hayley did. In the clearsighted, plain-spoken world of Smollett and Doctor Johnson he managed to be, and to remain, the complete "Man of Feeling," who shed the tear of sensibility at a beautiful prospect, who could not without emotion so violent that it made him ill revisit the scene of a former happiness, who would rather die than offend in the small-

est degree the delicacy of an elegant female, who would
starve sooner than stain his honor by receiving a gift,
whose heart was ready to thrill at any moment with filial
affection, love of solitude, and the "passion for freedom."

His mother—he had lost his father young—had intended him to be a lawyer. But to such a temperament
the idea of a regular profession seemed intolerably philis-
tine; and when he was twenty-one he announced that he
intended to devote his life to benefiting mankind by any
means in his power, but chiefly by composing literary
works of an improving character. It was very high-
minded of him, because he had no money, and philanthropy has never been remunerative. But Hayley was
optimistic, and had, as he characteristically put it, a contempt for money "romantic and imprudent." Nor was
he without grounds for confidence in his literary powers.
Had he not written an ode on the birth of the Prince of
Wales which had won the commendation of Doctor
Roberts, of Eton College? He started off, therefore,
with high hopes. Unfortunately Fate had endowed him
with bad luck as sensational as his aspirations. He
worked like a trooper, he laughed at failure, he was always ready with a new idea, he was delighted to modify
what he had done in the light of any criticism. But
somehow he never could make a success.

His first efforts were a tragedy, which he sent to
Garrick, and an epistle of compliment, which he sent to
the King of Poland. Garrick refused the tragedy, and
the epistle was lost before it ever got to Poland at all.
By 1771 Hayley ran short of money. Undiscouraged,
he retired to Eartham, in Sussex, where, amid the shades
of rural retirement, notoriously inspiring to poets, he
began to compose an epic about Stephen Langton, a sub-

ject which, he felt, would both give scope to his own passion for freedom and stimulate it in others. However, he
had hardly written a canto before he contracted an illness in his eyes and was forced to stop. A period of
idleness in the company of his wife and mother seems to
have persuaded him that there were other benefits of
which mankind stood in even more pressing need than of
the passion for freedom; for when he began work again
in 1781 it was at a poem entitled *The Triumphs of
Temper,* expressly designed to exhibit "the effects of
spleen in the female character" and to induce "his fair
readers to cultivate a constant flow of good humour."
For once he made a success. The poem went into several
editions; it gained him a place among the leading poets
of the day, and he had the gratification to learn from the
"good and sensible mother of a large family" that it had
entirely reformed the temper of her eldest daughter.

Alas! this success was not to last. His romantic and
imprudent contempt for money soon made away with
any that he had earned; and when he tried to make some
more, bad luck once again began to dog his footsteps.
He wrote a tragedy about a mad Javanese Sultan, but
on the very eve of its production George III went mad,
and the delicacy of a loyal subject compelled Hayley to
withdraw it. Then he wrote a novel designed to promote
the interests of religion, and dealing with the striking
subject of "an elegant young widow struggling between
her maternal affections and an attachment of the heart
to an engaging young infidel." It was dedicated to the
Archbishop of Canterbury; but there is no record that he
read it nor any one else either. An opera adapted from
the German fared no better, though Hayley had em-
bellished it by a transformation scene in which "magical
personages" congratulated the British defenders of the

Rock of Gibraltar. Finally, despairing of success on the English stage, he wrote a play in French, and somehow managed to get it produced in Paris. Paris must have been a very different place from what it is now. The play failed because it contained among its *dramatis personæ* a courtezan, and the public representation of such a character proved insupportable to the modesty of a French audience. Even Hayley's hopes were checked by this rebuff, and he stopped writing for the stage.

His private life had not proved more successful than his public. With his mother—"a lady," he tells us, "noted chiefly for her majesty"—he got on well enough; but before he was twenty he had fallen in love, and, true to the tradition of the sentimental novel, corresponded wih the object of his affection, a Miss Fanny Page, clandestinely, with the help of a friend of hers—Miss Eliza Ball. But other friends made trouble, and Miss Page broke the connection off. Hayley was, however, as ready to cut his losses in love as in art, and without more ado transferred his attentions to Miss Ball. Her mother was mad, and Mrs. Hayley sought to discourage her son from his new love-affair, saying, no doubt with her usual majesty, that such afflictions were hereditary, and Miss Ball might go mad too. "In that case," replied Hayley magnificently, "I should bless my God for having given me courage sufficient to make myself the lawful guardian of the most amiable and pitiable woman on earth." And he married her.

He lived to regret it. For the first few years, indeed, Eliza was a charming wife, as full of sensibility as himself, and so liberal in her views that she agreed to adopt and bring up as her own a child of his by a woman of Eartham village. But by 1781 she began to change; by 1783 she was in a confirmed state of nervous collapse.

Poor Hayley was very far from thanking God he was her guardian. Indeed she was intolerable—sometimes silent and moodily suspicious, sometimes in violent fits of hysteria. Her sensibility became so acute that she would not come near him when he was ill, for fear of ruining her eyesight by the amount of tears the sight of his sufferings would cause her to shed. And when she did feel equal to seeing him, she did not make herself pleasant. "You were the most agreeable man in the world," she remarked one day, with an innocent sincerity which must have made the remark doubly mortifying, "but you seem to have lost all your talents."

He became unable to stand life with her for long at a time, and sent her, "with affectionate solicitude," on visits to Bath. But this was very expensive; besides, she came back between whiles. And even a day of her grew more than he could bear. There was no doubt they must live apart. Mrs. Hayley, now always alluded to as "my pitiable Eliza," was quite willing to go; she found Hayley as trying as he found her. But it was not so easy to arrange. Where was she to go to? She liked Bath; but Bath, as he knew to his cost, encouraged her to be extravagant. At last he made arrangements with an old friend of his, Doctor Berridge, to take her in as a paying guest. Just when he thought he had got her settled there Doctor Berridge died, and she came back. It was not till 1789 that he had her safely established with "a respectable circle of friends" at Derby.

Even after this, there came an awful moment when she heard he was ill and she wrote to say that she felt it her duty to come back and nurse him. He rushed to his writing-table and with a desperate eloquence besought her not to come. His only wish was for her happiness; and it might make her ill; let them rather communicate "by the frequent intercourse of affectionate letters." Their language to each other had, indeed, grown more high-flown as their feelings cooled; and by the time they were living apart it was of a rhapsodical silliness that must be seen to be believed. They vied with each other in declarations of devotion in order to keep each other away. Eliza achieved the masterpiece in this kind when she implored Hayley to write less often, as the excitement of reading his letters was so great that it prevented her from sleeping.

Repeated setbacks had not quenched the fire of Hayley's spirit. There was something heroic in his incapacity to profit by experience. Plays might be damned, books fail to sell; after each successive blow he reappeared with eyes still bright and bearing still erect, undismayed and enthusiastic, ready with a new scheme for the benefit of mankind, confident that this time it would succeed. The world he looked on was still the world of sentimental literature; he himself was still the "Man of Feeling."

Even the ironical comedy of his own career he managed to re-stage in the theater of his memory as a drama of sentiment: its hero "The Hermit of Eartham," a man of genius who retires undefeated by the blows of an unworthy world to a life of contemplation; its heroine, his wife, brilliant and elegant, but too exquisitely sensitive to stand the rough friction of common life. In this guise his past could be contemplated without dissatisfaction, even with complacency.

In plain fact his life at this time did have its compensations, apart from the fact that he had got rid of Eliza. There were other ways of benefiting mankind than writing tragedies. All his life Hayley had promoted schemes—a new and nobler edition of Shakespeare, or the erection of a statue to Howard, the philanthropist—

and he continued to do so now.  Nor had he stopped writing poetry.  It was mostly occasional verse, but still designed to further some good object.  Epitaphs, for instance—he was always ready to write an epitaph, whether he knew the man it was about or whether he did not, in order to soothe the sufferings of the bereaved by publishing the virtues of the deceased.  And almost every day saw the composition of a lyric designed to reconcile an unhappily married couple of his acquaintance, or to promote charity to decayed musicians, or to encourage Mr. Wright, the painter, to disregard malicious criticism.  One day Hayley read some of his poetry aloud to Gibbon.  At the end Gibbon remarked with great animation, "When you began to read I was suffering from gout, but you have charmed away my sense of pain."  Such is the only recorded occasion when Hayley's poetry did succeed in benefiting mankind: it was unlucky that it was also the only recorded occasion when it was not intended to.

The mention of Gibbon brings one to Hayley's main source of happiness at this time.  His longing to be an ornament to the race inspired in him a hero-worship of any one who was; and he had always sought to get to know such men, with such effect that he became the intimate friend of Romney, Flaxman, Blake, Gibbon and Howard.  The strange thing is that they should have liked him.  But his admiration, though, like everything else about him, rather silly, was, also like everything else about him, sincere.  And no one dislikes sincere admiration.  Besides, all his virtues, his enthusiasm and generosity and disinterestedness, went to make him a good friend; he was always ready to listen, to appreciate, even to give practical help.  As a result Eartham became a minor center of the world of art and letters.  He had spent a large part of his meager earnings in building himself a library, adorned with portraits of geniuses whom he knew, and presided over, appropriately enough, by a large picture of Sensibility watering the sensitive plant, by Romney. There of an evening would the great men sit and take their ease; and sometimes one of the painters made a sketch, and sometimes one of the writers read his latest work, and all the time Hayley hovered round and rhapsodized and admired.

It was this enthusiasm for genius that made him scrape acquaintance with Cowper. And he had no difficulty in making Cowper like him. After a year's anxiety, sharpened by self-distrust, shadowed by a conviction of impending damnation, it was wonderfully soothing to spend the day with some one who thought all one's work of the first value and who was convinced it was only a prelude to greater things. Hayley had too, in supreme degree, that quality of vitality which Cowper had always looked for in his friends, which had drawn him to people as different from one another as Newton and Lady Austen and Mary. Since Mary's illness he had been without such support, and now he reposed on Hayley as a tired swimmer on a buoyant wave. In addition to this, Hayley was the first professional literary man Cowper had met since he became a poet, the first friend he could talk to about his work on equal terms. And talk they did, and read each other's works and criticized and admired. It was no wonder that within a few weeks Cowper's liking had warmed to strong affection.

Hayley, for his part, had even less difficulty in feeling enthusiastic about Cowper than about other things. Never, among all the geniuses of his acquaintance, had he met one so courteous, so modest, so gentle. Cowper's love for Mary and his intense desire that the visitor should appreciate her, especially moved him. "It seems hardly possible to survey human nature in a more touching and satisfactory point of view," he remarked.

The growing friendship was soon strengthened by a tenser bond.  One morning, as Hayley and Cowper were coming back from a walk, they were met by a messenger who told them Mary had been taken by another attack. Cowper rushed home to find her speechless, helpless and almost blind.  It was a second stroke—far worse than the first.  In a moment of terrible illumination he realized that his darkest fear was now a practical possibility, that his hopes had been delusive, and she might be going to die.  At once all his most somber convictions crowded back into his mind, and he saw this new disaster as the last inevitable act in the course of his tragedy.  How could he have expected anything different?  Was he not the cursed of God?  Surely therefore the most disastrous event was always the most likely.  Beside himself with anguish, his face working, his eyes wild with sorrow, he tottered from the room.  Hayley met him outside. "There is a wall of separation," cried Cowper, "between me and my God."  "So there is," replied Hayley instantly, "but I can inform you that I am the most remarkable mortal on earth at pulling down old walls, and by the living God I will not leave a stone standing of the wall you speak of."  He spoke without thought, from a mere impulse to say something that would comfort Cowper.  His words had an immediate and formidable effect.  Eagerly Cowper scanned his face for a moment; then a serene calm overspread his features, and taking Hayley by the hand, he said, "I believe you."  Hayley's words of comfort, striking his ear as they did at such a crucial moment, had inspired him with the conviction that he was a heavenly messenger sent to help him.  And from that moment he submitted himself to Hayley's direction with the unquestioning trust due to an angel of God.

Hayley assumed his new responsibilities with his usual sanguine energy, recommended electric treatment for Mary, showed how to administer it, wrote for further advice from a doctor in London. By the end of May she was a little better, and he went away. Cowper felt his strength was leaving him. "Farewell," he said, pressing Hayley's hand with passionate tenderness, "farewell, I ne'er shall look upon thy like again." Actually he was to see him again very soon. Hayley had urged him to bring Mary to Eartham if she was strong enough for the journey, as he was sure the air there would do her good. By August she was well enough, and they started.

Cowper could have shown no greater proof of the ascendency Hayley had acquired over him. He had never gone back on that decision to retire from the world made at St. Albans thirty years before. Indeed, except for his visit to Cambridge when John was dying, he had only traveled twice, and neither time back into the world. He had moved from one sequestered sanctuary at Huntingdon to another at Olney, and once again to Weston, and each time he had intended the move to be a final one. Now, at the age of sixty-two, when his health was failing, he took a three days' journey to stay for a short time with a man he had only seen for the first time three months before, whose house was a stirring intellectual center of the day.

Nor was re-entering the world a more drastic change in his life than leaving Weston. Long associations and love of Nature had combined to weave his surroundings into the texture of his life in such a way that without them he felt as awkward as without his skin. To take him from them was like rooting up a tree from its soil. If at any time he was asked to stay away, he had replied, with the brief finality of one declaring a law of Nature, that it was impossible. Now, however, the object of his whole life was to cure Mary, and Hayley, the messenger of God, had said that such a change might aid her cure. There was no question that he must go. Indeed, her relapse had so deranged the whole order of his existence that nothing seemed impossible any more. Actually, as the time drew near he experienced qualms. In order to confirm him in his decision he asked Teedon to inquire the divine will in the matter. Teedon duly reported that he had received a message: "Go, and I will be with him. . . . And he went to Bethel to inquire of the Lord, who said, I will go down with thee into Egypt and will bring thee up again." This, if uncomplimentary to Hayley, was favorable to visiting him. Trembling with agitation, therefore, Cowper steeled himself to go.

The journey went more easily than he could have expected. They had Johnny and three servants to look after them, and Mary felt little fatigue. Cowper was only once disturbed: when they crossed the Surrey hills at night. To his untraveled eye they seemed as tremendous as the Himalayas, and as they loomed up bare in the baleful moonlight, a thrill of elemental terror ran through him.

All was forgotten, however, in the excitement of arriving at Eartham. It must have been an extraordinary moment for him. Twenty years before he had fled from the world, wretched, broken, obscure; now, in his old age, he returned famous, to receive the homage of his distinguished contemporaries. Hayley had only asked a few people to meet him, but they were all distinguished—Romney, Mrs. Charlotte Smith, the novelist, and later Hurdis, the poet. They were struck not unfavorably by Cowper's modesty, his awkward and punctilious courtesy, as of some Rip Van Winkle survived from a former age. Shy and awkward, Cowper stood blinking his eyes in the unaccustomed sunlight of their attention. He soon became happy enough in their company as long as he was not expected to talk too much. All the same, he was really happiest, because most at his ease, in the mornings when he and Hayley worked together at Milton. He had translated some of Milton's Latin poems, and Hayley suggested corrections.

The loyal heart of Johnson was outraged by such impertinence. It is to be feared neither he nor Lady Hesketh altogether approved of Hayley. Who was this stranger who had assumed so sudden and so complete a sway over their "bard"? A professional literary man, a friend of Gibbon—Lady Hesketh had heard rumors that he was an infidel. These proved untrue; but Johnson was disquieted to notice that he never went to church, and he wondered whether such a friend would promote Cowper's happiness. Anyway, it was intolerable that he should presume to correct his poems. Cowper did not mind himself. No amount of admiration could make him vain; he even welcomed the criticism of Hayley's son Tom, a boy of twelve. He was a pompous child, already the true son of his father in the way he expressed himself. "Be assured that among all my young and sprightly associates you are not forgotten," he wrote to his father from school. But Cowper was disposed to feel more at ease with a child than with the other people at Eartham, and Thomas Hayley finally won his heart by the kind way in which he wheeled Mrs. Unwin out in a chair. When Cowper parted from him they both shed tears.

But he had not come to Eartham just to make friends, and they occupied a small part of his time. Except for the early part of the morning, he was with Mary; and at bottom his mind was concentrated on the state of her health. At first the change seemed to do her good; her voice grew stronger, her step firmer. But a delicate woman of seventy is not likely to recover from a second stroke. And as the days went by Cowper gradually became convinced the change was doing her no good and that the journey had failed in its object.

With the realization, the gust of preternatural energy that for the last three months had supported him, subsided. It had been called out, it could only have been called out, to help Mary. When it failed to help Mary it collapsed, and his old inhibitions and prejudices reappeared, all the stronger for their brief eclipse. Talking to strangers seemed an intolerable strain, the unfamiliar landscape intolerably alien; he became consumed with a desire to go home. Early in September they went.

# CHAPTER VIII

## NIGHT

HIS return to Weston is momentous in Cowper's life; for with it the curtain rises on the last act in its weary tragedy. Alas! it was to end on no classic note, "in calm of mind all passion spent," soothing and reconciling even while it saddens. No, in the Elizabethan manner, amid shriek and blood-boltered specter and wild infernal darkness, was the scene to close. For the last time the forces of madness were to rise and overwhelm him.

The events of the last year had rendered them irresistible. Ever since 1787 he had, as we have seen, only kept them at bay with the utmost difficulty, and already, a year ago, they had begun to gain ground on him. Anything like a severe blow, and the battle would be irretrievably lost. Actually the blow he did receive would have been fatal to him had he never begun to weaken at all. Mary's collapse was far and away the greatest disaster Cowper could have sustained at any time in the last thirty years. For it meant the collapse of the foundation on which during that thirty years the whole order of his life had been erected. Always dependent on some one, on no one had he ever depended as on her. The illness of 1773 had irremediably bent the stem of his existence; but by clinging to her he had managed to train it to an upright position again. Afterward, it is true, he had erected an elaborate structure of occupation and habit on which to maintain his mental health. But he could never have got well enough to begin to put it together without her. Finally under the strain of his third madness it had fallen to bits, and he was left clinging to her once more. For she remained. Alone in all his experience, she stayed with him in light and darkness; and though all his faith in God had vanished, he kept a sort of blind, instinctive faith in her. Now at a time when his health was beginning to fail, she was suddenly stricken with a mortal illness, and soon she needed support as much as he did. His only defense was gone; though he might still struggle, the battle was decided.

Of course if he had left her and made his home with other people in another place who knows that he might not have managed to stave off the evil day indefinitely? But even had such a course of action entered his head, his whole nature would have risen up to repudiate it. How often had she stood by him during his illnesses; and how patiently, how self-sacrificingly had she done it! Was it not her care for him, indeed, that had brought her to her present case? Now it was his turn to help her. And if to do so were to risk his life, it would only be a small recompense for what he owed her.

But it needed no obligation of gratitude or loyalty to keep him at her side. Every other consideration was swallowed up in the great tide of compassion which welled up in him at the sight of her affliction. Mary, his Mary was suffering; his only thought was to relieve her. And recklessly, unhesitatingly he poured out any drop of vitality that remained to him in order to do it. By the inscrutable decrees that govern mortal destiny, his devotion was his destruction. There can be no doubt that it was the strain of nursing her that finally confirmed his doom.

It was no longer possible even for a moment to pre-

serve that precarious balance which by desperate efforts
Cowper had managed for the last three years to maintain
between sense and madness. His incongruous double
life was at an end. From now on, inexorably, unfalter-
ingly, night began to gain on day, the world of sense to
be obscured by the world of vision. Already in the early
summer, the time of year when he was usually safe from
worry, his sleep had been disturbed by nightmares, fearful phantoms of death, carcases and churchyards; and,
more dangerous, he had once more begun to hear spirit
voices. While at Eartham he had experienced those fits
of depression when he woke in the morning that had
tormented him in 1763.

These, however, were only intermittent mutterings of
the oncoming storm. When he got back to Weston it
broke in good earnest. The particular circumstances of
his life there, were, indeed, the very worst for him in
every possible way. For one thing, he was so much
alone. Now that Mary could not be a companion to
him he was in double need of visitors. And no one came
to stay in the house for months; so that there were hours
in the day when he had nothing to take his mind off its
own thoughts. Then again it was autumn, and to any
one with Cowper's sensibility to environment every
shortening day, every sallowing leaf, spoke ominously of
mortality. He was conscious, too, that after autumn
would come winter, fatal period; and his spirits grew
heavy with melancholy anticipation.

Nor could he, as in earlier years, stave off his depression by working. From the middle of the morning he
was always with Mary; and as she was not able to use
her hands, he did not like to use his in front of her, for
fear of making her more painfully conscious of her in-
firmity. So that he had only time to write if he began by

candle-light, at six or seven in the morning. Besides, the work he had on hand happened, most unluckily, to be a commentary on the first books of *Paradise Lost.* And as these were all about hell and its fires, they tended rather to deepen than to dissipate his depression.

But, anyway, even if he had enjoyed his work, and even if he had been able to give more time to it, it would have made no difference. For he was too tired to do it. Time and again he would get out pen and paper and sit down at his table, and then an hour later get up without having written a word. The exertion of the earlier part of the year, the strain of nursing, the violent alteration in his ordinary routine and the constant anxiety, had been too much for his already failing constitution. And now he simply had not got the physical strength to make the effort of concentration needed for his work.

On his general morale his exertions had not proved less disastrous. He had tried so hard and with so little effect that now he felt helpless and without hope. The visit to Eartham had given him especial cause for dejection. He had hoped so much from it, and not only for Mary. Buoyed up by the excitement of the struggle, half-formed hopes regarding his own disorders had begun to stir within him. If Heaven were intervening through the means of Hayley to save Mary, might it not also save him? Besides, supposing there was something in what people had always said to him, and that his own sufferings were, in part at least, the result of physical causes. Then the change might alleviate them. It was a faint hope, and he hardly admitted its existence even to himself: but he could not banish it from his mind. It proved as vain as his hopes for Mary. And the fact that he had hoped now added all the pangs of disappointment to his usual depression. Here was only another proof, so he told himself, that his troubles were incurable and he must carry them to the end.

Solitude, idleness, exhaustion, disappointment and the time of year—all the circumstances of his situation had combined against him. It was no wonder that he took a rapid turn for the worse. A persistent depression took possession of his spirits, a depression which gradually identified itself with two subjects. One was, of course, his old fear of Mary's death. Now that he had acknowledged to himself that she would not get well, he felt she might die at any moment. And he was proportionately agitated. His other fear came from his inability to finish Milton. The task had been commanded by God; and now God had rendered him incapable of carrying it out. What could this portend? Was God once more forcing him to commit a sin in order to damn him for it? Convinced as he was of his damnation, this new proof of it sent a thrill of horror through him. Again and again in desperation he nerved himself to make another attempt to get it done. And with each successive failure suspense gnawed more cruelly at his heart. They were terrible days.

Hour after hour he would sit silent, with Mary silent on the other side of the fireplace, brooding on his fears till they obscured his whole horizon. And the nights were worse than the days. No longer did nights of terror come spasmodically and far between, infrequent black patches on the pleasant-colored surface of his existence. There was hardly an evening now when his candle did not light him up that quiet staircase into hell, hardly a night when he did not close his eyes to be haunted by horrible visions. In fitful, incoherent parable, they mocked the fears that tormented his waking hours. That destroying fire which is the symbol of damnation flared

luridly through his dreams. "Friday, Nov. 16th. . . .
Dreamt that in a state of the most insupportable misery,
I looked through the window of a strange room being all
alone, and saw preparations being made for my execution. That it was about four days distant and that then
I was destined to suffer everlasting martyrdom in the
fire, my body being prepared for the purpose and my
dissolution made a thing impossible. Rose overwhelmed
with infinite despair, and came down into the study,
execrating the day I was born with inexpressible bitterness." Another time he dreamed that he was in his own
room waiting to be led out and burned alive. Seized
with a desire to carry some remembrance with him, he
picked up a piece of the door plate. A strange and horrible thought struck him. The fragment he held was of
metal and, growing red-hot in the fire, would only exacer-
bate his agony. Once again, cold with horror, he awoke.

But waking was as bad as sleeping. For then the
voices would begin. He heard them almost every night
now. Generally their purport was hostile, to warn him
of Mary's death or his own damnation. But they
clothed themselves in some short sentence, often a saying
he had heard or a quotation. Once, for instance, he heard
the words: "The wonted roar is up among the woods."
It was a line from *Comus,* and no doubt it stuck in his
head when he was working on Milton. But it was
fraught with a new significance. The picture it conjured
up before his inward eye was of no florid Comus rout,
but of wrath and supernatural danger, a demon-hunt
rather, of German legend, Walpurgis rider and baying
hell-hound afoot after his soul. It was as if his obsessed
mind involuntarily twisted any bit of experience present
or remembered into a reference to the subject of his obsession.

After the voices came a fit of dejection which lasted all the morning. Only in the afternoon did the peaceful daily life round him penetrate his spirit sufficiently to lift it to a listless torpor. And soon night would come; and with night the fearful cycle began again.

The strain of such an existence was more than Cowper could bear. And, in a paroxysm of misery, he would at times curse the God that had made him. But a moment later he would realize that by the curse he had added one more to the tale of sins that were leading him to damnation. Beside himself with misery, once more he cursed God, to be stricken once more with an intolerable remorse. Caught in a vicious circle, his horror of damnation seemed only to make that damnation more certain.

But though the battle was irretrievably lost, he could not even now give up the fight. In the recesses of his being a last spark of his marvelous vitality still flickered. And with the desperate energy of a man snatching at his only remaining chance of life, he rallied in a final superhuman effort to achieve that faith which alone, in his view, could save him. He knew, none better, what it felt like to have it. To revive the palest glow of that feeling—this, and this alone, was the object of his every thought. He knew of only one man who could help him to it. With abject, hungry hope, he turned anew to Teedon. To Cowper's yearning eyes he shone out—poor, fussy, seedy Teedon—aureoled in all the glory of an angel of salvation. He was pleased to find himself in this splendid and unaccustomed rôle, as who would not be? And he threw himself into it with a will. He prayed for Cowper assiduously, and generally with most favorable results. A comforting message would be revealed to him; at once he would come hurrying over to Weston to deliver it. He also gave Cowper advice as to how to stimulate his faith.  Let him say one collect over and over again; if that had no effect, let him paraphrase it and say it once more.  He, Teedon, had often tried both methods, and found them most helpful in inducing spiritual emotions. With a pathetic docility, Cowper accepted the messages and set himself to follow the advice.

At first both did him good.  He slept more calmly; and at moments, notably when he was walking in the fading autumnal garden, he was visited by a faint gleam of religious emotion.  But these hopeful signs were not fulfilled.  The gleams vanished, not to return, and his sleep began to be disturbed once more.  Nor did Teedon's subsequent messages and advice repeat the good effect of his initial ones.  How, indeed, should they? Teedon had not the slightest understanding of the nature of Cowper's malady, and so could not attempt to cure it. His methods and messages by their novelty had managed to revive the feeble remaining glimmer of Cowper's capacity for religious feeling.  When, however, he grew accustomed to them, they produced as little effect on him as reading the Bible or going to church.  And the consequent disappointment after hope now added to his dejection, just as his disappointment after his visit to Eartham had.  A revulsion against Teedon and his advice took possession of him, which grew until, as usual, it found expression in his dreams.  In February, 1793, he dreamed God had declared to him that all the encouragement He had given him through Teedon had been meant in mockery.  It was the end of Cowper's connection with Teedon.  He continued his pension: and if Teedon wrote to him, answered politely in order not to hurt his feelings.  But he looked for help to him no longer.

His last hope had failed him.  And now at length he resigned himself to disaster.  Disappointment had quenched that last spark of vitality; he could fight no more. He grew worse rapidly. As his despair grew wilder, his anxiety about Mary and Milton gave place to more immediate and sensational terrors. He became convinced that some fearful disaster was going to overtake him at once. It was not hard to fancy what form it might take. He dreamed one night that he asked a doctor for a remedy against madness. The doctor replied he knew a sure one, death. Death or madness— these were the two alternatives that faced Cowper; and daily he waited for one to strike him down. Spring was coming on, and in the ordinary way he would have felt safe till the following winter. But it is the measure of his decline that spring no longer stirred any response in him. The trees might grow green in Weston Park, the birds twitter along the alleys of the Wilderness; they cheered them as little as the drizzling rains of November. The darkness that swallowed in turn his hope and his resistance had now come between him and the visible world he had loved so long.

Meanwhile he had more mundane troubles to contend with. Mary was growing steadily worse. When they had got back from Eartham she had still been able, after a fashion, to walk and talk and take an interest in what was happening round her. Now she could hardly see; her conversation was an incoherent mumble; and it was with infinite difficulty, at a snail's pace, that she could drag herself round the garden with two people supporting her. The change in her spirits was even more marked. Nine months ago, hopeless though she must have known her case to be, she had still managed to keep up a gallant pretense that she was getting better. "She always tells me so," said Cowper tenderly, "and will probably die with the words on her lips." And when he

had come into her room, wild-eyed, from some awful
nightmare, she would notice and strive to stammer out
some sentences of comfort.  Pathetically, indeed, the two
old friends had sought to bear each other's burdens, he
to ease her body, she to soothe his mind.  Now all that
was over.  She was far too infirm to notice much about
Cowper or any one else; while under the pressure of
disease and of the enforced idleness, so intolerable to one
whose life had been exclusively devoted to practical
things, even her iron self-control had begun to give away.
She rose, hardly knowing how she would drag through
the day, sat sunk in a gloomy lethargy longing for it to
end, and from time to time broke out in vain lament.

Living with her must have been a terrible strain, especially to one in Cowper's condition.  But he allowed
no sign that he was conscious of this to escape him.
Deathly ill, his every night an ordeal of unspeakable
horror, expectant every moment of final catastrophe,
he continued to nurse her, to feed her, to read to her, to
comfort her.  Nor did he for an instant relax his care,
lose patience, utter a word of complaint.  Even a
thought of it, indeed, he would have suppressed as a
disloyalty.  If her illness had changed her, that only
added fuel to the flame of pity which consumed him.
What must she have gone through that she should succumb!  His consciousness of the change showed, if at
all, in an added assiduity of tenderness.  Only once, as
he looked back down the years of their friendship and
thought of what had been and what now was, his full
heart overflowed in a strain of mournful pathos.

> The twentieth year is well-nigh past
> Since first our sky was overcast ;
> Ah, would that this might be the last,
>           My Mary!

Thy spirits have a fainter flow,
I see thee daily weaker grow—
'Twas my distress that brought thee low,
    My Mary!

Thy needles, once a shining store,
For my sake restless heretofore,
Now rust disus'd and shine no more,
    My Mary!

For though thou gladly wouldst fulfil
The same kind office for me still,
Thy sight now seconds not thy will,
    My Mary!

But well thou play'd'st the housewife's part,
And all thy threads with magic art
Have wound themselves about this heart,
    My Mary!

Thy indistinct expressions seem
Like language uttered in a dream;
Yet me they charm, whate'er the theme,
    My Mary!

Thy silver locks, once auburn bright,
Are still more lovely in my sight
Than golden beams of glorious light,
    My Mary!

For could I view nor them nor thee,
What sight worth seeing could I see?
The sun would rise in vain for me,
    My Mary!

Partakers of thy sad decline,
Thy hands their little force resign;
Yet, gently prest, press gently mine,
    My Mary!

And then I feel that still I hold
A richer store ten thousandfold
Than misers fancy in their gold,
      My Mary!

Such feebleness of limb thou prov'st,
That now at every step thou mov'st,
Upheld by two; yet still thou lov'st,
      My Mary!

And still to love, though prest with ill,
In wintry age to feel no chill,
With me is to be lovely still,
      My Mary!

But ah! by constant heed I know,
How oft the sadness that I show
Transforms thy smiles to looks of woe,
      My Mary!

And should my future lot be last
With much resemblance of the past,
Thy worn-out heart will break at last,
      My Mary!

Once Cowper was strong and happy and brilliant; now he was sick and miserable and crazy. But his devotion to Mary makes it perhaps the crowning moment of his life.

Mary's decline could not fail to hasten Cowper's. Throughout the summer and early autumn of 1793, helped by a visit from Hayley, he managed to maintain his existing condition. But with November events began to rush headlong to the final catastrophe. Swiftly the darkness began to eat up such shreds as remained of the world of daylight. The nights became even more terrible than those of last year. Higher blazed the phan-

tom fires of torment, fiercer and more insistent clamored
the ghostly voices. And now their activities were not
confined to the night. Out of the solitary bedchamber
where they had lurked so long the demons of his terror
began to creep; stealthily they descended the stairs, and
took possession of the world of day below. And soon
there was no place, no time of day when he was safe
from their attack. At meals, on walks, working in his
room, he heard their voices; sitting with Mary by the
fireside, suddenly they would steal into his thoughts and
clutch with icy hand at his heart.

And, as the world of spirit grew more present, so the
world of matter grew more insubstantial. He could
scarcely see his ordinary surroundings in the infernal
light which now quivered round his every step; the
sounds of daily life grew thin and inaudible beside the
supernatural wailings that dinned incessantly in his ears.
As for the world outside his immediate experience, it
had lost all significance for him whatever. It was 1793,
and every day the newspaper was full of the terrific
events of the Terror in France. But though Cowper
read of them he could not muster up the slightest feeling
of revulsion or pity. Indeed, all the bloodshed of the
guillotine might well seem trivial to him beside the
nameless and stupendous spiritual horrors which were
now the habitual element of his thoughts.

In January, 1794,—once more January,—his sufferings came to their crisis. He had never lost his sense
that a catastrophe was impending over him. But as the
world of flesh gave place to the world of spirit, once
again the object of his terror changed. Madness and
death were earthly ills, and as such the prospect of them
no longer alarmed him. In their stead a new and appalling idea presented itself to his imagination. He began

to wonder if death, so far from being a disaster, was not to be the last mercy denied him by a wrathful God. Could it be that the supernatural visitations which had pursued him during the last month were only the precursors of a more formidable attack, and that the demons of hell were going to carry him off like Faustus, while he was yet alive? In his shattered nervous state, the sheer horror of the idea was enough to make it irresistibly convincing to him. With the conviction his remaining vestiges of sanity forsook him. His dual existence was finally at an end. The last streaks of normal daylight had vanished from his mental horizon, and nightmare darkness held dominion over all.

It was never to lift again. For the last time his lifelong enemies had gathered to the attack; for the last time they had overwhelmed him. His body lived on for six years more, but his spirit inhabited another world. Weston, familiar Weston, was become to him only a fragment of space beleaguered amid the wastes of primal darkness, where the fiends howled and beat their wings and gnashed their teeth, greedy to snatch their prey. If his old friends came to see him, he shrank from them. What were they doing far away from the old homely earth? Most likely it was not them at all, but devils again, cunningly disguised in the shape of those he loved, to entrap him. The devils were coming to seize him; amid the confused cloud of fear and misery in which his brain now reeled that was the one fact that stood out with a dreadful, persistent clarity. Not for a day, nor for an hour, not for a minute during six long years did he forget it! Not a day, not an hour, not a minute passed which he did not confidently believe to be his last in the world.

Sometimes he would make wild attempts to circumvent his enemies; refuse to leave his room lest they should take possession of it, and he should find them there, ready to leap on him at his return. At other times, in a desperate effort to obtain redemption, he would impose strange penances on himself: sit for long periods without moving, refuse to eat for days together. But generally he just waited. Rigid with fear, his breath coming in short gasps, his eyes keen to discern any oncoming shadow, ears agog to hear any approaching rustle, he would stand for hours; then, unable to contain himself, he would pace the room like a caged tiger; then sink into a chair inarticulately moaning, or perhaps rush to the writing-table and unburden himself in a torrent of words. "I cannot bear the least part of what is coming upon me," he scrawls in 1794, "yet am forced to meet it with eyes open wide, to see it approach and destitute of all means to escape it." Passionately he protests against the cruelty of his destiny, rehearses the long tale of Heaven's injustice to him, and at length relapses into a fatalistic dejection. "I was a poor fly entangled in a thousand webs from the beginning. . . . My despair is infinite, my entanglements infinite, my doom is sure." And finally, his feeling once more rising, in a strain of tragic eloquence he bids a last farewell to the God who has so strangely recompensed his devotion. "Farewell to the remembrance of Thee forever—I must now suffer Thy wrath, but forget that I ever heard Thy name. Oh, horrible! and still more horrible that I write these last lines with a hand that is not permitted to tremble."

One would have thought that Cowper's sufferings had reached their zenith. What, indeed, was there left for human being to suffer more? But a final horror was yet to be added to his existence. In May of 1794 Mary had another stroke. Once again she rallied from it; but this time it had touched her brain, and when she rose from her bed it was perceived that her personality had undergone a terrible change. The old Mary, stoical and selfless, with her calm eyes and quiet ways, was gone, and instead, hideously travestied in her shape, though with face distorted by disease, stood another woman: selfish, querulous, suspicious and exacting. To that same Cowper to whom she had dedicated her whole life she was now a peevish tyrant; never let him leave her for a moment, forced him, weak as he was, to drag her for hours round the garden. The little house, which she had managed to invest with an atmosphere that, even at its saddest, was sober and dignified, now echoed with sordid scenes of her own making. Losing all control, in mowing imbecile fury she would scream out that Cowper's relations and friends were plotting against her, that they were taking him away, that they had designs on her property, even that she had caught them trying to get possession of her silver.

It was the last drop in the cup of Cowper's anguish. To lose the support of his good angel had been sorrowful indeed; but to see her degraded into something physically and mentally repulsive was ten thousand times more painful. Even now he was always gentle to her, submissively obeyed her most unreasonable demand. Sometimes he thought that she, like his visitors, was really a demon in disguise. For once this delusion may have been less unbearable than the truth.

Indeed, the change in Mary makes life at Weston during these years too painful to contemplate. No story, however tragic, is wholly depressing in which the virtue of the characters is untouched by what happens to them. There is even something exalting and consoling in the spectacle of human integrity triumphing over adverse circumstances. But that this integrity can fail, and through no act of conscious human will, but irresistibly impelled by physical causes, strikes at the root of any confidence one may hold in existence.

But even this, the blackest period as it was of all Cowper's story, is relieved by a ray of light, the devotion of his friends. Round the somber pyre of his supreme agony hover the figures of Hayley, John Johnson and Lady Hesketh. There is something comic about them. They are so wonderfully unsuited to understand, let alone alleviate the psychological intricacies of Cowper's disease; their busy, mundane silhouettes stand out in such incongruous contrast to the apocalyptic flame and dark of their background. But there is nothing comic about their love. During one time or another of the next seven years each shows himself prepared to subvert the whole order of his life in order to relieve Cowper's affliction. It was a credit to them; but it was also a credit to him. That a normal, conventional, prosperous Georgian lady like Harriet Hesketh, and a normal, conventional, prosperous Georgian divine like John Johnson should have been willing to give up a considerable part of their lives to him is the most striking testimony possible to the extraordinary beauty and charm of Cowper's character.

It is not so odd that Hayley should, for he was prone to fits of unbalanced enthusiasm. Nor, as it turned out, was he called upon to sacrifice so much as the other two. But the circumstances of his life at this time made it extremely good of him to exert himself on Cowper's behalf as much as he did. For his domestic difficulties had begun again. The pitiable Eliza had deserted her respectable friends in Derby and established herself in London, where she filled the ears of all and sundry with complaints of the inadequate financial provision which, she asserted, Hayley made for her. Such accusations were peculiarly distressing to a man of his sensibility, especially as he was now, as ever, very hard up. However, when in the spring of 1794 he heard of Cowper's collapse, all his personal worries were forgotten, and traveling, with characteristic disregard of convention, alone with his housemaid, he hurried over to Weston to see if he could be of any help. With admirable ardor and patience, he sought to comfort Cowper and to re-awaken his interest in Milton. His efforts were vain. But in administering to Cowper's material wants he met with more success.

Two years before Hayley had been profoundly shocked to find that Cowper was in financial straits. Surely, he thought, a man of genius who had benefited mankind ought to be supported by a grateful country. With him to think was to act; and early in 1792 he had immediately set to work to procure Cowper a pension. At first it seemed likely that his attempt would share the fate of most of his other schemes. For, as usual, the almost supernatural indefatigability with which he pursued his end was only equaled by the eccentricity of the means by which he sought to achieve it. At a critical period of English history he thrust himself upon eminent statesmen whom he hardly knew, harangued them for hours in a high-flown style, and when he could not see them, bombarded them with letters both in prose and verse.

The first man he applied to was Cowper's old friend, Thurlow. He listened to Hayley in silence, then ushered him out, earnestly assuring him he would do everything he could. Two years passed, and nothing happened, though Hayley had reminded Thurlow in a series of

lyrics increasingly severe in tone. He therefore turned
to Pitt himself, and set out Cowper's situation to him in
a long and eloquent letter, culminating in a sonnet. What
was his horror to receive the letter back unopened.
With great difficulty he procured an interview with him,
and one morning, in June, 1793, fortified by port wine,
he arrived at Downing Street and poured out his story in
a speech even longer and more eloquent than usual. The
effect was the same as it had been on Thurlow. Hastily
and earnestly Pitt ushered him out, assuring him that he
would do what he could. "In a tumult of sensibility"
Hayley kissed his hand and burst into tears. The game
seemed won. But once again the months passed and
nothing further happened. Hayley was dismayed, but
he was undefeated. He managed to enlist a new and
powerful advocate, Lord Spencer, to assist him; and himself mustering all his literary powers, composed a letter
to Pitt which should compel him for very shame to recollect his obligations.

"It is not often," it began, "that a Hermit can be deceived by a Prime Minister; yet I am an example that
such an extraordinary incident may happen." Vigorously
it rehearsed the details of Pitt's perfidity: and then, "I
write in the frank and proud sorrow of a wounded
spirit," it concluded, "with a cordial and affectionate
wish that Heaven may bless you with unthwarted power
to do good and with virtue sufficient to exert it. I re-
tain a lasting sense of the very engaging kindness with
which you allowed me to pour forth my heart to you on
this interesting subject, and I am most sincerely, my dear
sir, your grateful though afflicted servant, W. Hayley."

Alas! the hearts of Prime Ministers grow hard to resist even darts such as these; Pitt did not reply. Hayley's hopes at last began to flag. But meanwhile Lord

Spencer had been busy, and in March, 1794, news came
to Weston that his good offices had procured Cowper a
pension of three hundred pounds a year. By Hayley's
efforts Cowper was relieved from material difficulties for
the rest of his life.

Lady Hesketh's was a harder task. She was at Weston at the time of Cowper's final collapse. Overcome
with anxiety, she suggested he should go to a home kept
by Doctor Willis, the most famous mental doctor of the
day. Surely the man who had cured "the dear excellent
King" was likely to benefit her poor cousin. If there
was a difficulty about the expense, she would make that
all right. But Mary in her present state of mind would
not hear of Cowper going away. The "enchantress," as
Lady Hesketh now bitterly called her, said that if the
Archangel Gabriel were to persuade her to let him leave
her, she would not comply. Clearly, however, it was
impossible to leave him without care. So, without hesitation, at the age of sixty, Lady Hesketh left her comfortable, cheerful home in London and settled in the
depths of the country to take the solitary charge of two
lunatics.

It was not an easy life for her. She tried to occupy
Cowper by teaching him netting and mat-making, and
she read aloud to him. But he was liable to think anything done for him was meant as an injury, and any kind
word concealed an insult; suddenly when she was reading
aloud he would leap up in a fit of passion and rush from
the room. She had never been one to conceal her feelings; nor did she now. The post brought John Johnson
page after page of lamentations over "the poor dear
soul, my cousin," intermingled with denunciations of the
"enchantress." But her old vigor of spirit never deserted
her, and though she complained, she never gave in. With

the consequence that at the end of two years her health was seriously impaired.

This presented a problem. Bereft of Lady Hesketh and unable to go to Doctor Willis, what was to happen to Cowper? At this juncture it was the turn of John Johnson to throw himself into the breach as unhesitatingly as Lady Hesketh had done. Of course, Cowper must come and live with him. He could imagine no greater pleasure and privilege than to look after his dear bard, and Mary too. It was true that his house was small, but he was sure he could manage to get them in.

"As for ourselves, my love," he wrote to the unfortunate sister who kept house for him, "I know you will have no objection to the garrets."

We do not know how she received this proposal; but his other relations protested with a growing acrimony against the burden he had so quixotically shouldered. However, he paid no attention; and in July, 1795, he took Cowper and Mary to Norfolk. Nor were they parted from him till death. He looked after Cowper with unremitting, solicitous affection, gave up his curacy at East Dereham, and moved his house from place to place in the neighborhood, from village to open country, from open country to the seaside, trying to find somewhere that seemed likely to help his recovery.

But Cowper, far sequestered in his nightmare world, was impervious to his surroundings. How could any variation in that infinitesimal piece of matter called the earth make any difference to one who expected to be flung at any moment into bottomless abysses of perdition? As a matter of fact, a few days before he left Weston, when he was taking a last look from the window of his room at his beloved garden, he was visited by a moment of emotion. His departure from the home of so many

memories seemed the symbol and confirmation of that
more irrevocable departure from the world of ordinary
human hopes and fears.   As with a gesture of valediction
he wrote on the window shutter:

> Farewell, dear scenes forever closed to me,
> Oh, for what sorrows must I now exchange thee!
> Me miserable!  How should I escape
> Infinite wrath and infinite despair,
> Whom death, earth, heaven and hell consigned to ruin
> Whose friend was God, but God swore not to aid me?

But this impulse of feeling soon passed.   Throughout
the long journey to Norfolk and those shorter journeys
that succeeded it, Cowper followed Johnson as docile
and oblivious to all around him as a blind deaf mute.
The sudden change from sheltered Bedfordshire to the
skyey levels of Norfolk, the return to a district poignant
with memories of childhood, into what a tumult of feeling would two such events have cast him in the days of
his sanity!   But now he could only be roused by some
fact relating to his present condition.   In his Aunt Bodham's house at Mattishall he caught sight of a portrait
of himself painted in former days.   The contrast between the mood in which he remembered to have sat for
the picture and that which now possessed him sent a
twinge of horror through him.

"Oh," he broke out, clasping his hands in hopeless
yearning, "if I could be as I was then."

As for the scenery, it did not stir the slightest response
in him any more.   Only the sea had not lost all its power.
As he wandered on the stretching sands, his ears filled by
the monotonous thunder of the breakers, his anguish was
lulled as it had been at Brighton and Southampton years
ago.

But even this solace was reft from him. Brooding incessantly, as he did, on the subject of his torments, one day the idea flashed into his mind that Providence had brought him there in order the better to fulfil its awful purpose; and that over the limitless ocean, sailing from no one knew where, a phantom ship manned with demons might bear down on him as he was pacing the sands and carry him off. From that moment with staring eyes and trembling limbs he scanned the horizon for a sail.

For his fears dominated him, if possible, even more than at Weston. Sometimes he would welcome Johnson in the morning with a loving look; but as often with gloomy, terrified eyes, for he thought him an evil apparition. And every brief note he scribbled at this time contained a sentence to say that these were the last words fate was ever going to let him write. The feeling of foreboding about his journey which he had experienced that morning in his bedroom at Weston turned out to be in a sense justified. His spirit had long ago taken leave of its surroundings. But with his departure from his old home the last worn threads that had bound him even in memory or by association to the world of his sanity snapped; and the unfamiliar background known only in madness tended to confirm his confused mind in the impression that his old life was completely vanished. He felt Heaven had transferred him to a strange and remote place, there to inflict on him his supreme ordeal; and such shreds of his old self that might still adhere to him slipped off.

Even to look at, lean, livid and distraught, he was hardly recognizable as the plump, placid Cowper of a few years back. And the few letters he wrote after he got to Norfolk read like the letters of another man. For one thing, the handwriting, small, deliberate and shaky, is different; but more startlingly different is the style. It is not imbecile or degraded; not at the height of his delusions were the processes of Cowper's brain impaired. But he writes no longer in the easy flexible prose of his prime, or even in the Hebraic phraseology of his Evangelical phase, but in a new style, naked, throbbing, orchestral, falling in lamenting cadence like the cry of the gulls that hovered and swooped round the Norfolk cliffs.

"Adieu," he concludes a letter to Lady Hesketh, "I shall write to you no more. I am promised months of continuance here, and should be somewhat less of a wretch in my present feeling could I credit the promise. But effective care is taken that I should not. The night contradicts the day, and I go down the torrent of time into the gulf that I have expected to plunge into so long. A few hours remain, but among them not one that I should ever occupy in writing to you again. Once more, therefore, adieu—and adieu to the pen forever. I suppress ten thousand agonies to add only William Cowper."

Yet changed though he was, he was not yet wholly unrecognizable. All the madness in the world could not root out the love and constancy which were the strongest qualities in his nature. Sunk in despair, he could never forget where he had once loved; cut off as he felt himself by an immeasurable gulf from his old life, still at times memories would stir in his breast and he would cast a longing, lingering look behind to Weston and all he had loved there.

"I shall never see Weston more," he wrote; "there indeed I lived a life of infinite despair . . . but to have passed there the little time that remained to me was the desire of my heart."

In a pathetic letter he besought the clergyman for news. "Gratify me with news of Weston," it begins, and finally, after many inquiries, "tell me if my poor birds are still living. I never see the herbs I used to give them without a recollection of them; and sometimes I am ready to gather them forgetting I am not at home." Nor, confident though he was that his time on earth was short, did he cease from attaching himself to those around him. He grew very fond of a Miss Perowne, whom Johnny got to take care of him, while to Johnny himself he clung with a wild intensity of devotion. He would be ill with agitation for a whole day before Johnny went on a journey; and if he went away on Sundays, as he sometimes did, to take the service somewhere in the neighborhood, Cowper used to stand in the evening, a bent wistful figure at the garden gate, striving to catch the barking of a dog at a cottage farther along the road which he knew betokened his return.

So passed a year and a half; and in 1796, since change of scene seemed to do Cowper no good, Johnny settled permanently at East Dereham in a house overlooking the market-place. Not that he had given up hope concerning Cowper's recovery, nor had Hayley or Lady Hesketh. Absent from Cowper, they continued to think of him much as ever; were always writing letters, in Hayley's case varied by sonnets, demanding news and expressing hope. The trio of Cowper's active friends was now become a quartette by the addition of the conscientious Rose; he was found useful since he lived in London for the purpose of extracting Cowper's pension from a dilatory exchequer. Shy and awkward, he was not naturally fitted for such a task.

"With all the little Rose's, *Sense, Genius* and *Learning,*" declared Lady Hesketh on one occasion, "he was quite at a *standstill* in a very plain, simple affair and had not that *bold, courageous animal,* Lady Hesketh, made a

*Row* about the matter . . . we might all have gone a-
begging together."

Her activities on Cowper's behalf were not confined
to harrying Rose. She also recommended remedies.
They were of a simple kind. Restored as she now was
to a normal life, she had returned to her normal frame of
mind, which was not one appreciative of the mysteries of
lunatic psychology. And she tended to think Cowper's
a physical disorder arising, she ingeniously suggested,
from checked perspiration. Let him, therefore, try warm
bathing, or, if that was not possible, eat peaches, figs,
sago and large quantities of ass's milk. In the flood-tide
of her reaction from the gloom of Weston, she began to
think that such a diet, consistently adhered to, might
very likely cure him completely. Indeed, her chief
anxiety on his behalf did not relate to his illness. The
French war was at this time raging, and Lady Hesketh
wondered if Norfolk was safe. It was so near to France
that it might well prove to be the landing-place of an
invading army; could not Johnny move Cowper inland?
At any rate let him collect as much gold as possible. She
did not trust this newfangled paper money; one could
not be sure that the French, so diabolically cunning to
ruin honest English people, might not by some despicable
trick render it valueless at any moment. In 1798 news
that the French army was safely involved in the Egyptian
campaign raised her spirits. "Don't you long to be
*certain* that the dear Arabs have swallowed Bonaparte
and made mincemeat of his army?" she exclaimed in an
ecstasy of patriotic fervor.

Hayley was also optimistic about Cowper's illness,
and he also had his remedies. But they, as might have
been expected, were of a more sensational kind. Indeed, a scheme he originated in 1797 provides the one

melancholy gleam of comedy that lightens the blackness
of Cowper's last years.  On June twentieth he received
a letter from Cowper, the first he had written to him
since he had left Weston.  It was in his customary strain,
and the benevolent Hayley, horrified by the condition it
betrayed, set to work with even more than his usual
ardor to devise some method of relieving it.  The result
of his frenzied cogitations expressed itself in a letter to
Cowper, the most extraordinary composition that even
Hayley ever made accessible to an astonished world.

"My very dear dejected friend," it began, "the few
lines in your hand, so often welcome to me and now so
long wished for, affected me through my heart and soul
both with joy and grief, joy that you are again able to
write to me, and grief that you write under the oppres-
sion of melancholy.

"My keen sensations in perusing these heart-piercing
lines have been a painful prelude to the following ecstatic
vision: I beheld the throne of God, whose splendour,
though in excess, did not strike me blind, but left me
power to discern on the steps of it two kneeling, angelic
forms.  A kind seraph seemed to whisper to me that
these heavenly petitioners were your lovely mother and
my own. . . . I sprang eagerly forward to enquire your
destiny of your mother.  Turning towards me with a
look of seraphic benignity, she smiled upon me and said:
'Warmest of earthly friends!  Moderate the anxiety of
thy zeal, lest it distract thy declining faculties, and
know that as a reward for thy kindness my son shall
be restored to himself and to friendship.  But the All-
merciful and Almighty ordains that his restoration shall
be gradual, and that his peace with Heaven shall be preceded by the following extraordinary circumstances of
signal honour on earth.  He shall receive letters from

members of parliament, from judges and from bishops
to thank him for the service he has rendered to the
Christian world by his devotional poetry.  These shall
be followed by a letter from the Prime Minister to the
same effect; and this by thanks expressed to him on the
same account in the hand of the King himself. . . . Hast-
en to impart these blessed tidings to your favourite
friend,' said the Maternal Spirit, 'and let your thanksgiving to God be an increase of reciprocal kindness to
each other.

"I obey the vision, my dear Cowper, with a degree of
trembling fear that it may be only the fruitless offspring
of my agitated fancy.  But if any part of the prophecy
shall soon be accomplished, a faint ray of hope will then
be turned into strong, luminous and delightful conviction
in my heart, and I trust in yours, my dear delivered
sufferer, as completely as in that of your most anxious
and affectionate friend, W. H.

"P.S.—If any of the incidents speedily take place
which your angelic mother announced to me in this vision,
I conjure you in her name, my dear Cowper, to communicate them to me with all the kind despatch that is
due to the tender anxiety of sympathetic affection!"

The rest of Hayley's plan is sufficiently apparent from
the letter.  It is a curious fact that his plans always did
seem to involve entering into communication with eminent men; and he proposed, without of course saying
anything about the vision, to ask the leaders of English
public life referred to in it to write letters of sympathy to
Cowper, who, convinced by this fulfilment of the Maternal Spirit's prophecy of the certainty of his salvation,
would be immediately restored to health and sanity.  It
was an ingenious plan; but it was marred by one important defect.  Hayley did not know any of the public men;

it was unlikely that he ever would; and even if he did manage to scrape acquaintance with some of them, there seemed not the smallest reason to suppose they would agree to write an uninvited letter to a total stranger on a delicate personal question just because Hayley asked them to. However, his optimistic spirit, intoxicated by the fertility of its own invention, brushed all this aside. He was sure all that would come right in the end; Providence could not fail to assist any scheme for the cure of a man of genius.

Accordingly he sent the letter off to Cowper, and communicated the plan to Johnny. Poor Johnny, rendered desperate by two uninterrupted years of Cowper's society, welcomed the idea enthusiastically. But Lady Hesketh, to whom he explained it, was more doubtful. Of the general scheme of "the charming vision" she approved; but its details shocked her moral susceptibilities. These were peculiar. She did not mind the whole thing being a lie, but she did disapprove of Hayley saying he had seen the throne of God, when he had not. And the fact that he could do so reawakened her old suspicion of his orthodoxy. "I fear he is a stranger to the Great Truths of Christianity," she said. In addition to this, her practical mind saw very clearly the difficulty of procuring the required letters. However, she too was glad of any scheme which might help Cowper, and she volunteered to get into communication with some of the public men.

It was thought unwise to attack the most exalted straight away. So, as a preliminary attempt, overtures were made to Mr. Wilberforce, a Member of Parliament, Lord Kenyon, a Judge, and three bishops, Doctor Beadon, of Gloucester, Doctor Watson, of Llandaff, and Dr. Beilby Porteus, of London. Their responses were

318 The Stricken Deer

only partially satisfactory. Lord Kenyon, who was approached through Rose, did not answer at all, and Doctor Beadon wrote angrily, by the hand of a third person, to say that he could not think of granting such an extraordinary request. On the other hand, Mr. Wilberforce, Doctor Watson and Dr. Beilby Porteus all wrote off admirable letters to Cowper immediately, and Mr. Wilberforce even sent him a book he had written. Fortified by this support, Hayley made one more attempt on Lord Kenyon. This time, again saying nothing of the vision, he persuaded Thurlow to speak for him. But Thurlow's pleadings had no more effect on Lord Kenyon than Rose's had done. They were not, indeed, ardent. "I have been pressed," began his letter, "by one mad poet to ask of you, for another, a favour which savours of the malady of both."

Meanwhile the unhappy object of their schemes had not reacted satisfactorily to them. To Hayley's original letter and to that of Mr. Wilberforce, Cowper had listened in gloomy apathy. And when that of Doctor Porteus was read to him he had interrupted in a tone of anguish: "It was written in derision—I am sure of it." "Oh, no, no, no, my cousin," protested Johnson, in shocked tones. "Say not so of the good Beilby, Bishop of London." Cowper's feelings were made yet more explicit after Watson's letter arrived. Johnson and Miss Perowne, anxious to see what effect it had had on him, carefully steered the conversation at dinner round to the subject of Hayley's vision, and Johnson said, as if by chance, that in this last letter there seemed to be signs that its prophecies were being fulfilled. "Well," said Cowper, "be it so. I know there is and I knew there would be, and," he added significantly, "I knew what it meant."

If Hayley and Johnson had listened more carefully to Cowper's ravings, they would have known too. Was it not one of his chief causes of misery that he had been explicitly told by God that any promise of hope he might receive was given in mockery? So that even if he believed Hayley's vision to be genuine, it would be no comfort to him. But whatever their diagnosis of his despair, it was clear to his friends that the letters had done him no good, and the scheme dropped. To the end of his days, however, Hayley would never admit that it had failed. Cowper, he insisted, would have been worse without it.

But the time for remedies, good or bad, was past. Cowper's sufferings were nearly at their period. Mary was already dead. In the winter of 1796 she had begun to sink rapidly, and on the evening of December seventeenth it was realized that she could live only a few hours. "Is there life above stairs, Sally?" Cowper asked the maid who came to call him in the morning. She said yes. He dressed, came down and quietly asked Johnson to go on with the book he had been reading to him. A few minutes later Johnson was beckoned from the room to be told Mary was dead. He came back, resumed reading, and after a few pages stopped and broke the news. At first Cowper remained calm; but a few hours later he was seized with a violent agitation. Wildly he protested that he was sure Mary was not really dead, that she would be buried alive and then wake in her grave, and that if she did it would be his fault, as he had been created to cause her every imaginable suffering; and he demanded to see her. Johnson took him up to her bedside. For a moment he continued to protest that he could see her stir, then, as he looked more closely, he grew still. The distortions with which

disease had disfigured her countenance were smoothed
away, and she lay there, calm, strong and benignant as
in former days.  At length she had been given back to
him, by the hand of death.  For a long moment he gazed
at her, a supreme, unwavering look.  Then, for the first
time since he had left Weston, his self-control completely
forsook him, and he flung himself down in a torrent of
sobbing.  It did not last; after a few minutes he asked
for a glass of water, and recovered his composure.  Nor
did any one in the four years that remained to him of
life ever hear him mention her name again.  He was not
told about her funeral, for fear of reviving his agitation.
A few nights later her body was secretly hurried down
the hill and buried in Dereham Church by torchlight.

It is not likely that Cowper would have broken down
again even if he had known.  For under the continued
pressure of misery the excitement which had characterized his state of mind at Weston had now given place to
a dull apathy.  It is beyond the capacity of human nerves
to continue in a state of violent agitation for several
years, even if faced by the prospect of damnation.  Cowper was acquainted with sad misery as the tanned galley
slave is with his oar; and if custom had not made his
suffering easier, it had at least made him numb.  As a
consequence, he began to appear more like his former
self, tidier, fatter, rosier; he had taken up some of his
old occupations, revising Homer, translating, and he
asked to be read aloud to.  Johnson proposed reading
his own poems to him.  Cowper refused to hear *John
Gilpin;* the contrast between his present condition and
the care-free mood in which he had composed it was too
painful.  But to the rest he listened calmly enough.
More striking, during the last months of Mary's life he
had volunteered to read the Bible to her if she wanted.

And when the servants trooped in for family prayers he no longer left the room.

But of course none of this meant that he felt any happier. Now his nerves were quieter he needed distraction to make the day pass. But none of the distractions gave him any satisfaction. "My thoughts," he writes, "are like loose and dry sand, which the closer it is grasped slips the sooner away. Mr. Johnson reads to me, but I lose every sentence through the inevitable wandering of my mind." And "Wretch that I am," his servant would hear him mutter to himself, "thus to wander in quest of false delight." As for his attending prayers and reading the Bible, far from being signs of religious hope, they only meant that he was now so hardened to the thought of God's wrath that references to it no longer accentuated his suffering.

Nor had his visionary torments abated. He told Johnny how his bedroom was every night the battleground of a struggle between good and evil spirits, and how in the end the evil always vanquished the good, and then "Bring him out!" they would cry, "bring him out!" And even in the day when he was sitting alone he would often look up and see a spectral figure advancing on him, who, with menacing gestures, announced some fearful and immediate doom. His disordered fancy played round his woes in whimsical flourishes. One morning he told Johnson that a spiritual voice had spoken this message to him:

> Sadwin, I leave you with regret,
> But you must go to gaol for debt.

"Do you know the meaning of Sadwin, my cousin?" said Johnson.

"Yes," replied Cowper, "the winner of sorrow."
Thus for four years longer dragged on the days.

From them one extraordinary incident stands out.
Long ago at Olney Cowper had read a story in *Anson's Voyages*. It told how a sailor had fallen overboard in the Atlantic; how his companions had vainly attempted to save him; and how, after a long struggle, he had succumbed. Now one day in March, 1799, as he was sitting lost as usual in aimless brooding, the story strayed by chance into his mind, and immediately arrested his attention by the analogy it presented to his own life. Had he not fallen early in life from the ship which carried normal mankind from the cradle to the grave? Had not his friends tried to save him in vain? And now, after a lifetime of struggling, was he not sinking exhausted to death? He, too, was a castaway, the castaway of humanity. The story lit up his past like a sudden flash of lightning; stimulated by it his old powers of mind reasserted themselves, the incoherent, lethargic muddle that was his thoughts fell once more into order; and he turned to survey, as from a high mountain, the whole rugged path over which his steps had wandered since they left the Berkhamstead vicarage sixty-nine years before. As he looked, the accumulated anguish and despair of his life of unparalleled disaster caught fire and blazed up in a last towering flame of poetry.

> Obscurest night involv'd the sky,
>    Th' Atlantic billows roar'd,
> When such a destin'd wretch as I,
>    Wash'd headlong from on board,
> Of friends, of hope, of all bereft,
> His floating home for ever left.

No braver chief could Albion boast
Than he with whom he went,
Nor ever ship left Albion's coast
With warmer wishes sent.
He lov'd them both, but both in vain,
Nor him beheld, nor her again.

Not long beneath the whelming brine,
Expert to swim, he lay;
Nor soon he felt his strength decline,
Or courage die away;
But wag'd with death a lasting strife,
Supported by despair of life.

He shouted; nor his friends had fail'd
To check the vessel's course,
But so the furious blast prevail'd,
That, pitiless perforce,
They left their outcast mate behind,
And scudded still before the wind.

Some succour yet they could afford;
And, such as storms allow,
The cask, the coop, the floated cord,
Delay'd not to bestow.
But he (they knew) nor ship, nor shore,
Whate'er they gave, should visit more.

Nor, cruel as it seem'd, could he
Their haste himself condemn,
Aware that flight, in such a sea,
Alone could rescue them;
Yet bitter felt it still to die
Deserted, and his friends so nigh.

He long survives, who lives an hour
   In ocean, self-upheld;
And so long he, with unspent pow'r,
   His destiny repell'd;
And ever, as the minutes flew,
Entreated help, or cried—Adieu !

At length, his transient respite past,
   His comrades, who before
Had heard his voice in ev'ry blast,
   Could catch the sound no more.
For then, by toil subdued, he drank
The stifling wave, and then he sank.

No poet wept him: but the page
   Of narrative sincere,
That tells his name, his worth, his age,
   Is wet with Anson's tear.
And tears by bards or heroes shed
Alike immortalize the dead.

I therefore purpose not, or dream,
   Descanting on his fate,
To give the melancholy theme
   A more enduring date:
But misery still delights to trace
Its semblance in another's case.

No voice divine the storm allay'd,
   No light propitious shone;
When, snatch'd from all effectual aid,
   We perish'd, each alone :
But I beneath a rougher sea,
And whelm'd in deeper gulphs than he.

The verses are written in his characteristic, simple
measures, in his characteristic, formal language; but the

passion which informs their every line raises and sustains them at a height he never touched before. It is Cowper's final considered and terrible judgment on his own life: it is also the unique occasion on which he enters the realm of great poetry. By the last and most baffling caprice of that destiny whose plaything he was, those afflictions against which he had exhausted his life in struggling, now, in the very moment of his defeat, revealed themselves as the instrument of his greatest achievement. If Cowper had been victorious in his struggle, if he had vanquished his deformity and his delusions he might never have been quickened to that intensity of feeling in which alone the greatest art is born. Experience taught him to repudiate life; but in that repudiation his own life found at last its highest fulfilment.

He lived for only a year more. In January, 1800, his health began to exhibit alarming symptoms; by March he was confined to bed. He lingered another month, watching the daylight wax and dwindle along the dark-wainscoted walls of his bedroom, the brass sphinx heads on its door. In a final dedication of his affection Johnny threw himself into the task of nursing him; and, with a passionate desire that Cowper should once more see light before he died, and at least leave the world in hope, he sought with ardent words to convince him of his salvation. But the evil fate which so early had sworn itself Cowper's comrade kept faith with him to the end. He was to look his last on a world on which no thinnest ray of hope had penetrated the pervading shadow. He listened with his usual apathy when Johnson spoke of the general truths of Christianity; but when he mentioned God's love for Cowper himself, the certain happiness that was preparing for him in the next world, he interrupted and besought him to speak no more. One

day the doctor asked him how he felt. "Feel," he replied,  "I feel unutterable despair."

On the nineteenth of November he was observed to
be weakening.  Throughout the following night he lay,
conscious and still.  Once Miss Perowne asked him if
he wished for a drink, but he refused.  "What does it
signify?" he said wearily.  They were his last words.
At five in the morning he became unconscious; twelve
hours later he ceased to breathe.  Then, and then only,
was Johnny's wish granted.  As he took a last look at
the still face, he noticed with awe and amazement that
on Cowper, as on Mary, the healing hand of death had
wrought a change.  The strain and the apathy which so
long had marked his wasted features were gone, and
instead they lit up with a rapt, unearthly wonder, "a
holy surprise."  Was it a mere chance effect of dissolution? or could it be that during those hours of uncon-
sciousness a momentous event had taken place in the
unseen territories of Cowper's spirit: that on the very
threshold of the grave it was vouchsafed to him, for the
second time, to behold the supreme vision of St. Albans;
and gazing with unveiled eye at the Beatific Glory, he
learned that, after all, his despair had been founded on
delusion?  We shall never know.

He was buried in Dereham Church by the side of
Mary.  And it was universally agreed among his friends
that his grave should be marked by a memorial.  Memo-
rials, however, are notoriously the subject of controversy;
nor was Cowper's an exception.  Lady Hesketh wanted
a plain slab of marble; anything ornate, she said, "tho'
quite in character for a *grocer* or a *soap boiler* who had
acquired Immense Wealth, would be degrading to the
Memory of Our Cousin."  Hayley, on the other hand,
anxious, no doubt, to do honor to two geniuses at once,

was in favor of a more elaborate monument to be designed by Flaxman. His proposal carried the day; and though in general he can not be looked on as a trustworthy arbiter in matters of taste, we can not regret his success. For the memorial was so characteristic of the period in general, and in particular of the little group of people who erected it. There in a transept of the quiet well-kept church, with the sunlight shining mildly down on it through the unpainted windows, and decently protected by a neat railing, it still stands, a block of dark marble. On the top, carved in pure white, are disposed two volumes, the Bible and *The Task,* across them a classical palm branch; below is Cowper's name, and yet below that, on two medallions, are those of Mary and Miss Perowne. Underneath each is engraved an epitaph in blank verse by Hayley.

It is the light of Cowper's fame which has irradiated the little circle of people round him; and so rescued them from that darkness of forgotten time, in which most of their contemporaries lie buried. When he dies, it is withdrawn. But we have traveled so far in their company that it may be permitted us, before we say farewell, to watch the figures of his friends as they grow dim and are lost in the encroaching shadows of oblivion.

Little Rose is the first to disappear. He had never swerved from the road of conscientious self-improvement which he had marked out for himself so early in life. He had worked conscientiously, and not unsuccessfully, at the Bar, conscientiously married, and was, by the time Cowper died, already the conscientious father of several children. But in 1804 he contracted consumption; and early in December of that year he learned from his doctor that he had only a few weeks to live. In these tragic circumstances his conscientiousness as-

sumed heroic proportions. He was already supported
by a religious faith; but he had always doubted whether
it rested on a sufficiently strong intellectual foundation.
The last days of his life, therefore, he dedicated to reading Paley's *Evidences* and the works of Loudon. He
was gratified to find their arguments completely convincing. After this he took a suitable farewell of his
family; and, composed to the last, died on the twentieth
of September.

Three years later he was followed by Lady Hesketh.
Hers was a happy nature, and in spite of Cowper her
last years were very happy ones. She divided her time
between Bath, Clifton and Weymouth, had a great many
friends, wrote a great many letters, held a great many
strong opinions and took an interest in everything. Two
events in particular gave her satisfaction. For one
thing she actually got to know the King and Queen.
One would have thought that to meet George III and
Queen Charlotte in their unlovely old age must have
damped any loyalty, however ardent. But Lady Hesketh's was of a kind that burned all the higher for the
intractability of the fuel which it was forced to consume.
The Queen's face, she said, was "full and convincing
proof of the triumph of *Countenance* over *features*"; and
as for the King, he was "so good, so pious, so kind and
benevolent to everybody that one cannot look at him without wishing he might live forever!" Her other source of
especial pleasure was Hayley's *Life of Cowper,* which
came out in 1802. There were two points in it, indeed,
to which she took exception. It emphasized Cowper's
Whig views in a manner which she felt would put the
King against him, and the fact that she herself was
mentioned in it by name offended her sense of the decorous privacy which should shroud an English lady.

Surely, she said, Hayley could have called her Lady Dash. But these small defects were overwhelmed in the flood of the delighted enthusiasm into which she was thrown by the rest of the book.

"Oh, my dear good Johnny! how can I ever express or *describe* to you what I think of *Cowper's Life!*— You, indeed, do right to call it The Life—it is indeed The Life, and I hope there never will be another of anybody—no one, indeed, should attempt writing one who has not all the happy Talents and all the Sensibility of our friend Hayley." In 1807 her end came peacefully from mere old age.

Hayley's was a stormier voyage. Poor Hermit! Fate had treated him with an unmerited severity during the last few years. Such fame as he had possessed was diminishing; he was still in want of money; and he, whose happiness depended so much on those he loved, had lost Gibbon, Blake, Cowper and his adored little son. For such disasters, the departure of Eliza in 1797 from a world for which she was unfitted was not a sufficient compensation. Still, he had a gallant spirit; within a short time he had pulled himself together; and a little battered, but still undisillusioned, was soon hard at work, as we have seen, celebrating the virtues of those whose loss he deplored by composing their epitaphs, writing their lives, and promoting the erection of their monuments. In 1809 he had so far recovered his optimism as to marry again, a girl years younger than himself, but "willing to enliven with the songs of tenderness the solitude of a poetical hermit." Alas, his luck in domestic matters had not turned; within four years his wife had parted from him. He survived to write his memoirs and die in 1820.

There remains Johnny. And of him there is little to

be said. When he saw Cowper laid in his grave, the work which had made his life memorable was done; and he retired to the uneventful, useful life of the prosperous country clergyman he was. He married, had five children and lived till 1833. Before he died Cowper's popularity was already on the wane. In the thirty years that had elapsed since his death a revolution had taken place in English letters: the monarchs of Augustan tradition had been cast from their thrones. And in their stead a new race of poets—youthful, lawless, hag-ridden with genius—commanded the homage of the inconstant hearts of men.

THE END

INDEX

# INDEX

Abraham, 167
Adam, 17
Adams, Parson, 94
Addison, 23
Africa, 134, 137
Aldwinkle, 129
Andrews, Mr., 174
*Anson's Voyages,* 322
Apollo, 15, 239
Austen, Lady, 283
  and John Gilpin, 223
  and Lady Hesketh, 238, 240
  and Mrs. Unwin, 212-213, 217,
    219, 221, 227, 241
  and William Unwin, 213, 218,
    220-221
  anger of, 217, 218
  at the Rectory, 221
  attitude toward Cowper, 211-212,
    214, 216, 226
  correspondence with Cowper,
    213-214, 215-217, 228
  Cowper's attitude toward, 212,
    214-216, 225
  effect on Cowper's life, 229
  first visit to Orchard Side, 209
  leaves Olney, 228
  picnic with Cowper and Mary,
    210
  qualities of, 210-211
  sickness of, 219-220
  stimulates Cowper, 223-225, 234
  *See* Chapter V
Austen, Jane, 23, 252
Austen, Sir Robert, 209

*Authentic Narrative of Some In-*
  *teresting Particulars in the*
  *Life of John Newton, An*
  Newton, John, 131

Bagot, William, 234-235, 256, 257
Ball, Mrs., 265
Ball, Eliza
  *See* Hayley, Mrs.
Ball, Geary, 185
Barbauld, 23
Bartolozzi, 20
Bath, 280, 328
Bayreuth, 190
Beadon, Doctor, 317
Bean, Mr., 256, 257
Beaton, Cardinal, 184
Beattie
  *Church History,* 131
Beaumont, 84
Bedfordshire, 243, 310
Bedlam, 39
*Beggar's Opera, The*
  Gay, John, 20
Bellamy, Mrs., 224
Berkeley, Bishop, 94
Berkhamstead, 30, 33, 36, 37, 59,
  131, 176, 322
Bess, 172, 173
Blake, 282, 329
Bodham, Mrs., 36, 265
Bologna, 19
Bourne, "Vinny," 38
Brighton, 310
Brown, Capability, 19

Browne, Robert, 184
Browne, Simon, 201-202
Buckinghamshire, 129, 189
Bull, Reverend William, 183-185, 194, 201, 248, 257
Burke, 23
Burney, Fanny, 213
Burton, Robert, 184

Cagliostro, 23
Calvinism, 96, 98, 126
Cambridge, 86, 107, 108, 110, 112, 153, 154, 262, 285
Canterbury, Archbishop of, 278
*Captain Cook's Voyages,* 197
Caroline, Queen, 202
Carteret, 19
Casanova, 17
Castres, 36
Catlett, Miss (Newton's niece), 187
Catlett, Mary
  *See* Newton, Mrs.
Chapman, Mr., 44, 46, 49, 50
Charlotte, Queen, 328
Chatham, Lord, 20
Chesterfield, Lord, 17
Chichely, 256
China, 13
*Church History*
  Beattie, 131
Clarendon
  *History of the Rebellion,* 197
*Clarissa Harlowe,* 22
  Richardson, 23
Clifton, 209, 218, 219, 220, 228, 328
Clinker, Humphrey, 97
Clumsy, Sir Tunbelly, 106
Clunie, Captain, 137
Colet, Mary, 125
Colman, 38, 45
Colman, Dick, 125
*Comus*
  Milton, 294

*Connoisseur,* 62
Cook, Captain, 21
Cornwall, 23
Cotton, Doctor, 89, 103, 105, 108, 109, 125, 151, 159, 167
  Doctor Cotton's Home for Madmen, 88
Covent Garden, 21
Cowper, Doctor, 31, 59, 76, 124
Cowper, Major, 70, 125
Cowper, Mrs., 123, 124, 151
Cowper, John, 86-87, 89-90, 107, 108, 110, 153-156, 159, 285
Cowper, William
  abnormality of, 43-44
  ailments of, 268-269
  and the Americans, 196
  and animals, 39, 172-173, 204
  and Lady Austen
    *See* Austen, Lady
  and ballooning, 197-198, 235
  and brother, 153-156
  and Mr. Chapman, 50
  and children, 254
  and the Clerkships, 70-82
  and concerts on Sunday, 198-199
  and the French, 196
  and the garden, 173-174, 193-195
  and Harriet
    *See* Hesketh, Lady
  and Hayley
    *See* Hayley, William, and Cowper
  and January, 201, 248, 265, 301
  and the moon, 265
  and Nature, 40, 172, 188-190, 191, 205, 264, 285-286
  and Newton
    *See* Newton, John, and Cowper
  and a pension, 306-308
  and politics, 45, 121-122, 195-196
  and rouge, 198
  and suicide, 75-82, 167, 250

Cowper, William—*cont.*
and Theodora, 48-50, 51, 59, 63, 128
and Mrs. Unwin
  *See* Unwin, Mrs.
as public figure, 259
at the Disneys', 36, 37
at Market Street, 33-35
at Middle Temple, 50-53, 55, 58
at Westminster, 37-39, 44
charm with women, 46-47, 212
day of, 119-121, 142, 145, 177-180
disciples of
  *See* Rose, Samuel
  *See also,* Johnson, John
disease in, 28
*Dog and the Water-lily, The,* 204
drawing of, 174
dreams of, 85-249
duality of, 28-29
family of, 30-31
father of, 31, 59, 76, 124
first book of, 208, 233
first madness of, 1862, 68-90, 166
fourth madness of, 301-326
goes to live in country, 107-109
goes to live with Unwins, 118-119
in 1763 and 1772, 160
*John Gilpin,* 223-224, 320
*Lady's Shoe Lost at Bath, A,* 39
last words of, 326
life at Huntingdon, 109*ff.*
mother of, 31-32, 41, 83, 115, 262, 263
part in life at Olney, 186
physical deformity of, 34
poor manager, 110-111, 124-125
portrait of, 27
reading of, 196-197
religion of, 63-66, 67, 101-105, 122, 146-157, 197-200, 256, 270, 273

Cowper, William—*cont.*
removal to Weston Lodge, 245-246
*Retired Cat, The,* 204
scholarship of, 38, 44-45
second madness of, 160-171
supported by relations, 124-125, 237
*Task, The,* 224
third madness of, 249-252
turning point in life of, 68
visit with Mr. Hesketh, 53-55
vitality of, 168, 171, 207, 252
writing of
  estimate of letters, 202-203
  poetry, 24-27, 203-207, 223-224, 230, 256, 324-325
  style, 122, 312
  translations, 234, 242, 252
  work on Milton, 273, 287
Cozens, 206
Crabbe, 22
*Cranford,* 26
Crashaw, 125
Cromwell, Oliver, 97, 141
"Croydon, Sir John," 263

Dante, 92, 100
  *Inferno,* 14
Dartmouth, Lord, 97, 130, 138, 145, 174
Dashwood, Marianne, 276
Defoe, Daniel, 15, 21, 140
Derby, 280, 305
Dereham Church, 320, 326
Devonshire, Duchess of, 198, 260
Devonshire, Duke of, 179
Disney, Mr., 36, 37
Disney, Mrs., 36
Doctor Cotton's Home for Madmen, 88
*Dog and the Water-lily, The*
  Cowper, William, 204
Donne, Dean, 30

Dostoyefsky, 89
Downman, 253
Drury Lane, 21
Du Deffand, Madame, 19

Eartham, 277, 282, 285, 286, 287, 288, 291, 292, 296, 297
East Dereham, 309, 313
Election, 148
Elijah, 99
Elizabeth, Queen, 37
England, 18, 19, 20, 23, 30, 45, 78, 121, 136, 139, 196, 198, 199, 205, 251
Erasmus, 141
Eton, 19, 277
Evangelicalism, 93-100, 148, 165
*Evidences*
    Payley, William, 328

Fielding, Henry, 20, 23
    *Joseph Andrews,* 37
Final Perseverance, 148
Flaxman, 282, 327
Fletcher, 84
Fop, 256
Fox, Mr., 179, 196
"Fox and Grapes," 186
France, 78, 211, 228, 301, 314
Frederick William I, 19
"Frog, Mrs.," 255

Gainsborough, 20
Garrick, 23, 277
Gay, John
    *Beggar's Opera, The,* 20
    *Hare with Many Friends, The,* 36
Gayhurst, 241
George III, 121, 195, 196, 278, 328
Gibbon, Edward, 23, 139, 282, 287, 329
Gillray, 20
Gilpin, John, 223-224
Girtin, 205

Gloucester, 317
Goldoni, 132
Goldsmith, 23
Gordon Riots, 195
Gray, 23
Greatheed, Mr., 257
Greece, 252
Grimston, 113, 115
Guido Reni, 19

Hampshire, 54, 237
Handel
    "Messiah, The," 199
Handel Festival, 199
*Hare with Many Friends, The,* 36
Harriet
    *See* Hesketh, Lady
Harwich, Dock, 133
Hastings, Warren, 38-39
Hayley, Mrs., 279-281, 305-306, 329
Hayley, Thomas, 287
Hayley, William, 275-283, 329
    and Cowper, 283-285, 286-287, 292, 300, 305-308, 313, 314-319, 326-327
    *Life of Cowper,* 328-329
    *Triumphs of Temper, The,* 278
Herbert, 52, 53
Herefordshire, 88
Hertfordshire, 30, 105, 123, 131
Hesketh, Lady, 257, 264
    and Cowper's first madness, 88
    and Cowper's grave memorial, 326
    and Hayley, 287, 317
    and Johnson, 263
    and *Life of Cowper,* 328-329
    and Rose, 261, 313-314
    and Mrs. Unwin, 116, 118, 241-242, 308
    and William Unwin, 242
    and vacation in Hampshire, 53-54, 55, 237
    and Weston Lodge, 245

Hesketh, Lady—*cont.*
 as a child, 36, 237
 **care** for Cowper, 305, 308-309, 314
 comes to Olney, 238-240
 correspondence with Cowper, 60, 85, 110, 114, 123, 237, 258, 268, 312
 Cowper's attitude toward, 48, 118, 123-124, 238, 240, 258
 death of, 329
 effect on Cowper, 240-241, 243-244, 247, 266
Hesketh, Thomas, 53
Hickey, William, 21, 23
Hill, Joseph, 114, 122, 176, 203, 221
Himalayas, 286
*History of the Rebellion*
 Clarendon, 197
Hobbes, 140
Hodson, Mr., 110
Hogarth, William, 20, 21, 121, 196
Holland, 110
Holland, Lord, 20, 73, 276
Homer, 45, 224, 234, 235, 242, 259, 263, 264, 269, 320
Horace, 45, 137, 140
Houghton, Lord, 187
Howard, John, 281, 282
Hume, 139
Huntingdon, 108, 112, 113, 115, 121, 125, 131, 143, 144, 147, 152, 177
Hurdis, 260, 287
Hutchinson, Reverend Alfred, 99
*Iliad,* 234
Impey, Elijah, 38
Inglesant, John, 125
*John Gilpin,* 223-224, 320
Johnson, Doctor, 19, 23, 51, 100, 276
Johnson, John, 262-264, 265, 287, 305, 308, 309, 310, 311, 313,

Johnson, John—*cont.*
 314, 317, 318, 319, 320, 321, 325, 326, 329-330
Jonah, 17
Jones, Mr., 217
Jones, Mrs., 209
Jortin, 21
*Joseph Andrews*
 Fielding, 37

Karamazof, Alyosha, 89
Keats, John, 189
Kenyon, Lord, 317, 318
Kilwick Wood, 266
King, Mrs., 259

*Lady's Shoe Lost at Bath, A*
 Cowper, 39
Langton, Stephen, 277
*Lass of Pattie's Mill, The,* 224
Latour, 20
Lazarus, 91
Legge, 39
Leonardo, 19
Life of Cowper
 Hayley, William, 328-329
Little Gidding, 125
Liverpool, 138
Llandaff, 317
Lloyd, 39
London, 19, 23, 37, 39, 45, 55, 62, 73, 74, 86, 88, 98, 106, 181, 198, 202, 210, 211, 213, 223, 236, 253, 259, 261, 265, 285, 305, 308, 313, 317
Longhi, 132
Loudon, 328
Luther, 141

Madan, Mrs., 148, 151
Madan, Martin, 87
Madeira, 134
*March in Scipio, The,* 224
Margate, 73, 74
Market Street, 33, 34, 42, 72

*Marriage to the Sea,* 142
Mattishall, 310
*Meditations among the Tombs,* 105
Mesmer, 23
"Messiah, The," 199
Methodism
　*See* Evangelicalism
Middle Ages, 13, 66
Middle Temple, 50-51, 55, 58, 68,
　76, 78, 88, 269
Milton, 273, 275, 287, 293, 294, 297,
　306
　*Comus,* 294
　*Paradise Lost,* 292
Mordaunt, Miss, 218
Morland
　*Pious Family in Four Plates,*
　*The,* 119
Morte D'Arthur, 13
Mozart, 15
Mungo, 173, 178, 191, 192

Neptune, 256
Newfoundland, 136
New Guinea, 133
Newport Pagnell, 183, 185, 257
Newton, Mrs., 133, 135, 137, 138,
　167, 182, 187
Newton, John
　and Miss Catlett, 133, 135, 137,
　138
　and John Cowper, 156
　and William Cowper, 129-130,
　142-145, 148, 151, 156-157, 162-
　163, 167, 170, 171, 174, 181-182,
　185, 187, 196, 204, 231, 233-234,
　242-243, 257-258, 276, 283
　and Lord Dartmouth, 138-139
　and Evangelicalism, 138, 141-142
　and Horace, 137
　and Mr. Scott, 183
　*Authentic Narrative of Some*
　*Interesting Particulars in the*
　*Life of John Newton, An,* 131

Newton, John—*cont.*
　character of, 139-141
　dream of, 132-133
　early life of, 131-132
　fear of moon, 266
　leaves Olney, 181
　on the Bananoes, 135
　on Platane Islands, 134
　on sea, 132-134, 137
　ordination of, 138-139
New Zealand, 21, 174
Nicholson, Mr., 110
Nineveh, 17
Nonsense Club, 62
Norfolk, 36, 49, 309, 310, 311, 314
Northampton, 145
Northamptonshire, 129
Norwich, 110

Olney, 129, 130, 139, 142, 144, 145,
　146, 150, 151, 153, 156, 157,
　158, 169, 174, 179, 180, 183,
　184, 185, 187, 190, 197, 207,
　209, 210, 213, 219, 235, 239,
　245, 252, 256, 260, 270, 285,
　322
Orchard Side, 130, 163, 164, 170,
　172, 173, 177, 183, 185, 186,
　187, 219, 220, 221, 238, 239,
　244, 245, 246
Ossian, 19
*Our Village,* 26
Ouse River, 110, 131, 190, 192
Oxford, 163

Page, Fanny, 279
Paley, William
　*Evidences,* 328
Palmer, the draper, 185
Pantheon, 253
*Paradise Lost*
　Milton, 292
Paris, 19, 196, 279
"Peasant's Nest," 193

Pelham, 44
Pemberton, Mr., 110
Perowne, Miss, 313, 318, 326, 327
Peterborough, Lady, 218
Peters, Reverend William, 22
Pertenhall, 259
Phaethon, 239
*Pious Family in Four Plates, The*
Morland, 119
Pitt, 307
Platane Islands, 134
Plumes, Captain, 97
Poland, 277
Pope, Alexander, 19, 224
Potsdam, 19
Porteus, Dr. Beilby, 317, 318
Powley, Mr., 163
Powley, Mrs., 115, 163, 187
Puss, 173

Quebec, 62

Ramsay, Allan, 19
Ramsgate, 204
Ranelagh, 44, 47, 198, 237
Raphael, 19
Reformation, 141
Renaissance, 13, 15, 65
Reprobation, 148
*Retired Cat, The*, 204
Reynolds, 20
Richardson, Samuel, 23
*Clarissa Harlowe,* 22
Richmond, Duke of, 38
Rivaulx, 129
Roberts, Doctor, 277
Roberts, Sam, 105, 125
Rockingham, Lord, 121
Romaine, Mr., 97
Rome, 253
Romney, 260, 282, 283, 287
Romney Marsh, 110
Rose, Samuel, 260-261, 262, 264,
265, 313, 314, 318, 327-328

Rossetti, Christina, 52
Rowlandson, 20
Rowley, Clotworthy, 58
Royal Academy, 14
Russell, 39, 45, 59, 63
Russia, 273

St. Albans, 88, 106, 108, 114, 125,
285, 326
St. Christopher, 137
St. Etheldreda's, 46
*St. James's Gazette,* 106, 110
St. Margaret's, 40, 75
St. Mary Woolnoth, 181
Sample, Nathan, 185
Sandgate Park, 73
Scotland, 184
Scott, Captain, 145
Scott, Mr., 183
Scott, Sir Walter, 14
Seed, 21
*Sermons*
Tillotson, 84
Shakespeare, 281
Sheraton, 17
Singleton, Captain, 21
*Sir Charles Grandison,* 62
Smith, Mr., 186
Smith, Mrs. Charlotte, 287
Smollett, T. G., 20, 276
Southampton Row, 46, 47, 49, 59,
114, 176, 237, 244, 259, 310
Spencer, Dowager Lady, 260
Spencer, Lord, 307-308
Stapleton, Miss, 255, 256
Steventon, 193
Stock, 163
Surrey, 286
Sussex, 277

Tardiff, Monsieur de, 228
*Task, The*
Cowper, 225, 230, 233, 236, 242,
272, 327

"Taureau"
See Bull, Reverend William
Teedon, Samuel, 270-273, 286, 295-296
Thames River, 51
Theodora, 47, 48-50, 51, 59, 63, 116, 118, 128
Thompson, 22
Throckmorton, Mr., 190
Throckmorton, Mrs., 236-237, 246, 253, 254-255, 256, 265, 266, 268
Throckmorton, Mr. George, 255
Throckmorton, Sir John, 235, 236, 244, 246, 253, 255, 265, 268
Thurlow, 46, 63, 177, 306, 307
Tillotson, John
Sermons, 84
Tiny, 172, 173
Tom Jones, 99
Tophet, 124
Torbay, 135
Tower Wharf, 78
Trianon, 190
Triumphs of Temper, The
Hayley, 278
Troy, 252
Trunnions, Commodore, 97
Tyburn, 37

Udolpho, 73
Unwin, Mr., 112, 115, 121, 127, 128, 129, 143
Unwin, Mrs., 112-114, 129, 144, 156, 173, 174, 175, 177, 178, 179, 186, 187, 195, 196, 197, 204, 209, 210, 225, 231, 235, 239, 241, 254, 266, 283, 287, 292, 293, 294, 297-298, 300, 301, 309, 327
and Lady Austen, 212-213, 217, 219, 221, 227, 241
and Cowper's second madness, 162, 163, 164, 167, 168-170
and Cowper's third madness, 250

Unwin, Mrs.—cont.
and Lady Hesketh, 116, 118, 241-242, 308
and John Johnson, 263-264
attitude toward Cowper, 128, 227
cared for by Cowper, 275, 290, 291, 298, 304
character of, 116-117
Cowper's attitude toward, 127-128, 227
death of, 319-320, 326
faith of, 169
intimacy with Cowper, 117-118
prayers for Cowper, 243
servants of, 145-146
strokes of, 274, 284, 303-304
support for Cowper, 127, 201, 222-223, 290, 291
taken to Eartham, 285-286
walks with Cowper, 120-121, 142, 180, 192
Unwin, Mary
See Unwin, Mrs.
Unwin, William, 112, 115, 120, 123, 163, 176, 187, 203, 208, 213, 218, 220, 233, 234, 242, 248, 249

Vaughan, Henry, 126
Vauxhall, 21, 44
Venice, 132, 142
Venn, Mr. 97, 145
Vestris, 196
Virgil, 234
Voltaire, 15, 17, 67, 100

Wagner, 15
Wales, 23
Walpole, Horace, 18, 19, 23, 37, 44
Walpole, Robert, 37
Watson, Doctor, 317, 318
Wesley, Charles, 125
Wesley, John, 94, 138

Westminster, 37, 44, 45, 59, 83, 235
Westminster Abbey, 37, 85, 199
Weston, 183, 241, 244, 245, 248, 252, 285
Weston Lodge, 244-245, 246, 265, 266, 273, 289, 295, 302, 304, 306, 308, 309, 311, 312, 314, 315, 320
Weston Park, 190, 235, 245, 253, 254, 255, 297
Weston Wilderness, 190-192, 235, 256, 297
Weymouth, 328
Whitefield, 94, 138
Wilberforce, Mr., 317, 318

Wildair, Sir Henry, 37
Wilderness
  *See* Weston Wilderness
Wilkes, Mr., 179
Willis, Doctor, 308, 309
Wilson, the barber, 185, 223
Winchester, 248
Witwould, Sir Wilful, 106
Woffington, Peg, 37
Wolfe, 62
Wordsworth, 189
Wright, 282

York, Duke of, 198
Yorkshire, 129